PATRICK HENRY BRADY

WITH MEGHAN BRADY SMITH

DEAD MEN FLYING

VICTORY IN VIET NAM

THE LEGEND OF DUST OFF: AMERICA'S BATTLEFIELD ANGELS

 WND Books

DEDICATED TO CHARLES KELLY, HIS FAMILY,
AND ALL THE KELLY TWIGS.

DEAD MEN FLYING

WND Books, Washington D.C.

Copyright © 2012 by Patrick Henry Brady

Written by Patrick Henry Brady with Meghan Brady Smith
Book Designed by Mark Karis

Paperback ISBN: 978-1-942475-60-6
E-Book ISBN: 978-1-936488-72-8

Library of Congress information available.
Printed in the United States of America.

WND Books are distributed to the trade by:
Midpoint Trade Books
27 West 20th Street, Suite 1102
New York, NY 10011

WND Books are available at special discounts for bulk purchases.
WND Books also publishes books in electronic formats.

For more information call (541) 474-1776 or visit www.wndbooks.com

17 18 19 LBM 5 4 3 2 1

CONTENTS

INTRODUCTION   I

PART I: SEMI-WAR

1	Meeting the Man	3
2	A Flying Christmas Tree	8
3	Red Clay, Rabies, and Titty Mountain	12
4	Lethal Patients	18
5	The Big Grandmother of Medicine	20
6	Death Spiral	26
7	WHAM	29
8	Duty in the Pearl of the Orient	33
9	Ghost Riders in the Sky	40
10	Portable Red Crosses	42
11	Geneva, the Dead, and Preventive Medicine	49
12	A Traitor in the 57th	53
13	The Genius of a Mad Man	59
14	An Atheist Is My Co-Pilot	63
15	Two Unlucky Irishmen	67
16	When I Have Your Wounded	72
17	The Kelly Way	80
18	Kelly's Krazies	87
19	Between His Ankles	96
20	Lesser Nobles and Butterfly Balls	110
21	I Gotta Get Out of This Place	120

PART 2: PREPARATIONS FOR WAR

22	The Flying Red A**hole	131
23	The Golden-Winged 54th	139

PART 3: WAR

24	Where the Hell Is Chu Lai?	157
25	An AO from Hell	160
26	Opening Week	176
27	OCTOBER: Man-Made Stars and an Epiphany	182
28	NOVEMBER: The Fog Is Lifted	198
29	Another Epiphany	202
30	DECEMBER: Doldrums	206
31	Father Don's Air Medal	212
32	JANUARY: New Year, New Life	219
33	6 January: The Feast of the Epiphany	221
34	TET: America's Greatest Victory in Viet Nam	232
35	FEBRUARY	236
36	MARCH: My Lai and Operational Definition	240
37	APRIL: The Man Without a Face	252
38	MAY: Mayhem	254
39	Viet Nam Golgotha	256
40	Where Is the Worm?	271
41	JUNE: Amazing Stats	275
42	JULY: A Wedding, a Medal, and My Last Mission	280
43	Dust Off Déjà Vu	289

PART 4: AFTER WAR

44	Why Soldiers Fight	297
45	America's Axis of Evil	306

EPILOGUE	314

THANKS AND THOUGHTS	319
ABOUT THE AUTHOR	321
GLOSSARY	323
INDEX	325

INTRODUCTION

SOME time ago I visited the battlefields of Viet Nam, many of which were littered with statues of dead and surrendering American Soldiers, testimonials to our "defeat." Certainly it is true that to the victor goes the spoils, but it is also true that the American soldier was never defeated on any battlefield in Viet Nam. Our defeat was at the hands of our elite in the courtrooms, the classrooms, the cloak rooms, and the news rooms: cowardly media-phobic politicians, an irresponsible dishonest media, and other cowards and spoiled brats and professors from Berkeley to Harvard.

Living with the scars of war is difficult, for some unbearable, but all veterans suffer. The Viet Nam veteran suffered physically as much, perhaps more than any veteran of the past century. But no veteran has suffered the mental agony of that veteran. The thing that makes Viet Nam so intolerable is what the elite have done to dishonor the source of those scars, to intensify the pain of the Viet Nam veteran and destroy their unselfish and honorable legacy. They opened a gash in the psyche of that veteran and then rubbed salt in it.

But not even the elite could guarantee total defeat. The American soldier still found victory—in humanitarianism. Viet Nam may be the only war we ever fought, or perhaps that was ever fought, in which the American soldier added to their heroism with humanitarianism unmatched in the annals of warfare. And the humanitarianism took place during the heat of the battle. The GI fixed as he fought, he cured and educated and built in the middle of the battle. He truly cared for, and about, those people. What other Army has ever done that? Humanitarianism was America's great victory in Viet Nam. And it goes on today as American medical personnel, many former military, teach and treat and contribute to the people of Viet Nam. During my visit I was treated wonderfully. What the GI did for those people is still there in their hearts and minds and it will always be. I never met anyone who didn't put America at the top of the places they wanted to visit. Clearly they remembered our selflessness.

As I looked down on the cement bodies of fallen GIs, it occurred to me that Viet Nam may have hosted the only war in which we fought that there are no memorials to the American warrior. When I got home I decided to do something about it. I wrote to two American ambassadors to Viet Nam and a U.S. congressman (a Viet Nam veteran, unfortunately now in prison) urging that something be done to recognize the humanitarian effort of the GI in Viet Nam, emphasizing that such a memorial would certainly have a positive effect on our relationship. I also wrote a cover article in a popular military magazine highlighting the omission. I got little meaningful response. I hope this book will further highlight the incredible humanitarian efforts of the American soldier in Viet Nam both during the war and since; and perhaps someday a monument to that effort will stand among the fallen images that litter those dismal battlefields. Such a memorial could do much to heal the salted wounds of many GIs and bring these two wonderful people closer together.

At the center of the humanitarian efforts were the air ambulance operations—the most dangerous of all aviation operations. About one third of all air ambulance crew members became casualties and the loss of air ambulances was 3.3 times that of all other types of helicopter missions. The air ambulance crew members, who made up a small percentage of the helicopter crewmen who served in Viet Nam, suffered a disproportionately high percentage of the deaths. Thus was born the oft repeated legend of a young soldier in flight school considering with his Instructor Pilot (IP) his choice of assignment. Would he opt to be a gunship pilot, would he fly troop transport, or would he choose aeromedical evacuation, called Dust Off? The IP cautioned about the latter as he pointed to another pilot and noted that yonder was a dead man walking. He was a Dust Off pilot. In another story, the IP is extolling the virtues of both naval and Air Force aviation but warns: Don't even think about Army helicopter aviation unless you have a pair larger than basketballs—those guys are completely crazy.

This is the story of those guys, one described as a mad man, another actually called Craze, and their crews when they were flying. It is also the story of faith in combat and the miracles it produces.

· PART I ·

SEMI-WAR

MEETING THE MAN

TODAY, after 53 years, I still remember in detail the first time I met him. I remember how he looked and I remember his first words. I have the same recollection of first meeting my wife when we were 16. I wonder why this is. I certainly did not have any idea at the time the impact both would have on my life; but this man has been with me these many years, in my decisions and in many of my efforts to sort out what kind of a man I wanted to be.

It was 18 January 1964. Dick Anderson and I flew in from San Francisco the day before after a 20 hour ordeal through Honolulu, Guam, and Clark Airbase in the Philippines. I had just graduated from flight school and volunteered for Viet Nam. I hoped a combat tour, nominal as the combat was, would help what was a decidedly mediocre, even disastrous, career to that point. We were joining the 57th Medical Detachment, HA (Helicopter Ambulance), the only helicopter ambulance unit in Viet Nam. The 57th covered the entire country with five UH-1B (Huey) Bell helicopters and was the first unit to use that magnificent bird in combat. The unit arrived in

Nha Trang, Viet Nam, in April of 1962 without operational definition, doctrine, or support. When the commander, John Temperilli,
asked the local medics if they knew where he was to be stationed
their answer was, "No, we don't know a damn thing about you." I
would have a similar experience five years later.

Their primary mission was U.S. casualties, barely 30 hostile
deaths to that point. Initially the 57th was forbidden to carry
Vietnamese patients, who were the only significant casualties at
the time. In 1962, the 57th flew a paltry 235 evacuations, hardly a
good day's work in future times. Their most difficult mission was
to keep other aviation units from cannibalizing 57th aircraft for
non-medical missions. On one occasion, Temperilli was ordered
to turn over key parts of three aircraft, rendering them unflyable,
for other aircraft engaged in an air assault. The assault had no aeromedical coverage. Some grunt commanders give little thought to
casualty needs—until they need help; and then they scream at the
medics. The 57th Medical leadership, usually a physician, was not
helpful. They initially tried to scatter the 57th all over the country
without any clue to the intrinsic logistical demands of an aviation
unit. They would actually be forced to turn down missions for
lack of fuel. In its first year in combat, not a single officer from the
Surgeon General's Office visited the 57th.

The 57th moved to Saigon in January 1963. It now had three
choppers at Tan Son Nhut, the major airfield in Saigon, with one
each up north at Qui Nhon and Pleiku. U.S. Forces at the time
numbered some 16,000, mostly in advisery and logistical support
of the Army of the Republic of Viet Nam (ARVN) which did
most of the fighting. The enemy was the Viet Cong or Vietnamese
communist guerillas who disguised themselves as the National
Liberation Front (NLF), posing as southern insurgents, nation-
alists fighting for freedom, not communism. Ho Chi Minh also
tried to hide his communist identity knowing that an informed
people would reject communism.

The Viet Cong were known as the VC, Victor Charlie or Charlie by the GI. Regular force North Vietnamese Army (NVA) troops were rarely encountered. Major Charles Kelly was the third commander of the 57th, in command one week when Dick and I arrived. The unit call sign was Dust Off, selected from a Navy operational list by Lloyd Spencer, the second 57th commander, because some choppers in the dry season disappeared in a cloud of dust. It caught on and became permanent for ease of communication; when someone cried Dust Off into a microphone (mic) everyone knew it was a cry for medical help. Dust Off was also given its own frequency, invaluable in the confusion that surrounds casualty situations. (Major Harry Phillips later developed Dust Off into the acronym: Dedicated Unhesitating Service To Our Fighting Forces; Phillips was killed on a night mission.)

We were picked up at the airfield and taken to our quarters in an old French villa by a sharp combat arms pilot, Chuck Schexnayder, assigned to the 57th. The heat was oppressive. When I stepped off the plane I felt like I was suddenly wrapped in a steaming-hot wool blanket. I could hardly breathe. I was not in bad shape but would lose 16 pounds in the next month. Dick and I were anxious to know what was going on and Chuck told us of a massive ARVN combat operation happening as he spoke. It was the largest heliborn assault in history. One Huey had exploded in mid air. Five helicopter crewmen were killed and three were wounded. Not good news for a couple of brand new chopper pilots.

The next morning while en route to the flight operations shack at Tan Son Nhut Airport, I saw a Red Cross helicopter clearing the end of the runway. It was Major Kelly departing to support the heliborn assault. I had heard a lot about Kelly. He was the only soldier who ever wore the four major badges of the Army at the time: The Combat Medic Badge, the Combat Infantry Badge, the Parachute Badge, and Flight Wings. He was an enlisted veteran of World War II and served in Korea. Viet Nam was probably his last assignment. I heard he had some skeletons in his closet and would likely not make lieutenant colonel. He was reputed to be a bit of a rascal to work with and believed the current generation was softer than the World War II guys. And he was getting weary of being separated from his beloved wife Jessie and their children.

We were at lunch when Kelly joined us. He was a small man, proud in appearance, perhaps a bit vain but still rather shy. He combed his hair toward his eyebrows to camouflage a receding hairline. His belt appeared too tight, and although it never affected his breathing, he seemed always to be holding his belly in and puffing out his chest. His walk was structured in the military way but rather graceful. His face was all Irish, freckled and round, dominated by large eyes that seemed to change size according to his mood. Those eyes moved more quickly than the rest of him and could be rather disquieting once they rested on you. Only rarely did I see them twinkle, and I never heard him laugh. He spoke with a soft Georgia drawl and never raised his voice regardless of his mood or the danger of the moment. You only needed to look at his eyes to know his frame of mind. This day they reeked of a deep helpless anguish.

The first words I heard from him were, "We never covered ourselves with glory today." During that morning's operation an American helicopter had gone down in the South China Sea. Kelly and his crew were overhead, heard the call for help, and almost beat the falling bird to the water. Miraculously everyone had gotten out before their chopper sank. They were in the water clear of the sinking helicopter when Kelly came down over them. He had no hoist and had to get within arm's length for his crew to pull the men out of the water. Kelly started to put his skids in the water but was stopped by his co-pilot. A wave could hit their blade and they might crash on top of the men under them. Kelly was the unit commander but having been in country only a short time, he had not yet qualified to be aircraft commander (AC). He had to obey the other pilot and was forced to hover over the downed crew and watch them drown one by one as his crew struggled to pull them from the sea.

The combination of rotor downwash, rough seas, and the weight of their clothes, especially the boots, was enough to kill all but one soldier who was pulled aboard with a litter. I will never forget the look on his face as he told us the story. I don't think he ever forgave his co-pilot for not allowing him to put the skids in the water. As risky as it was, it was the only way he could have saved them. If they had draped themselves over the skids perhaps he could have hovered them to the shore. That may have been the only time Kelly left undone anything that might have saved a life no matter how dangerous. Dick and I were not off to a good start; two days in country and seven dead helicopter crewmen.

When Kelly finally focused on me he said, "Don't unpack." That was it. No welcome, no pep talk, nothing, just don't unpack. He was sending us north, me up to Pleiku, and Dick Anderson to Qui Nhon. Both Dick and I were Medical Service Corps (MSC) pilots. Some pilots up north were Combat Arms pilots (i.e., infantry artillery armor), not medically trained, and Kelly was anxious to fill up with MSC aviators. Kelly saw a danger in non-medically trained pilots flying medical missions, something not of particular concern up to this time. In fact, some in the Surgeon General's office were actually assigning MSCs to combat aviation units to get them more combat time.

· 2 ·

A FLYING CHRISTMAS TREE

BACK at the villa that evening, a mission came in for a Vietnamese soldier with a crushed arm in the jungle just north of Saigon. I was excited and asked if I could go along. There was only one patient so space was not a problem. This was a night pickup, then considered the most dangerous of missions. The duty pilots looked at me somewhat surprised but agreed to let me go. Cargo space in the B model was tight but I could ride the water can between the pilots to keep out of the way as the crew attended the patient.

As a new guy, known as an f****** new guy (FNG), I was fascinated with everything that went on. I watched as the pilots carefully planned the route using large-scale terrain maps. We then drove to the operations shack 10 minutes away where we were joined by the crew chief and medic. They rechecked the map, plotted an azimuth and distance, and we drove to the chopper pad. The crew for a Dust Off mission consisted of the AC, a co-pilot, a medic to tend the wounded, and a crew chief who owned and maintained the bird. The medic and crew chief also served as door gunners covering the flanks of the helicopter on approach and take off. You cannot parachute out of a helicopter—our crew chiefs were our parachutes.

As we cleared the lights of Saigon and headed into the darkness, I experienced for the first time the peace and power that is unique to night combat flight. It was a feeling I would experience many times but one that never ceased to thrill me. The cockpit took on a surreal appearance with the red, gold, and green instruments reflecting off man and machine. Beyond the roar of the engine, the darkness inspired a deep calm, a peaceful quietness. And the cool of the night enhanced the machine, which was more responsive and powerful than in daytime. I would learn that if you flew properly, it was very difficult, almost impossible, for the enemy to kill you at night. That fact added immeasurably to the tranquility of night missions; but we did not fly properly this night.

We circled the assigned coordinates and spotted a bonfire which marked our pickup zone (PZ). As was required for night flights, all our outside lights were on: red, green, and white. The rotating beacon was flashing and the instrument and console lights were on bright. We landed using both the landing light and search light. The patient was loaded without incident but as we cleared the area on takeoff, I heard the sharp snap of small arms fire, a sound like popping fire crackers. Then the sky around our chopper filled with tracer fire. Both pilots ducked and the bird was yanked sideways. The pilots recovered and flew to altitude through the fire. We took the patient to the Vietnamese hospital and returned to Ton Son Nhut without further incident. Since this was my first combat flight, and we got shot at, the crew immediately marked me as a magnet ass, a term reserved for unlucky pilots who attracted bullets.

I experienced for the first time the sensation of being shot at. Some fool said it was exhilarating to be shot at and missed. It is not, not when you know you will be shot at again on the next mission. The bottom line was that if the bullets got lucky, and you got unlucky, there would be a period of time, horrible time, time without control, from altitude to the ground and certain death. Yet I did experience some excitement watching the tracers flash by. Tracers at night are bizarrely beautiful things. They seemed lazy and whimsical as they danced around the sky some distance away, but deadly serious, dreadful, and so fast when they blasted close by. The bullets buzzing the chopper snapped like firecrackers. And my ears burned during the time we received fire. I would experience the burning ears phenomenon many times and it was a feeling I did not enjoy.

That night in bed I reviewed the lessons learned. I began with a prayer that I would never experience the anguish I saw in Kelly that day. I was told that some pilots who went down at sea would wash up on shore with one boot on and one boot off. I would later hear of a Dust Off crew that crashed in the sea killing all but one pilot who was in the water with his boots and a broken leg, arm, and ankle who swam as far as he could then, totally exhausted, decided to just drown. He hit bottom and made it to shore. For this reason, many pilots wore zippers in their boots. I would get zippers the next day. I also got a rope. From then on, I never flew without one unless I was in a ship with a hoist. I could visualize pulling those poor drowning soldiers on board with a rope, or even towing them to shore.

It seemed to me that a lot of time was wasted getting the night mission off and I wondered why the duty pilots were not at the flight line. Time is everything in life saving and my vision of a mission was that of firemen going to a fire. The first hour after injury is known as the Golden Hour, 60 minutes from the time of injury in which the majority of critically injured patients can be saved if properly treated. The concept of the Golden Hour highlights the sensitivity of trauma to time, not a minute must ever be wasted. How fast we react is life and death for our soldiers.

And why use lights at night? They ruined every advantage we had. We must have looked like a flying Christmas tree landing in that jungle clearing. Why not fly blacked out? In a peacetime environment the lights are required, but this was combat. The rules should be changed. As a FNG, I never expressed my concerns after that mission but my education as a Dust Off pilot had begun. With those thoughts I dozed off to the chirping of what I thought to be birds. In the morning, I found my walls covered with lizards. They were the chirpers, reptilian rhapsodizers no less.

RED CLAY, RABIES, AND TITTY MOUNTAIN

PLEIKU was located in the hills and mountains of the central highlands. The dominant characteristic was red clay and the suffocating dust it produced. I arrived during the dry season and the wind blew continuously, scattering the red dust everywhere. It was not as hot as Saigon, averaging a pleasant 87 in the day and a cool 55 at night. We lived in Stilwell Hooches, named after Brigadier General Joe Stilwell, the commander of Army forces in Viet Nam. He was the son of the famous General "Vinegar Joe" Stilwell of World War II. We called him "Cider Joe," but not to his face. The hooches were essentially open bay huts with two lines of bunks and wooden shutters for windows that could be closed during monsoon rains. The roofs were tin and I enjoyed the music the rain gave to them. We covered our bunks with a mosquito net not just for the mosquitoes but also to keep the other critters that roamed the rafters at night out of our beds.

Our hooch was right next to the airfield, which facilitated our reaction time for missions but subjected us to constant dust storms as the choppers came and went. Soon all my clothing and bedding took on a rusty hue. A paper left on a bunk disappeared by nightfall as the blanket and paper took on the color of the dust. We had a hooch maid, a local Vietnamese lady, who did our laundry and shined our boots. In my travels, I noticed that each country had its own special aroma most evident upon arrival. Viet Nam had a strikingly aromatic signature influenced greatly by the human feces used as fertilizer in the rice paddies. We all adjusted quickly to the smell thanks, in no small measure, to the fact that the maid washed our fatigues in rice paddy water.

I was surprised at the size of the creatures in Viet Nam. The people were small and so were the animals. The elephants seemed no larger than moose I had shot in Alaska. The deer were like dogs, much smaller than the mule deer back home. Although I never saw a tiger, I was told they were also under-sized but still dangerous as some soldiers would learn. They originated a new category of casualty in the highlands. The wounded in action were WIA, the killed in action were KIA. At Pleiku they had the EIA. On occasion an unfortunate troop would surprise a hungry tiger and get eaten in action.

My co-pilot at Pleiku was a first lieutenant combat arms pilot. I was a captain and outranked him but he would be in charge until I got checked out in the area. He was a bit too cavalier for my tastes and seemed more curious than caring about the few patients we carried. He put on the air of an old-timer despite having been in the country only a few weeks. I would learn that we are veterans only of past missions; we are rookies on each new mission. I was always wary of any veteran who acted too much the part. And I found it annoying that my new co-pilot adhered to that sorry old adage that one gets used to the blood and carnage. This was not an uncommon sight but one I never understood. I never got used to it and most of the Dust Off people I knew did not either. It does get repetitive, but something is wrong if the feeling for the pain of others ever weakens. Once again, I was an FNG and I listened, but it did not take me long to realize he did not know much.

Finally, I was flying freely, unleashed from the chains of flight school. I loved it. I was fascinated by the view from the air. Pilots are privileged to see our gorgeous earth as God does. Some fixed wing pilots scoff at the chopper and those who fly them. They are suspicious of any aircraft where the wings go faster than the fuselage. They whimper that if something hasn't broken, it is about to. Everything about it, they believe, wants not to fly. In a sense, they are correct. If you listen too carefully, it sounds as if something is breaking all the time, especially at night, over water, over jungles, over mountains, and if you are flying instruments. I found the vibrations mesmerizing, their sound melodious. Everything rhymed. But if that rhyme and rhythm and vibration change, something probably is about to break.

In truth, there are two kinds of flying—flying and flying a helicopter. Actually, if you think about it, there is only one. You only truly fly a helicopter; you mostly ride in everything else. Flying a helicopter was an artform, the rest was science. In a chopper, and only in a chopper, man and machine truly bond. It can be as erotic as the union of man and woman in marriage. It was physical, even sensual. Anyone who has mounted a great and powerful horse knows the feeling. Feet on the pedals as in the stirrups, the cyclic and collective are the reins—two hands full of power; then lean forward for a great ride. Then experience the melodious mesmerizing sounds and vibrations, as of a galloping steed, which flowed from machine to man as blood flows through one's veins.

In most choppers of this era, every limb, every finger, every toe, your wrist, and all your senses were used, indeed required, to keep that thing flying. Up on the collective in with the left foot; down on the collective, in with the right foot, all while adjusting the cyclic with your right arm and twisting the throttle with your left wrist. And that left arm better be quick if the engine quits, after which you have a second or so to save your rotor RPM and find a suitable landing area, while ensuring the rotor does not leave the green which could cause it to leave the helicopter. Your eyes were your life especially at night, and smell was vital for the wayward bullet that went through the fuel cell, a hydraulic, or oil line.

The more I flew the more I became one with that machine. I loved to cuddle up to the controls, especially at night. I came to a point where I imagined my ears on each rotor tip and the tail boom on my tail bone. I could feel the leaves of a tree as they touched the hair on the outside of my ears and my tail bone twitched with the nearness of the tail rotor to anything hard. Later, when we were able to get music on our FM radio, I would try and dance that bird through the sky. My favorite song to fly/dance to was about a beautiful balloon, something like: "Would you like to fly in my beautiful balloon? We could float among the stars together, you and I. We can sing a song and sail along the silver sky." Beautiful! All in all, flying a helicopter in combat, in beautiful terrain, matched any experience in life save one—using it to save a life.

Only John Steinbeck, who as both a Pulitzer and Nobel Prize winner in Literature, had the words to properly and beautifully describes helicopter pilots. In 1967 he wrote the following to Alicia Patterson, Newsday's first editor and publisher after a chopper ride.

"I wish I could tell you about these pilots. They make me sick with envy. They ride their vehicles the way a man controls a fine, well-trained quarter horse. They weave along stream beds, rise like swallows to clear trees, they turn and twist and dip like swifts in the evening. I watch their hands and feet on the controls, the delicacy of the coordination reminds me of the sure and seeming slow hands of (Pablo) Casals on the cello. They are truly musicians hands and they play their controls like music and they dance them like ballerinas and they make me jealous because I want so much to do it."

The terrain around Pleiku was mountainous, rusty, and repetitive but still beautiful. There were open areas easily accessible but also thick-canopied jungles with confined areas, some suitable only for hoist rescues, others requiring great skill in landing. Forced landing areas were rare and much of the terrain was not a good place to lose an engine—especially at night. Navigation could be difficult. There were no navigation aids or water towers with town names, my salvation in flight school. But one terrain feature, actually two, named Titty Mountain helped in the navigation. It was here I began my study of terrain, the single most important factor in combat and also in combat helicopter rescues.

I was fascinated by the incredible variety of landscape, not only the beauty but also the disparity in the view from altitude and at ground level. To be able to see terrain from altitude and visualize what it is actually like at ground level is important; especially if you make that transition rapidly. It is also vital in working confined areas which demanded precise visual judgment (the longer the ear hair the better). I was only vaguely aware of how important this would be in my later flying. I also noted the unique requirements of solo missions. The Dust Off pilot was the sole planner and executer of every mission. There were no operations people to assist and no one prepped the Landing Zone (LZ) as with most helicopter operations.

Although I had a few hours in an A model Huey in flight school, I had never flown a B model and forgot how to start it in the month since flight school. I got checked out on combat missions. I was impressed with the B model and am to this day. Compared to our trainer, the wooden bladed H-23, known as "Hiller the Killer," this bird was a Rolls Royce. Other model Hueys would have more space and power, but none had the quickness or responsiveness and, most important, the flat attitude one could maintain on night approaches and high-speed daytime landings. All this and no need for the left wrist.

In the midst of all the improved technology, they neglected pilot protection. An armored helicopter is an oxymoron. We did wear a flack vest, which was psychologically comforting despite the fact that a .30 caliber easily penetrated the front and back of the vest— and the body in between. More comforting but probably equally useless was our hand gun which we snuggled between our legs in hopes it would protect our manliness. Essentially you were sitting in a sack full of JP4 (gas) that ignited easily and could turn the whole bird, and the crew, into a pile of ashes. The designers also forgot that pilots fly sitting down. The seat in the B model was rock hard and totally merciless—there was no escape from it. Sitting in that bird for several hours made you wish you could fly standing up. It reminded me of my time as an altar boy kneeling on marble stairs during a High Mass—God help the pilot with piles.

As a young boy I had saved two lives. I never got over the feeling and was thrilled to be able to do it again. But initially I had great fear about how I would react to the reality of human suffering and the graphic, bloody harshness of the battlefield. Flying across Viet Nam was not unlike driving through the American West where the highways were littered with road kill, unfortunate animals that got in the way of speeding vehicles. In Viet Nam, the road kill was human; unfortunate individuals who got in the way of speeding missiles.

I became a medic by virtue of the fact I was a psychology major in ROTC, a profession not involved in blood and gore. I had no stomach for a needle, much less for the sight of blood. I fainted the first time I gave a blood sample. I fainted when I saw the messy body of my first-born son. I broke out in cold sweats during the medical training films at Medical Officers Basic School. I had to put my head down and cover my eyes to keep from falling out of my desk. The hardest things I had done up to this point in my life was to donate my blood. One of my friends had actually died donating his blood. He was doing it for money but my donation was for a good cause and there was some shame attached to refusal.

It took all the courage I could muster to do it. I still have these problems to this day. But I never had a problem with the carnage on the battlefield and I cannot explain it—emotionally yes, physically no.

· 4 ·

LETHAL PATIENTS

MY first pickup at Pleiku was a sick young girl from a nearby village. She was sweating profusely and jerking so badly that the crew had to strap her down. We brought her to the dispensary at Pleiku. The physician took one look and ordered her isolated in another room. He said she had rabies and there was nothing that could be done. I was a bit shocked by his cold-blooded treatment of the poor girl. He then turned his attention to the crew. Had she bitten them or did they come in contact with her saliva? She had not. We had no idea what the young girl's condition was when we picked her up, or the danger she posed.

Later missions would involve leprosy and plague patients, grim serial killers from antiquity, or so I thought. I recalled that the plague, which is spread by fleas from infected rats, once known as the "Black Death," had wiped out a good portion of the human race. The central highlands were home to various primitive tribes known collectively as Montagnards, and rat meat was a key ingredient in their diet. There was an epidemic of the plague in Viet Nam at this time. It had gone from single digit cases in 1961 to thousands. At least five soldiers would be infected with the disease, but it was no longer the showstopper it was in the Middle Ages. We were told we could safely transport plague patients (hopefully sans the fleas). An added concern was an ongoing cholera epidemic.

A village near Pleiku, set aside for lepers, reminded me of the leper colony in Molokai, Hawaii, run by a childhood hero of mine, Father Damien called "The Leper." I remember the horrible descriptions of noses and other body parts rotting off. Some of the lepers lived in mausoleums in graveyards hanging blankets between tombstones as hammocks for their children. Our physicians called it Hansen's disease, which made it less fearsome. They told us it was not particularly dangerous. Yes, it could be contagious but it was very unlikely we would catch it in the short time we were exposed. But leprosy patients were unsettling. I could not forget that Father Damien caught the disease and it killed him.

If leprosy and the plague were not serious threats, rabies certainly was and we quickly learned its symptoms. Once they appeared, death was certain. This deadly disease was all too common in the Montagnard villages and we were very careful on the missions that followed. The slightest exposure required preventive treatment almost as horrible as the disease. I got a firsthand description of rabies treatment from a hooch mate. One night, a rat fell through his loose mosquito net (a definite no-no) into his bed and bit him on the chest. His screams woke us and we tried but could not catch the rat. With the rat's brain they could determine if it was rabid. Without it, treatment was the only option. The treatment was gruesome. My buddy said they stuck him in the gut some 12 times with a needle not unlike a larder. We all tightened up our nets. Clearly, there would be an added dimension to patient evacuation in this area. Beyond caring for our patients, we would have to take care they did not make patients of us.

THE BIG GRANDMOTHER OF MEDICINE

THE Montagnards reminded me physically of the American Indian. The men wore loincloths and were seldom seen without a clay pipe. Since they never stopped smiling, I wondered what they used for tobacco. They were short, powerfully built, very courageous, and loyal. The women were naked to the waist and dyed their teeth black as a cosmetic. They also filed their front teeth off so they would not appear animalistic and chewed beetle nut, a mildly narcotic root which gave their mouths a red glow which together with their black teeth presented a look some rock stars would die for.

The Montagnards were a family centered matrilineal society. The men were the hunter-gatherers but owned only the means to be breadwinners. The women owned the house and animals. The man often lived with the wife's family, a situation demanding great respect for his mother-in-law. If the male had enough money, he could have multiple wives, but the women could have only one husband. It was the women who proposed marriage and the eldest daughter inherited the estate. Some lived in houses up to 400 feet long. They had no word in their language for lying or for comfort; but they seemed never to stop laughing. Unlike many primitives, a good many were Christians but they could be intolerant of those who broke their rules. Infidelity was treated with a bamboo stick, notched and inserted into the offending member. Our GIs kept a safe distance from Montagnard maidens.

These cheerful, happy people were eager to sell us their wares which included rat traps, crossbows, and what was called a VC gong. The gong was a round beaten piece of copper used, I guessed, for communications. As I mentioned, rat meat was a big part of their diet and the rat trap was a bewildering configuration of bamboo pieces that would have mystified Einstein. I contributed to their economy by buying one of each as well as the horns of a buffalo, known to the GIs as a F*** Ox. Don't ask me why.

Montagnards were known affectionately as Yards by the Special Forces (SF or Green Berets) who lived and fought with them and considered them great warriors. Soldiers often equate one's courage to the size of one's gonads. The Yards needed a wheel barrow to carry their gonads according to their U.S. comrades. They actually hunted tigers with a crossbow. They did not like the communists and had been strong allies of the French against the Viet Minh. Their graveyards featured an occasional wooden statue of a French soldier in full uniform, a remnant of the French occupation. The Montagnards would eventually lose half of their adult male population in support of the Americans.

We took the first load of Montagnard patients to the Vietnamese hospital at Pleiku. We had no radio communications but were met at the pad and dropped the patients off. We returned some time later to find them still on the tarmac. I went into the hospital to find out why. We were not aware of any patient overload but regardless, they should never have been left out in the heat. We were shocked to learn that the Vietnamese did not treat Montagnards in their hospital. The Vietnamese considered them to be barbarians. We told them it was barbarian not to treat them but they still refused. This was not the last time I would see patient bigotry and prejudice. It was then I learned about Doc Smith's Montagnard Hospital at Kontum, some 27 miles north. In the future, we would take all our Montagnard patients there.

Dr. Patricia Smith, next to Kelly, was the most fascinating person I met in Viet Nam. I stopped in to meet her when I dropped off the Montagnard patients. She was a tall blue-eyed woman, attractive in a way we all find our mothers attractive. Her demeanor defined compassion. She was also very busy and not into idle chatter. Her patients were waiting. She personally saw 250 per day. And she set a standard of excellence that was painful for some subordinates. As it turned out, we had a lot in common and she gave me some time. We were both graduates of Seattle University. She was born at home in Ballard, a suburb of Seattle, one of four children of a butcher. My wife, Nancy, was raised in Ballard and she graduated from Holy Angels Academy in Ballard, as did Pat Smith. While at Holy Angels Academy, she became familiar with the works of the tragic Dr. Ignaz Philipp Semmelweis, known as the "Savior of Mothers" for his discovery of the cause and prevention of puerperal fever or childbed fever. In the mid-19th century, this disease killed about 30 percent of childbearing mothers. He would be vilified for his political beliefs, be committed to a mental hospital, and eventually die of the disease he, more than anyone, helped eradicate. Pat Smith's life would, in some respects, parallel that of this great man she so admired. She saved countless mothers and their children.

As an undergraduate at Seattle University, she started in journalism but ultimately could not resist the call to medicine and went on to medical school at the University of Washington. She did very well in medical school and could have any job of her choosing. But she could not resist the unfortunate and helpless and chose to begin her practice of medicine helping poor miners in a depressed area of Kentucky. Later she would meet an Australian journalist with Grail, an international organization of Catholic women, who recruited her with stories of the incredible misery and disease of the Far East, especially leprosy. She knew she must help those with this horrible disease and decided she would spend her life cleaning their sores.

She began a period of preparation under Grail, including study at the only leprosarium in the United States in Carlville, Louisiana. She also studied at a Seventh-Day Adventists hospital in Saigon and with the famed Dr. Tom Dooley in Laos. I remember a letter from Dr. Dooley to the president of Notre Dame posted at the Grotto there. He was greatly admired but I got the impression Doc Smith did not much care for him. Although she learned from Dooley, she did not agree with his appeasement of the sorcerers in his practice. She compared that to teaching children about the stork. Soon they would learn you were fibbing. In 1959, she joined the Catholic Order of Charity at their Ban-San Leprosarium near Kontum in the highlands of Viet Nam, 300 miles north of Saigon. She was paid less than $100 a month.

The Montagnards had the highest rate of leprosy in the world. Pat Smith was immediately attracted to these deprived and diseased people, a people despised by the Vietnamese; but a people Dr. Smith found to be honest and good beyond the norm. Their poverty was so extreme that ownership of shoes was a sign of affluence. The medical need was mind boggling. Only one in four reached the age of 18, many women dying in childbirth as they did in Semmelweis' time, and for the same reason. They used the filthy ashes from their camp fires on the umbilical cord during birth. They never celebrated a baby's birth until it was two years old. Forty years was considered a full life.

In addition to leprosy, the plague, and rabies, everyone had a strain of malaria imported by the communists from the north and resistant to existing drugs. And most of the children were full of worms, each of which sucks a cubic millimeter of blood from that child each day. Think what several hundred worms can do. (I would later see bodies moving because of the presence of worms, and heard that one woman actually reached into her eye and pulled out a worm.) These tragic people dearly needed her and she fell in love with them. Initially her love was not returned and they often refused her help. But she would help them whether they liked it or not. Her travels in the countryside, plus the refusal by the Vietnamese to admit Montagnards to their hospitals, convinced her to build them their own hospital. She left Grail and the leprosarium with two nurses, Joan Blonien and Jean Platz. They would form a medical three musketeers and work together on Pat Smith's dream of a hospital for her beloved savages.

They had no money and could not be sure that the Montagnards would accept them. Thanks to Catholic Charities they got the money. Fears about patient turnout were solved after word spread that she "miraculously" cured a dying child. The child had diarrhea and the miraculous cure consisted of an IV. Her hospital, named Minh-Quy, after a French priest Father Quy and a Vietnamese priest, Father Minh, both killed by the communists, opened in July 1963 after nine months of construction. It was full from day one, caring for 150–200 inpatients, mostly Montagnards, and 75–150 outpatients per day. Many families would walk up to 100 kilometers for her treatment. Although she was not a certified surgeon, she had to perform surgery often and once actually removed a spleen with only a medical book for assistance. This woman was a healer and nothing stopped her from healing.

She became known as the Big Grandmother of Medicine and was a goddess to the Montagnards. For that, the VC hated her. They hated any good perceived to be from the existing government. The vileness and cruelty of the communists was beyond belief. They actually fouled her well with feces. They even attacked the leprosarium and killed members of the World Health Organization who were making great strides eradicating malaria in the region. Her hospital was a good and she became a prime target for assassination. They overran her hospital twice.

During the first attack, shortly after TET 1968, they blew up the hospital's laboratory and X-ray and killed all the inpatients in their search for Doc Smith who hid in a bathtub during the blood bath. When she came out of hiding, she found the floor slick with the blood of her patients; many who died protecting her. One of her nurses was kidnapped by the communists and imprisoned for a year. Pat Smith was determined to stay despite the communists' hatred for her. If the communists came again, she said she would put on a nun's habit for protection. When she was told that the nuns would hide in lay clothing for fear that the habit would jeopardize them, she was incredulous. She rebuilt the hospital which only intensified the communists' resolve to kill her. They completely destroyed Minh-Quy three years later. She served those primitive people for 16 years; a female physician, unprotected in the jungle, surrounded by the enemy, fearlessly saving countless lives especially children and mothers in childbirth, which she told me, was her greatest accomplishment.

Doc Smith became a legend to all who served in the Kontum area, especially the GIs who worshipped her and helped her in every manner possible. Many wrote their families to contribute clothing and toys for the children. Doc Smith and her nurses were round eyes and that was an attraction to any GI in the area, but she had needs and the GIs scrounged their hearts out for her. She adopted two Montagnard children after their mother was killed by the VC. One of the children was found on the breast of her dead mother, the only creature the communists left alive in the village. She raised these primitive children; one became a dentist and the other a gifted musician.

I visited with Doc Smith and her 200-pound dog, Bear, shortly before her death. She still longed to return to those great people she had mothered for so many years. Her goal was to be buried as a Montagnard in a hollowed-out log among the wooden soldiers; surrounded by a people she loved. Pat Smith was a female Father Damien and I was grateful to have her for our Montagnard patients.

· 6 ·

DEATH SPIRAL

MOST of the patients we carried were Vietnamese or Montagnards. On occasion, there was an American adviser co-located with the patient but more often than not, we could not communicate with the troops on the ground. In addition to patient missions, we flew coverage for combat assaults, during which we followed the assault choppers to the LZ circling overhead while they dropped the Vietnamese combat troops in the jungle. The combat assaults produced few results. Indeed, it seemed that the war was not taken too seriously by the ARVN troops who often went into combat with squealing pigs and clucking chickens hanging from poles. We did all we could for the SF guys along the border but they generated few casualties. Except for the fact we were on duty 24/7, the flying was rather serene. We did pick up two U.S., wounded in a mortar attack on their officers club. I flew only one night mission at Pleiku and never took a hit. Nevertheless we did get calls for "hot" pickups, patients in areas under attack.

My first "hot" combat mission at Pleiku was for patients wounded in an outpost still under attack by the VC. Hot missions were rare at this time, although I had heard of one chopper being downed by a crossbow arrow which hit a vital part. My co-pilot was not available so I grabbed one of the other combat pilots and we headed toward the PZ. He was a short timer and I noticed him start to twitch as we neared our destination. The twitching increased as I set up the downwind leg of my flight school approach. When he could stand my flying no longer, he asked if I would mind if he showed me a combat approach. He was clearly the more experienced pilot but it was my bird. My feelings were hurt but I had never heard that term and so I consented. He then flew directly over the top of our target, beeped the engine down a few hundred RPMs and from 3,000 feet kicked it out of trim, bottomed the pitch, and dived for the area.

We fell like a rock at about 4,000 feet per minute in tight circles over the target. His combat approach was for me a death spiral. My IP at flight school would have been horrified. I was horrified! I had never been through such a maneuver and my heart was in my helmet about to quit as I saw the ground rushing up at us. I could see no way for him to stop our descent. But he did. At the bottom he flared it out; we went into a mushy wobbly float at about 50 feet. When we finally settled into the ground, I was completely blinded by a red dust cloud from the rotor wash that enveloped us.

The helicopter always raises a cloud of debris depending on the terrain but the cloud from the combat approach is especially thick because of the big power change at the bottom. I lost all visual reference on the approach and wondered how my co-pilot kept the bird under control. I knew that helicopters had been destroyed in such conditions and in snow. He explained later that at a certain point, you have to finish the landing through the chin bubble next to your feet where the ground first becomes visible.

His approach logic was simple: The only area we had any hopes of being secure was our PZ; therefore the shortest, fastest route in from altitude was the safest. It was hard to argue with his logic; a fast moving, briefly exposed target is harder to hit than a slow, lengthily exposed one. You are most vulnerable at the bottom of your approach. No matter how fast you come in, you must round off at the bottom and you are an easy target during that uneasy time. You must not be low and slow and in plain view of the enemy during that lonely period. I found this theory pretty common and mastered the combat approach. But I did not like the float at the bottom. I felt there must be a better way but what did I know, I was still just a FNG.

7

WHAM

IN any guerrilla conflict the primary goal, indeed the essence of victory, is to win the hearts and minds of the people—called WHAM by the GI. The support of the people is water for the insurgent fish that would die without it. I witnessed several elements in WHAM at Pleiku. The Red Cross helicopter was a great force in the battle for the hearts and minds and so were our Special Forces and Medical Civic Action Program (MEDCAP) teams. Another effort, the Strategic Hamlet program, initiated by the Republic of Viet Nam (RVN) was a disaster. Modeled after the successful British counterinsurgency effort in Malaya, the peasant was removed from his land into a fortified compound, a strategic hamlet. The idea was to protect the peasant and isolate the VC. Under the assumption that everything outside the hamlet was enemy, much of it became free fire zones. Anything that moved could be killed.

The free fire zones yielded few VC casualties but the critters there provided excellent practice for gunship pilots. On my first flight into a free fire zone in support of a combat assault, the lead chopper radioed that he had spotted an element of the Viet Cong transportation service and was going in for the kill. We broke off and followed him. I was a bit shocked to see him unload on a lone elephant ambling down a trail. I don't know to this day if the enemy used the unfortunate beast logistically but I do know we captured its tusks, sliced them in half and mounted them behind the bar of our WETSU (We Eat This Shit Up) club.

It did not take long for the propaganda-shrewd VC to label the Hamlets as prisons and infiltrate them. I agreed with the VC. To force someone from his home in the name of freedom made no sense to me. Thankfully, the program was aborted.

A great part of WHAM was our Special Forces (SF) or Green Berets. They traced their heritage to the famous Devil Brigade, a highly trained U.S./Canadian unit designed to operate behind enemy lines in World War II. They were organized in 1952 and introduced into Viet Nam in 1957. Initially they focused on training indigenous people to defend themselves from the communists. They worked with the Civilian Irregular Defense Group (CIDG) who were local civilian volunteers paid to fight the Communists. The SF eventually spread throughout Viet Nam with many posted along the borders to monitor the Ho Chi Minh Trail. In the Pleiku area, most CIDG were Montagnards. The Green Berets were a favorite of President John Kennedy and his administration later moved them into an offensive posture. They were embraced by the local people as they used their exceptional expertise to enhance the quality of life for all those they supported. Not only did they protect the peasants from communists' terrorism, they built roads and schools, dug wells, and provided medical care and supplies. I was at first alarmed and then amazed to see a SF enlisted medic amputate a gangrenous finger of a young boy.

(An SF friend related an unusual Montagnard "medical" procedure. A Montagnard mother, to relieve the distress of her crying baby, "sucked on his peter"—it worked! Although my friend feigned similar distress, no similar RX was forthcoming.)

They provided both the fish and the fishing pole for these backward people and dealt a serious blow to the VC fish who tried to swim in their waters. They were a jewel in the counter insurgency effort and captured the hearts and mind of the people wherever they served.

One of my missions at Pleiku was to fly the MEDCAP personnel to remote villages and camps in our Area of Operation (AO). The purpose of the MEDCAP was to provide outpatient care to those isolated from medical facilities. Many of these people had never seen a physician, let alone a dentist, in their life; nor had our medical personnel ever seen such hygienic squalor and medical need in their life. These two came together with wondrous results. The MEDCAP would eventually treat up to 225,000 civilian outpatients per month. They also vaccinated 17,000 per month, mostly children, and vaccinated and treated their livestock as well. I deeply admired the young doctors, dentists, and enlisted medics who risked their lives to care for these poor people. They cared for all, enemy and friendly, Vietnamese and Montagnard—no ID required. Their philosophy is best summed up by then Captain Keith Markey, a MEDCAP medic: "A helping hand should not be based on reciprocation, but only on the heart of the giver." I would fly them to a village or camp deep in the jungle and leave them there until night fall when I would pick them up—if the weather permitted. On occasion they were left overnight surrounded by the enemy, and the fleas, unprotected and sitting ducks for the VC who hated them for the good will they generated in the cause of freedom.

It is surprising how knowledge of the truth can do so much good; and how often the truth is resisted by custom or ignorance. The children suffered from a severe protein deficiency and the adults were stingy with their rat meat. The MEDCAP solved the problem by planting peanuts.

And although the adults resisted any new form of hygiene, the children could be taught to brush their teeth. And of course, this is the answer to much of the problems in the world. There is nothing we can do for most adults; terrorists simply have to be killed. Change will come, but only following a proper education of the children.

I had been at Pleiku less than two months when Kelly came to visit. The teamwork of the Montagnards and Special Forces had subdued the communists' activity in the Highlands. We were carrying few casualties and things were heating up in the Mekong Delta south of Saigon. Kelly decided to move the choppers at Pleiku and Qui Nhon to Soc Trang in the Delta in anticipation of an increase in casualties there. The two choppers would make up Detachment A of the 57th. Kelly would go to Soc Trang and set things up beginning 1 March. Once the detachment was operational, I would come down and command it. I was ecstatic, not only at the chance of increased combat flying, but because Kelly was putting me in charge. It was not as if he handpicked me for the job, I was the ranking pilot available, but I was still delighted. Dick Anderson would go with Kelly to the Delta. In the meantime, I would fly out of Saigon. My Pleiku co-pilot went on to distinguish himself as a gunship pilot, a duty better suited to his disposition.

Pleiku had not been a total loss. I had improved my flying skills not only in executing the death spiral and landing through a cloud of dust, but also in dealing with the vagaries of terrain. I also learned a great deal about the kind of war we were fighting and how valuable our red crossed helicopters were to victory. I would not return to Pleiku until my second tour and then under tragic circumstances. I picked up my cross bow, my VC gong, my rat trap, and the F*** Ox horns and headed for Saigon.

8

DUTY IN THE PEARL OF THE ORIENT

SAIGON was a breath of clear air after the red dust of Pleiku.
The pilots got some time off and could experience the culture
unique to this pearl of the orient. My dear friend and stick buddy
from flight school, Bill Cawthorne, visited me on his way to assignment up north. Together we explored this shopper's Garden of Eden
and learned the language, essentially number 1, good; number 10,
bad. I was amazed to see people relieve themselves in public. One
field was an open-air latrine and could be smelled for blocks. We
initially snickered about males who wandered about holding hands.
But it was a culturally natural custom of a wonderful loving and
hard-working people.

The exchange rate between dollars and piasters, Vietnamese cur-
rency known as P, was excellent. The French influence was ubiquitous, excellent food and everything was cheap. We could afford the
cabs, ride the cyclos, and buy or have custom made about anything
at Cheap Charlie's on the famous Tu Do Street. You could get a
haircut, massage, and manicure for a few cents. The massage ended

with a neck snap which hurt like hell. In my life, only the rich could afford such luxuries. I promptly stopped biting my fingernails so I could experience a manicure. I could actually afford to tailor my fatigues and design my own and my wife's clothes, more rich people stuff. It would be years before society caught up with some of my designs. But my wife did not like them. I was shocked to discover in later years that she used a house fire as an excuse to get rid of the elephant, snake, and alligator shoes with matching purses and belts I sent her. Not even the black leather coat with bright yellow lining and a collar and belt of genuine Jaguar that I personally designed and loved, impressed her. I noticed them in the closet *after the burning*, but never saw them again.

Elephant foot ottomans, ivory objects, endangered animal furs, and other items that would drive the animal rights folks nuts were abundant. Exotic pets unaffordable in the states were plentiful and inexpensive. I bought a beautiful Myna bird for $3, monkeys were $4, and beautiful baby ocelots went for $5 (it occurred to me then that if we took all the endangered animals and put them up for sale, they would be plentiful). It was quite a city. A GI could buy some pretty exotic things cheap—and catch some as well. In one colorful shopping site, known as Hundred P Alley, the ladies sold their wares for one hundred P—or 80 cents U.S.

The streets were full of the most beautiful panhandlers in the world, petite flower girls. I soon had my very own flower girl, beautiful to behold, who sold me flowers for which I had no earthly use. I wanted to adopt her but my wife reminded me that we already had four of our own. Still, it was a thrill to visit with her as a substitute for my own children who I dearly missed.

Our operations and supply shacks were on Tan Son Nhut airfield close to our three Dust Off aircraft. We got excellent maintenance from a nearby aviation unit. The terrain around Saigon and to the south was flat, checkered with rice paddies, a few jungles, and some rubber and tea plantations. Typically canals and rivers surrounded the rice paddies which were crisscrossed with dikes, narrow roads, and trails. It was essentially a gigantic forced landing area.

As you flew north, the forced landing areas decreased and the dense jungles increased. The terrain there was dominated by a 3,000-foot mountain called Nui Ba Den or Black Virgin Mountain, named for a young woman who died on its slopes while in search of her lover. All of a sudden there it was, out of nowhere, a serious problem as some Dust Off pilots in search of the wounded on dark nights would learn.

There were some dusty LZs but nothing like the rusty clay dust of Pleiku. And, hallelujah, there were few if any plague, rabies, leprosy, or other exotic patients. We had an excellent Navy hospital in the middle of the city as well as a Vietnamese hospital conveniently located next to a soccer field. The route into the Navy hospital took us right over a massive public swimming pool. It was a bit eerie to fly over a pool full of frolicking happy swimmers with a load of suffering patients from a nearby battlefield.

There had been a military coup since I left for Pleiku. There would be seven coups in 1964 and it would be some time before we knew who was in charge. In the meantime, each new leader was labeled a puppet by the communists. Unfortunately the Kennedy administration had been involved in the murder of the one significant South Vietnamese leader, Ngo Dinh Diem. At the time, I was in flight school with several of Diem's pilots. They were heartbroken. Regrettably many in the media and elsewhere celebrated the death of Diem and his brother. Shortly thereafter, when Kennedy was killed, and many of us were devastated, the Vietnamese pilots reminded us of how they felt over Diem's death.

During this time of coups, the city was dangerous, especially the bars. One night Bill and I were having a drink when the waitress dropped a tray. The place emptied in seconds. We would sit at dinner on the top of the Rex Hotel and watch firefights across the countryside; and lie in our bunks at night and hear bars blow up. They also blew up a floating restaurant and sunk a ship, the USS *Card*, in the Saigon River. They could have dropped a bomb anywhere. We worried more about bombs than bullets, which had hit few Dust Off aircraft up to this time. While bullets can be annoying, often scary, bombs are always terrifying.

One day three of us were in a jeep on the way to work when suddenly there was a loud pop and a sizzle, and then smoke filled the jeep. The driver hit at the brake and jumped out and so did everyone else but me. I was trapped in the middle in the back seat. I noticed that the problem was from a live wire on the radio that came loose and was jumping wildly and sparking. The good news was that there was no bomb; but the jeep was still moving, in fact straight at a deuce and a half-ton Army truck. I reached over the driver's seat to steer it past the truck until I could climb in the front and get it stopped.

The unit was transitioning to Kelly. Most of the combat arms pilots were gone and we were filling up with inexperienced young MSC pilots. There was some friction over who would be in command on missions. Kelly, although he was the unit commander, was subject to the command of a unit pilot on the mission when the troops drowned under his skids. The other pilot would not allow him to put his skids in the water. Aviation is unusual in that command can shift from the ground to the air. On the ground, there is no question that the colonel in the jeep tells the driver what to do. The colonel in the helicopter may have no say about what the pilot does. Only after extensive check outs and orientations can a new pilot be a pilot in command or AC, and even then he may be under the command of a lower ranking pilot who had more flying hours or time on station.

I had spent three years in command positions in a battle group in Berlin, surrounded by some of the finest troops in the Army. I had a different idea of command. My belief was that the pilot was just another equipment operator, albeit pretty skilled, but as such should be subject to the same rules as the rest of the Army. Certainly there should be an orientation period before missions but there was little time for that in Viet Nam. I had no orientation and, as noted, could not even start the Huey when I arrived in country. But none of that affected my judgment or ability to command which should be based on my rank, not my hours in the air. If the captain was not as capable as the warrant officer in the air, never mind if he was an FNG, something was wrong with the captain.

I recommended that pilot in command orders be published on every pilot and that the ranking pilot be in charge of the mission. I will say that my view is not the norm and was the subject of much criticism. But Kelly bought in and the FNGs loved it. There were some spats after this but there was never any question about who was in charge. And we never had any crashes as the pilots fought for the controls (which did happen).

Although my crew said we were shot at several times in Pleiku, I could never tell who was shooting at whom when everyone was shooting. (Some crew members said they could tell the difference between enemy and friendly fire. I could not. And some crewmen used enemy weapons as well as those from other countries.) Saigon would be different. The communists were much busier than at Pleiku. Within a week of my arrival, a colonel who lived next to us was shot down. All they found was his hand and one of his eagles. Tragically his wife was living with him at the time. Another Huey went down in a river and two crewmen drowned. They were flying escort for McNamara during a visit in which he declared that we would stay as long as it took for victory. We had seven ships hit in one week, which was more than in the previous two years. Two of them were mine.

Equally tragic, we were losing people in accidents. One friend on a mission with 12 souls on board lost his entire tail boom at 2,200 feet. The loss of torque protection sent the fuselage into a violent spin, slinging six poor souls through the door of the bird to their death. He managed to streamline the aircraft a bit and actually landed upright. He was the only survivor of the crash but died soon after. Many of these accidents resulted in severe burns and identification of the remains was a serious problem. When two other friends crashed and burned, the morticians called me in to identify the remains. What I found was two balls of black flesh, which smelled exactly like burned steak, with a mortician chipping at them for information. I was urged to sign a paper specifying the identity of the dead. It would have solved his problem. Although the names of the crew were known, and I knew both pilots, there was no way I could say who was who. I refused to sign. I left realizing that there may be a few widows putting flowers on a stranger's grave.

Our losses were nothing compared to the carnage of Vietnamese caused by the terrorist tactics of the communists. In one day I carried more Vietnamese patients than an entire week at Pleiku. One mission took us to the Plain of Reeds southwest of Saigon near the Cambodian border. An outpost had been attacked the previous night and there were many civilian casualties. The enemy had actually hid in a drainage ditch and inched his way toward the camp after dark. As we flew into the camp I noticed what looked like a pile of arms and legs. It was not, it was babies stacked like fire wood. I had never seen anything like it. Why were they stacked? Why were they killed? My crew was shocked. I was also but less so. Those children were slaughtered by communists. In Berlin, I had watched communists of a different race, but same evil, build a wall around their own people and shoot those who climbed the wall. They would not allow our maid through the wall to attend her parents' funeral. And our baby sitter, who was engaged to an East Berliner, never saw him again. A Dust Off pilot recalled another village over run by the communists. The children were soaked with gas, set on fire, and the parents forced to watch them running and screeching as they burned to death. As Dust Off pilots we would witness many such communists' atrocities.

Tragically, the enemy was not the only source of fatalities. Enemy caused casualties are easier to live with than those killed accidentally by friendlies, often because of ignorance but more often because of poor communication. On one horrifying pickup, we landed behind a low hill. The ARVN were positioned to our front firing over the crest of the hill. Among the patients was a baby. I noticed a young woman on the hill to the front crying, her arms stretched toward the baby as we loaded it. She struggled to get up but was held down by a soldier. Suddenly she broke loose and ran toward our bird. I watched in horror screaming as her former ARVN captive shot her—right under our blades. She fell and never moved. I yelled at my medic, who held her crying baby in his arms, to check her. She was dead.

I could not understand what in the hell happened. Did they think she was a VC? I could not find out. But we learned that she had been told she could not go with her baby. Why? Because she was not wounded and the ARVN thought we were there only for the wounded. This was nuts. We never said that. But someone did. There is no telling how many people are dead because of such tragic failures to communicate. From then on, we briefed those in the PZ that we wanted a responsible adult with every child. Otherwise how would that child ever get home? Additionally, the hospitals were overcrowded and any extra help was priceless.

· 9 ·

GHOST RIDERS IN THE SKY

I had been flying out of Saigon about three weeks when I experienced the strangest flight of my life. Late one evening Si Simmons and I were en route to the small village of Cao Lanh to pickup three patients when the crew signaled that we were being tracked by another aircraft slightly above and to our left. We flipped on the rotating beacon but the other bird remained steady on our tail. Two days earlier, one of our L-19s had been shot down by a T-28 out of Cambodia. I was not aware of the incident but Si was and made the connection immediately. He took the controls and began evasive action. The crew then began to scream that it was making passes at us. We were not a match for a T-28 in the air and Si dove for the ground as the crew screamed that other bird was close behind us, first on one side, then the other. Si rode that bird to a fare-thee-well, pitch black on the deck, zig-zagging across the rice paddies, jumping the trees too often at the last moment. An amusement park would pay a ton for that ride, but I was not enjoying this trip.

Suddenly the crew screamed that we were on fire. I checked the fire detection light and looked back at the engine. I saw no fire but did see the flashing beacon. I switched it off as we neared the river north of Vinh Long. We jumped the river and landed at Vinh Long all of us completely exhausted and our crew terrified by what they had seen. Other aircraft monitored our verbal anguish but no one saw the other aircraft and it did not register on radar. Night does strange things to people. I did not see the other bird but did see lights behind us. And there was no question about the panic of the crew. They must have known about the L-19 shoot down also.

We wrote up statements and flew home. Humor is an inescapable part of tragedy, indeed, often an escape from tragedy. But one man's comedy is another man's calamity. Our fellow troops had a ball with this one. Brady and Si chased by ghost riders in the sky—or could it have been aliens? Surely it was a UFO. Kelly wanted to know what the hell happened and threatened to never again let Si and I fly together. We were not laughing and neither was our crew, but to this day we do not know what the hell happened.

PORTABLE RED CROSSES

SHORTLY after his arrival, Kelly began an historic a battle with his boss, General Stilwell. "Cider Joe" was a combat hungry character and a damn tough one. I heard he survived a jump when his parachute failed to open. He was not an aviator but he flew—or tried to; and when he wasn't flying, he rode as door gunner. Later he would be lost at sea in an ancient Thai airplane, probably with him at the controls, illegally. Some folks waited a long time for him to walk up off the ocean floor.

General William Westmoreland (Westy), who took command of all forces in Viet Nam on 20 June, identified Stilwell as one of the most colorful characters in the Army. He tells the story about an inspection trip with Cider Joe. At one company they found the unit bulletin board surrounded by female pin-ups. Westy rebuked the commander for posting required reading in a background which could be distracting and to which some GIs might object. The truth be told, Westy, who was a gentleman's gentleman, was probably personally offended. At that point Stilwell broke in: "By God, sir, you are right. I never thought of it that way. We'll poll the unit, and if we find somebody who objects, we'll have him transferred." Westy was aware that Stilwell flew as a door gunner and did not think such was proper duty for his generals. It may have been the reason Stilwell never got a second star although his replacement wore two stars. It was in his capacity as a door gunner that Kelly and Stilwell met.

Kelly was called into a rice paddy to transfer some patients from a gunship. The door gunner in the gunship was helping to move patients to Kelly's bird who he complained were bleeding all over his chopper. The door gunner was Stilwell. Unlike too many commanders in combat, they could not get him out of the field. He hated an office and so did Kelly. They were a lot alike, both brown-shoe-black-and-white types. But Stilwell was a problem. He wanted Kelly's aircraft.

The year before Kelly took command, the 57th had evacuated a miserly 1,972 patients. Their birds spent a lot of time on the ground and that bothered Stilwell. The Huey was originally designed for aeromedical evacuation but it was the crème de la crème of rotor aircraft and was modified for guns and troop lifts. Stilwell wanted our ships available for those missions. Stilwell's concept was to use the slack time for missions of his choice and then slap a portable red cross on them when a Dust Off came up. He told Kelly's predecessor that the medics with Temperilli spent a lot of time sitting on their asses and he was not impressed with their performance. (He failed to mention that it is difficult to fly when someone takes parts off your birds.) He had taken their A model Hueys away and gave them to the Utility Tactical Helicopter Company (UTT), the Army's first gunship unit. He would later put the 57th under the control of a transportation unit, a scheme that was doomed to fail—which it quickly did. The transportation guys were not trained as medics; that's why they were called transportation soldiers.

Stilwell did not have a clue about aeromedical combat operations. But neither did anyone else at this point. Aeromedical evacuation was in its infancy and, despite some good experience in Korea, there was no doctrine or special training for Dust Off pilots other than their basic medical training. But, worst of all, Dust Off had no champion. Control could go in any direction. The Marines had no red-cross marked aircraft. Their patient evacuation was essentially a logistics mission which was what Stilwell's plan would do to the Army. A rational person would wonder why anyone would put portable red crosses on a ground ambulance and use it for ash and trash until someone got hurt and then slap on a red cross. No one would dream of putting a part time red cross on them. Dust Off was no different than a ground ambulance except that it flew. Kelly was appalled. The two of them went toe to toe.

"How about part-time flight line fire trucks, General?" Kelly asked, "They spend a lot of time on their ass, but it is damn nice to have them when your ass is on fire." Kelly was not intimidated by anything, much less rank. We heard that the staff would suck their heads into their necks when Kelly and Stilwell were in the same room. Stilwell boasted that the Surgeon General was a personal friend and would rule in his favor. Kelly replied that the Surgeon General might be his friend but he was no damn fool. One of Stilwell's colonels, a strong proponent of portable red crosses, was appalled at Kelly's belligerence: "Kelly, when I write your efficiency report, it will be lower than whale shit on the bottom of the ocean." To which Kelly replied, "Colonel, you just scare the dog shit out of me."

Stilwell was no different than many commanders. He wanted control, control of everything and everybody in his AO, whether he understood what they did or not. And there was some logic in his reasoning. Down time happened especially if Dust Off was confined to direct support of one unit or class of patients, i.e., only Americans as was the case when the 57th arrived. The pilot was essential in patient regulation, which required medical training; but the medic was the key to patient treatment en route to the hospital. In truth, for many missions, any pilot could be at the controls and the 57th was living proof since some of our best pilots were combat arms and later warrant officers. But a medically trained pilot could be handy in mass casualty triage. Although I experienced many mass casualty events, I only got out and helped triage once. And that was once too much.

In any mass casualty situation, it is essential that the commander be relieved of his wounded as soon as possible. Prolonged involvement with casualties is sure to generate more casualties. Therefore, we would do all in our power to get the WIA and KIA out of the battle zone quickly. This often involved dropping them in a safe spot in the field where the medics could triage them for backhaul to a hospital. In my one experience, the physician asked my entire crew to help him after we had dropped our last load from the battle zone. Dead and wounded were scattered all over the place. The area reeked of the unmistakable, indescribable, unforgettable smell of blood. This was my first experience with up-close and personal carnage. Amazingly I did not faint. I was surprised at the spectrum of colors on the inside of a human body—and the thickness of the flesh around the skull. I was near the physician as he treated a soldier with a severe belly wound. Both hands were in the belly. He shouted at me to get him a hemostat. I looked. Where? He nodded to the skull of another soldier. A missile had split the soldier's head which was severely swollen. His eyes were bulging and he looked as if his face was about to detonate. A lone hemostat was holding it all together. His breathing was ghastly but he was alive and looking right at me. I hesitated. The doctor asked again with urgency. Get it. I did. The man was still looking at me as his head exploded. I can't count the dead faces I have seen on the battlefield, but this face, and a man without a face, are faces I will never forget.

Another patient was equally unforgettable. Both his eyes were open, one wider than the other, and a misty white color. His face was yellow except for the blotches of red all over it. His mouth was open and all his gold teeth stared out at me. I thought he was dead but noticed his Adam's apple twitching, not another thing on his face moved except the Adam's apple and it twitched all the way to the hospital.

After meeting with Stilwell, Kelly called us together and said quite simply that the folks in headquarters did not wish us well. He was not sure when the issue would be decided but if the 57th was to survive as a medical resource under medical control, we would have to prove that no one could do what we did as well as we did it and that what we did was vital. If we failed, the welfare of the wounded soldier would be changed forever. None of us were sure just what this meant. There were only 16,000 U.S. troops in the country. They were our primary mission and they suffered few casualties. We also carried Vietnamese if their helicopters were not available or "broke," as they reported. Their birds were frequently "broke" not only because they flew the maintenance demanding H-34s but because Charlie would cut off the head of any ARVN pilot he caught. It was mostly a five-day war. Some officers actually had their families with them. (After he took command, General Westmoreland sent all families home.) One of our pilots sang in downtown nightclubs. We were not a very visible asset, certainly not one anyone would miss. But Stilwell was taking a medical resource away from medical command and control, something unprecedented in American combat operations since the Civil War. What he was doing would seriously jeopardize the availability of helicopter ambulances for the patients. While Kelly plotted to save Dust Off, the rest of us wondered if we would become gunship or slick ship (troop carrying) pilots.

Kelly wasn't the only one trying to prove something. Earlier agreements between the Army and Air Force imposed on the Army two dimensions and gave the Air Force the air. Contrary to the agreement, the Army saw a combat air role for themselves in the development of the armed helicopter for close air support. Viet Nam could be a great laboratory to develop and test gunships to be known as "Hogs." The Army formed the UTT Company for this purpose. Many in the Air Force considered the helicopter Neanderthallic but did not challenge the Army's development of armed choppers.

The UTT was led by the legendary Pat Delavan, at one time possibly the most decorated soldier in Viet Nam. He ended his tour with seven Purple Hearts (PH) and two Distinguished Service Crosses (DSC). He knew the Air Force would one day challenge the Army on the close air support mission and was out to prove the superiority of the helicopter for this mission. Delavan's men, like him, were hard chargers, totally fearless, the match of any pilot ever. Delavan, like Kelly, was in unmapped territory and a close relationship developed between them. In one of the many times Delavan was shot down, Kelly went in to rescue him and the two of them then stood shoulder to shoulder and destroyed the downed bird with their rifles (to deny its use by the enemy). On many other occasions, Delavan's Hogs protected Kelly and Dust Off as they landed under fire to rescue the wounded.

As Kelly worked to prove the worth of Dust Off, the UTT did the same. They continually rigged and re-rigged the Huey with various armaments and then tested it in combat. They actually used a grease mark on the windshield for gun sights—a notch below Kentucky windage for accuracy. I had watched them chase and miss VC in open rice paddies and take several runs to hit a VC hooch. I must say I was initially not impressed with their grease mark wet finger accuracy. But I did meet one gunship pilot who did very well with his grease mark, thank God.

Late one afternoon we were called out to the Laotian border to rescue the crew of a downed C-123. We would need a guide to ensure we did not fly into Laos. It was getting dark and the ceiling was low when we met the guide in a field near the Laotian border. We had to expedite before the weather and darkness closed in but he said we were only a 1,000 meters from the crash. He would lead us in with Dust Off in the slot and a gunship on each side.

We flew, and flew, and flew; far more than enough time to go a click. I was sure we were in Laos or worse—lost. I tried to radio my concerns but could not raise anyone. Suddenly an outpost appeared to our front containing several tin roofed buildings. We were almost on the compound when it opened up sending a sheath of red fire up into the clouds. The guide ship was hit and broke off. There was nowhere for me to go. I dared not go up in the clouds in the mountains and I could not turn either direction or I would hit a gunship. I was headed right into the wall of fire. Then our bird shuddered as the gunship on my right cut loose with his rockets. The next thing I saw was tin roofs going up toward the clouds. What a shot!

The firing stopped but not before we got hit and a gunship pilot was shot in the arm. Luckily, the bullets hit our box of C rations (C rats) and saved the bird from being seriously damaged. We had enough Cs left for a meal and spent the night in the field. The next day we went another direction and found the tail of the C-123 on top of a deep gorge, the fuselage was at the bottom. The crew had died in the crash and someone had thoughtfully buried them, albeit minus their wrist watches.

GENEVA, THE DEAD, AND PREVENTIVE MEDICINE

I had my only serious confrontation with Kelly soon after I arrived in Saigon. Brian Conway, our supply officer, and I were called out on a mission near Phan Thiet, a former residence of Ho Chi Minh, a.k.a. Uncle Ho, about 45 minutes from Saigon. Ho's disciples were active and the ARVN were in a serious fight. We flew east along Route 1, known as the Street Without Joy, and landed at the airfield four clicks south of the city. We met with the advisers and made arrangements for the patients. We would pull them out of the jungle and other aircraft would backhaul them to the hospital. The fight was in thick jungle a few clicks west of the airfield. Initially, things were quiet. Our first load included a Vietnamese civilian (or Viet Cong, it was hard to tell the difference) who was shot in the leg. Our medic checked him and rewrapped the leg. As we touched down the medic yelled that the guy was dying. We jumped out to see what had happened. The patient was foaming at the mouth and gasping. Brian bent over to give him mouth to mouth despite the mess. Thankfully we had an airway tube which was more sanitary and Brian worked hard to resuscitate him. But he died.

We were both puzzled and upset that a simple leg wound could kill him. We did not want the roof of our chopper to be the last earthly vision of anyone—especially if it was unnecessary. Our job was to save lives. No one should die from a bullet wound to the leg. The lesson was that we had to be more careful in monitoring our patients. We knew that you had to check the entire body, front and back, but we had missed something and the man was dead. I was beginning to realize how important routine and details and procedures were. I was determined this would not happen again and as far as I know, this was the only patient who ever died while in my chopper unless they were shot.

Things began to heat up and we got busy hauling patients into the Phan Thiet airfield. An L-19 fixed-wing reconnaissance bird, call sign 23 Enjoy, was in the area directing artillery and helping us find the patients. Almost every pickup was in tight confined areas in deep jungle. We had to come to a stop over the site and hover straight down. At that point, we were vulnerable but unless the enemy was in friendly lines, we were safe as we went down through the trees. In due course, we got too high, or some of Uncle Ho's supporters were mixed in with the friendlies, and we took hits, some in the fuel cell. Thankfully the fuel cells in the Hueys, unlike earlier aircraft, had improved and were virtually self sealing. They seldom blew up during a crash. In another chopper, the rounds, especially tracers, could have blown us out of the sky or, if we were shot down and lived through the crash, we would have then had to escape from a burning aircraft.

We were at the airfield checking to see if our bird was still fly-able when a U.S. adviser walked up and asked if we would take some ammo in on our next trip. Brian and I looked at each other. The bird was flyable but there was a serious question about using a red cross marked resource for hauling ammo. Brian had been in the country longer than I had but had not faced this issue before. I sensed some uneasiness in him. I was the ranking officer and had to make a decision. The adviser made it clear that the friendlies were in serious trouble and in desperate need of ammo. There was no other way to get it to them. The bullet holes in our Red Cross aircraft were proof that the enemy was ignoring the Geneva Accords and I decided that we would also.

We flew the ammo in as we flew the patients out. Suddenly 23 Enjoy cried out that he was hit in his fuel cell. The L-19 fuel cells were not self-sealing and he was on fire. I had him in sight. His next transmission was that he was going in. We watched him dive into the trees and marked the spot with his smoke. There was an open area within a few hundred yards of where he crashed. I immediately landed hoping to get to the pilots before they burned. Brian took the controls with the understanding that he would leave if things got hot. I grabbed my shotgun and ammo and headed into the jungle. I grew up in the woods and felt comfortable in that terrain. I worked my way through the dense undergrowth to the smoking crash site breaking out right on the L-19. It was still on fire in the bank of a creek right in front of me. The first thing I saw was the pilot in the back leaning over on the pilot in front. He had been trying to get out. They were both on fire and had burned together. They toppled toward me as I approached the plane. I verified that they were dead and ran back to my bird.

There was some shooting in the area but Brian held on for me. We flew back to the airfield and reported the fatalities. American combat deaths were rare, 100 or so at this point, and got a lot of attention. The ARVN agreed to divert to the crash and recover the American bodies. Although the patient flow stopped as night fell, and the dead were not an authorized mission, we decided to wait for the recovery and bring the American remains home with us. It took some time to recover the bodies and it was late at night when we headed for Tan Son Nhut. Much to my discomfort, I got word that Kelly wanted to see me when we landed. I was surprised to find that many of the 57th pilots were also waiting for us. They had been monitoring our missions.

Kelly took me to one side, a certain sign I was going to get a severe ass chewing; something not properly done in the presence of others. In his slow, measured, menacing manner he drawled, "Brady, what in the hell were you thinking of, carrying that ammo?" I had no idea how he knew, but I knew I was in trouble. "Sir, I was practicing preventive medicine," was my reply. "And the dead?" "Sir, they are now angels, how could I refuse them?" I did not know it then but Kelly had a thing about angels. I did, too. My angel is named Terry and he has looked out for me my whole life.

He looked at me, his mouth dropped a tad, his eyes seemed to twinkle a bit, and we returned to the group. He then told them that the missions we flew that day were the kind of missions he wanted to see the 57th fly. We had flown seven and a half hours of missions, rescued a lot of patients, took some hits, and made a hit with the guys on the ground. He never said exactly that he was proud of us but I sensed he was, and I was able to sleep that night. I never heard a word about the ammo from him again and never again hesitated to carry it, or anything else that would help the grunts, including their dead.

Kelly showed me something. I instinctively liked this man. I knew that I would not get the lash for the ammo; as the commander he would. He knew that also. The Red Cross ammo Geneva connection could have easily been blown up by some starched headquarters type, or the media. It is easy to find a boss who will stand by you when the buck stops with him, not so easy when it stops at his boss. He thought it over and agreed with me and to hell with the bureaucrats. This man was a match for Stilwell or anyone else who tried to mess with us. But I was not a match for Stilwell.

A TRAITOR IN THE 57TH

I was terrorized when Stilwell called me in shortly after this mission. No reason, no subject, just—the general wants to see you. It was Saint Patrick's Day and I was looking forward to falling off the wagon and celebrating. The 17th fell on a Tuesday, a day of phobia for me. Up to this point, I had never talked to a general and had no desire to do so. When I reported in, I found two other officers also waiting for me. One was the G2, the intelligence officer for Stilwell's command. The other was his deputy, a white-haired colonel who was highly respected by all. He epitomized the officer gentleman from the old school and was a World War II veteran.

The G2 opened the meeting by stating that he had revoked my security clearance and was recommending that General Stilwell dismiss me from the theater and I be processed for elimination. I was stunned. This could not be happening, not after all the disasters of the past year. As I sat there listening to the G2 denounce my character and pronounce that I was a security threat, my thoughts went back a few months to a rainy winter day in a cemetery in Maryland as my wife and I and our three children watched in anguish as my fourth child was lowered into a grave.

I had recently been reassigned stateside from my first Army duty station in Berlin, Germany. I was in the Intelligence School at Fort Holibird, Maryland, studying to be an Imagery Interpreter. My career was not off to a good start. Shortly after arriving at Holibird, I got a "Buck Up" letter from the Surgeon General's Office. The letter stated that my Officer Efficient Reports (OERs) from Berlin were subpar and I should use my new assignment to buck up and get on the right track. The letter noted that my superiors had found me to be headstrong, opinionated, inflexible, and not inclined to cooperate; none of which are desirable characteristics for a lieutenant.

The consequences if I did not improve would be removal from the Army. I was staggered. I thought I had done well in Berlin and felt any report to the contrary was not fair. My unit certainly performed during the time the Berlin Wall was being built in a unique situation, surrounded by communists. (In fact, my company was rated tops in the command.) Needless to say, that letter lowered my morale but I resolved that I would prove them wrong no matter how hard I had to work to do so.

Shortly after school began I was called out of class and told to report to the dispensary. I could get no details over the phone and rushed to the dispensary where I found my wife sobbing uncontrollably with three of our children. Our youngest, baby Terry, was not there. The physician motioned me to come with him to a room where he pointed to Terry lying on a slab. He was dead. I cannot describe the feeling of hopelessness, of helplessness. I refused to believe it, demanded that he be sure. What had happened? I was beside myself. There is no way to describe the horror of such a moment. I have never experienced anything like it since. No matter the circumstances, you never get over the guilt and to this day, I have not. That poor baby is in your care. He depends on you for everything. He is dead. Somehow you let him down, there can be no excuse.

The worst part was that you could not just stop and grieve. You had to move on; I had to go back to school. And I had to bury my son. I had no idea how I would be able to pay for the funeral. We lived from paycheck to paycheck. There was nothing that resembled savings. It was then I discovered The Army Emergency Relief. They were organized to help soldiers like me. They called me in and offered to help pay for the funeral. And they did. I have tried to pay them back over the years but there is no way I can ever fully do that. The Army really does take care of its own. This experience made me more determined than ever to be a good soldier.

After the funeral, I put everything I had into the classes. I was sure things would get better. They certainly could not get worse—but they did. I had seen the Army at its best when Terry died; now I would see it at its worst.

Shortly after my baby's death, the spooks called me in. During my background investigation they discovered I had a record, some arrests I had not reported in my applications for the security clearance required of all officers. I was sure they had made a mistake. Some members of my family did have criminal records but not me. Both my brothers would die as ex-convicts being convicted of murder, attempted murder, and various drug and assault charges. Two of my uncles also served time. There was no mistake, it was me. I did have some minor scrapes with the law but was told at the time, and during my commissioning process at ROTC, that none of them resulted in my having a reportable record and there was no need to include them in my official record. And I didn't.

They decided to give me a lie detector test to see if I was telling the truth, if I was intellectually honest, and whether or not I was a security risk. The result was that I was not intellectually honest and would be dismissed from the intelligence school as a security risk. But I would not be kicked out of the Army. I was not allowed to return to class even to get my notes. The down from that experience was second only to Terry's death. A minor security breach is enough to end a career. Getting kicked out of Intelligence School is beyond the pale. It was a minor miracle I was not boarded out immediately.

Now what? I called the Surgeon General's office. They knew of my dismissal. The voice on the other end was sympathetic but he had no place to assign me. I asked about flight school. I applied twice previously for flight training but there were no slots. He said he would check. It turned out there were no openings in the next class but they could put me to work in the Hospital at Camp Wolters, Texas the Army helicopter basic school, until a slot opened up.

Camp Wolters was a hot desolate place and my family settled into housing that featured an occasional scorpion in the front room and a yard full of tarantulas. At this time, a large percentage of each class washed out. Although I always knew I would fly someday, my IP was not impressed with my aviation abilities and bombarded me with pink slips. I had no doubt what the Army would do to me if I busted out of flight school. Throughout this ordeal, my stick buddy, Bill Cawthorne, who was doing well and soloed early, coached and cajoled and encouraged me. Flight school was tough and in any tough situation you become close to those who share it with you. I think I would have given up were it not for him. I was within one hour of the mandatory solo time when my IP announced he could not solo me. He said I was dangerous. But he would turn me over to another IP for one last chance before I was washed out.

The new IP took me around the flight pattern once without a word, then told me to set it down on the grass next to the runway—and got out. I soloed minutes from the washout time. The solo splash in the pond was one of the happiest moments of my life. Bill was as happy as I was. I earned my wings, a three-year obligation, and immediately volunteered for Viet Nam.

As I came back to the present, I felt a crush from all the calamity of the past year. How could things get worse? But they did. Here I am Lord, where are you? I sat there choked up and numb as the G2 finished assassinating my character. He was adamant that I be removed from the command immediately and be boarded for elimination from service. Then the deputy began.

He detailed the "preventive medicine" mission. How did he

know? He said I had risked my life by going alone into a jungle full of VC to rescue the downed L-19 crew after ordering my crew to leave me at any hint of danger. He praised me for providing ammo for surrounded troops who would have otherwise perished. He noted that I did all this under fire with an aircraft that had been damaged by enemy fire. Wow! I certainly never would have described the action that way, but I had to admit it sounded good. He certainly had Stilwell's attention. Stilwell loved combat, he was all about combat, and this was a combat story.

The deputy said there was a psychiatrist in the command experienced in the use of some new drug that could determine if I was honest. He could use that expertise to determine my trustworthiness and whether or not I was suitable to remain in Viet Nam. I guess they didn't have a lie detector. After the deputy finished, Stilwell decided to delay the recommendation of the G2 and ordered that I be evaluated by the psychiatrist. I was so sick after this meeting I forgot to celebrate St. Patrick's Day.

The psychiatrist, LT A. V. Khayat, a Navy guy, was a warm and wonderful person. After several sessions he declared that I was endowed with considerable leadership potential, an asset to the Army, fully worthy of trust and a full security clearance. He did not believe I would desert to the communists. Stilwell then decided to let me remain in his command. My career, such as it was, would continue.

The G2 was not happy. He was a handball player, as was I, and he called and asked if I would meet him at the handball courts. After acknowledging that I must think he was a SOB, he offered some advice. For my own good and the good of my family, I should resign my commission. He had carefully examined my record, read my "Buck Up letter," and was certain I had no future in the military. Someone down the line surely would take note of my discharge from the Intelligence School and seek to board me. I should get out as soon as my obligation was up.

In truth, I did not believe he was a SOB but was amazed when he told me he never minded a man who stole or drank or shacked up but I had lied about my past and that was unforgivable. I could not understand how a man could do all those things and not also be a liar. But I was sure he was doing his job and seemed to be sincere in his concern for my future. I just felt helpless throughout the entire nightmare. I did not think I was deliberately dishonest, nor did I feel I was a security risk. I would never betray my country no matter the cost. And it hurt that so many feared I would. My concern was my family and what I would do if I got boarded out of the Army. I could get a less than honorable discharge. Who would hire me? I had no place to go. We then went in the handball court and although I did not bear him ill will, I did beat the shit out of him.

The white-haired deputy made it a point to call me and encourage me to continue my career. He would later write and congratulate me on my awards. I am ashamed to say I do not recall his name but he is one of the heroes of my life and I pray for him to this day. It was clear in my mind that his comments on the mission influenced Stilwell. But where did he learn of the mission? Kelly?

After the meeting with Stilwell, I went to Kelly to explain what had happened. As my commander, he must have known of the G2 accusation and my record, and I did not want him to think I was hiding anything. He stopped me: "Brady, you don't need to explain anything to me. Just let me know how I can help you." At that moment, I felt affection for this man that I had never felt for another man. I learned later that he was recommending me for an award for the preventive medicine mission. I have no doubt he told the deputy about that mission; they were World War II buddies. He knew it would impress Stilwell. Many commanders would not want the risk of having someone with a record like mine in their command. Not Kelly. He would stick by me until I proved unworthy. Although he never showed favorites, and I don't believe he had any special feelings for me, he knew we had much in common in our backgrounds and careers—his skeletons were much like mine. I knew little of those similarities at the time but I did know I would fly down the tubes of a quad .51 for this man.

· 13 ·

THE GENIUS OF A MAD MAN

SOC Trang was in the middle of the Delta, a vast region of canals and rice paddies south of Saigon. It was the hottest fighting area in Viet Nam when Kelly and Detachment A arrived. Patient evacuation was handled with local resources which included Viet Nam Air Force (VNAF) CH 34 helicopters. The H 34 was durable piston engine helicopter that had served honorably for many years but it was not in the same class with the Huey. The VNAF seldom, if ever, flew at night and frequently reported their birds "broke" and called the 57th an hour away in Saigon for help. The delay was not helpful to patient survival. Kelly and Detachment A would reduce the delay.

Kelly immediately set about raising the visibility of Dust Off in the Delta. If Dust Off was to survive, patients were the key, saving lives no matter the circumstances; get them out—during the battle, at night, in weather, whatever. Get those patients, the more the better. And that included the enemy wounded. Dust Off never discriminated against a hurt human, no matter his cause. And what could be a better contribution to WHAM? After the daytime missions were cleaned up, Kelly started a nightly round robin. He would circle the Delta radioing the troops to let them know who he was, that he was in the area and available if they had any casualties. He did not want anyone else carrying patients. Kelly took owner-ship of all patients, Vietnamese as well as American, enemy as well as friendly. From now on, they were his.

Kelly was dead serious about his ownership of all patients and we all knew it. On one day of heavy casualties, I was en route to help him when my 20-minute fuel warning light came on. The one thing you could be sure of with that light—you did not have 20 minutes before the engine quit. I radioed Kelly that I might be delayed in getting to the patients while I refueled. He told me to do what I had to do but don't let anyone else get those patients. A pilot can overcome a lot of blunders. Running out of fuel in the field is not one of them. The only time a chopper pilot has too much fuel is when you are on fire. You may live through the autorotation, but you will not outlive the ridicule. The nearest fuel was from 55 gallon drums, lying in a field. We had to hand pump the JP4 and filter it through a chamois cloth—a time consuming operation if one was to avoid the dangers of fuel contamination not uncommon at the time. I decided to defer refueling to ensure no one else got our patients. We got the patients and the engine graciously waited until we got over the runway before it quit.

Kelly's frequent co-pilot was Second Lieutenant (2LT) Ernie Sylvester. Ernie loved to fly, shared Kelly's enthusiasm for night flying, and was an outstanding navigator. He had his finger on the map following the exact track of every flight in case they went down. Kelly had Ernie diagram the various landing areas for future night pickups. The troops were initially shocked to hear rotor blades at night. Many were American advisers hunkered down in remote areas surrounded by the enemy, not sure who their friends were. In combat or in death and near-death experiences, loneliness is a soldiers' great adversary. They often feel isolated and wonder if anyone cares. The sound of Kelly's friendly southern voice was a great comfort. They knew this man cared.

Major Kelly's marketing and ownership efforts soon bore fruit. The ARVN incidents of "broke" engines increased, especially at night and casualty requests began to increase. Many aviators, and others, thought it was insane to fly single engine aircraft, alone, over hostile terrain at night. There were few navigation aids. The other aviation units frequently flew two ships on night missions after they had done everything possible to avoid the mission. Most believed that if you lost that engine at night, you certainly were dead. Even if you landed safely, they warned, Charlie would get you before sunup. Kelly knew that the key to lifesaving was time—the time from injury to medical care, not necessarily to a hospital. Dust Off had highly competent medical care on board. The helicopter destroyed the time obstacles of terrain. It made no sense to waste lifesaving time waiting for the sun to come up.

Night flying was nothing new to Kelly. In Korea, he had been a pioneer of night flying (although he was color blind—not an asset in night flying) in the flimsy unforgiving H 13, of MASH fame, far more dangerous at night than the Huey. Kelly would lead the way in making Dust Off a 24-hour resource in Viet Nam. Many actually thought Dust Off was specially trained for night flying. One commander ordered a staff study of how we did it. The staff study concluded that experience at the time did not warrant night operations; natural obstacles, anti-helicopter devices, setting down in marshy ground, and the lack of a landing control team among other challenges made night operations too dangerous. Dust Off defeated these challenges every night. Today's military, of course, owns the night. In the early days of Viet Nam, only Kelly owned the night.

He soon become known as Mad Man Kelly but it was not just the night flying. He flew through enemy bullets as well as darkness and weather to get the patient. Kelly was, for the first time, demonstrating the incredible lifesaving potential of that great bird in the hands of someone who cared—and was fearless. He also demanded new Hueys since ours were at the 800-hour level. And he got them because of the appreciation everyone had for what we were doing. Maintenance gave us such good support the other units fought for our castaways.

The pilots at Detachment A worked hard to keep up with Kelly. In his first month in the Delta, the 57th evacuated more patients than ever before, double the previous high. Night missions increased fourfold. The pilots were soon exceeding what was then considered the safe amount of monthly flight hours. When the higher headquarters tried to slow him down, Kelly either ignored them or asked simply if they would want to be left in a rice paddy because a pilot had reached some arbitrary time limit? Some pilots simply stopped recording their time when they reached the limit. In Korea, Kelly once had to turn down nine evacuations because his unit lacked the flying hours to fly them. That would not happen here. The truth was that no one knew what a safe time was. The regulation, adopted from an obscure Air Force regulation, said 90 hours in 30 days. Kelly was setting new standards. Ernie would leave Viet Nam with over 1,000 combat hours, more than any pilot in the history of Army aviation up to that time. Ernie could have safely flown many more hours and would gladly have done so.

During this time, we philosophized a lot and not everyone in the unit agreed with everything we were doing. I worried that we had no definite system or doctrine. But I believed we were doing a lot for WHAM. (Kelly asked me to write an article on this, which I did.) One of our assigned combat arms pilot believes to this day that Kelly was a nut. But all of us followed his example, albeit for some out of fear. But fear is a part of respect. I think my greatest fear next to leaving someone to bleed in a paddy, was to let Kelly down. We were taking a lot of hits and the question came up as to what to do with our patients if we went down. Did you leave the patients and save the crew? Did you stay and fight? Kelly's position was simple—the patient came before all else. Our mission was to protect and care for him, not abandon him. This position is debatable and there may be exceptions. But not for Kelly. Thank God we never faced such a situation.

· 14 ·

AN ATHEIST IS
MY CO-PILOT

I AM a person who wears my faith on my sleeve. It has always been a vital part of my life. I could never understand, and do not to this day, why we are so often admonished not to discuss politics and religion. Why not? What is there in life more important? I attended 10 different schools the first nine years of my schooling. Our parents were divorced and my brothers and I were herded from relative to relative and in and out of boarding homes and schools. While boarding with the Christian Brothers of Ireland, an Irish-founded teaching order, I grew close to my faith. Without parents and only transient friendships, the Brothers became my mentors. They taught me to bring my troubles to the Lord and encouraged me to talk to Him. And I did, often casually in the heat of competition or in time of need. I do to this day (even on the golf course, no...especially on the golf course).

My faith became even more important in Viet Nam. The prospect of sudden death will do that to some but not all. It did me. I knew I needed to do more than just talk to the Lord. I decided to stay on the wagon while in Viet Nam as a kind of a token of sacrifice, if you will. I won't drink, God, if you don't get me shot. Not drinking was as tough for me as anyone of my ethnicity. I never drank for emotional or psychological reasons, I had the curse of the Irish; I liked the taste of the stuff. And there was no other way to get drunk. St. Patrick's Day was, of course, an exception and I gave myself a special dispensation on March 17th (ruined by the G2 this year). God knows all and would see this as a serious sacrifice on my part. I was certain He would do His part, but just to make sure I went to daily Mass whenever I could—another don't get me shot deal.

Now this may sound like over-kill but I also carried two holy medals, one from my wife which I wore around my neck and called my .30-caliber medal. It also covered glass in the ice, punji traps and other such devices. Punji traps were shallow holes filled with sharp stakes or nails, often covered with feces. One model closed around the foot of the victim driving the stake into his ankle. The other medal, in my pocket, was much larger, a real beauty from my mother, and I called it my .50-caliber medal. (I never knew it at the time but the VC actually had .51-caliber, or 12.7 millimeter (mm), weapons; thus they could use our ammo but we could not use theirs). We worried a lot about .50 calibers and this medal took care of those worries for me.

As a back up to cover any other threats, I carried a holy card sent to me by the nuns at my children's school. There was a false alarm at the school that I had been killed and they wanted to ensure that I got home safely. On the card was a prayer to St. Joseph given to the Emperor Charles by the Pope as he went into battle. It promises that "...whosoever shall keep this about themselves shall not die a sudden death or be drowned, nor shall poison take effect on them nor shall they fall into the hands of the enemy or be burned in a fire." That was a card I never left the ground without. I carry it to this day.

Of course, my buddies thought I was whacko and I took a lot of good-natured gas. They said the only reason I went to Mass was to ask forgiveness for my sins of the night before. But one friend, an avowed atheist, especially enjoyed ridiculing my medals. We hear that there are no atheists in foxholes. That may be true. I have never been in a foxhole in combat, but I did have an atheist in my cockpit and he stretched my medals to their limit.

We flew together often and although he outranked me and was the AC, he seldom took the controls. Usually the pilot not at the controls ran the radios. He liked to talk on the radio; he sounded cool and probably knew it. We were flying one day near the end of June when ARVN were taking mass casualties. We flew 13 hours this day and night to help clean up the mess. We had taken some hits but nothing serious. In one pickup site, the combatants were in tree lines north and south of each other with the friendlies to the south. The terrain that separated them consisted of the usual squares of tall grass, rice paddies, and berms. In a paddy south of the trees behind the friendlies on their west flank was a dead buffalo. The poor beast had been killed earlier and was mostly on its back, bloated with all its legs outstretched, very easy to spot.

The southwest corner gave us trees on two sides and the buffalo was a perfect registration point. I could low level in from the east, take a right at the buffalo, skim over the trees, do a 180 at the patients and depart the same way. The friendlies agreed to the scheme and organized their patients as we directed. It was fun. I doubt if the enemy ever saw us and if he did, had little time to get us in his sights. As we loaded the last wounded from this area, the atheist said he would fly us out. He had been busy on the radios regulating the patient flow and informing the friendlies where we were; but there was no way he could not know how I had been flying and why. Yet, to my shock, he picked up and headed directly at the enemy tree line to the north.

By the time I saw what was happening and started to scream at him, it was too late. We filled up with bullets, including .51 calibers which came up through my side and scattered shrapnel across the cockpit. He was hit by flying shrapnel and it must have knocked some sense into him as he headed east and then south back to the tree line—with my assistance. By this time, I was on the controls cussing him for all I was worth as we tried to dodge the bullets blasting by. (Lord, I know I should not be cursing but surely there is no excuse for what this idiot has done.) My head was bursting with fire-crackers and my ears were about to burn off. We made it to the ground where his smiling face further darkened my mood.

The aircraft was riddled with holes. Three rounds actually went through the leading edge of the tail rotor. The air had to be jam-packed with bullets for that to happen. He proudly showed me his wound and predicted he would get a Purple Heart. He did. I told him that if it weren't for my holy medals they would be pinning it on his coffin. He allowed that we had been lucky but faith had nothing to do with it since there was no God. The difference between him and me was that I had someone to thank. Such a situation must be tough for an atheist who must certainly be thankful to be alive—but had no one to thank. The one good thing to come out of that mission—he never touched the controls again when we flew together.

· 15 ·

TWO UNLUCKY IRISHMEN

ABOUT a month after the preventive medicine mission, Brian and I were called out on a pickup for some wounded Vietnamese troops. Just before the mission, Brian had been in his supply room where he was getting a tutorial on the Purple Heart, a medal thus far never awarded to a Dust Off crewman, from Captain James "Doc" Ralph, our faithful flight surgeon and one of the finest flight surgeons I ever knew (to this day, he sends us health advice). That conversation proved to be prophetic.

We met at the flight line and were joined by a new medic who would be flying his first mission. After failing to get #8589 started we jumped in #8591 (this bird would have a tragic end) and headed out. The PZ was 20 minutes NNE of Saigon in an area five clicks south of the Hobo Woods and 10 clicks west of the Iron Triangle, both known VC strongholds. We were having great difficulty finding the pickup site when suddenly the hydraulic light flashed on and the controls started to convulse. I instinctively flicked the hydraulic control switch off. This was supposed to capture enough hydraulic fuel to enable safe flight. The procedure then was to shoot a running landing.

We should have been able to return to Saigon. But I found that it was taking every muscle in my body to keep the thing level. I worried about getting in an unusual attitude and not being able to straighten it out. The hell with Saigon and the fact that we were over Viet Cong territory, we searched for a smooth place to make a running landing. We found a grass strip and began an approach from 2,000 feet. The slower we got the tougher it was to control. We secured the crew and Brian came on the controls with me. We were moving rapidly when we hit the ground and it took both of us to stop #8591 before it hit the trees at the end of the strip. My first image was of bamboo cages and we immediately set up a perimeter around the bird.

In short order, to our delight, a large white man in swimming trunks stomped out of the jungle. It turned out we had landed at Trung Lap and there were friendlies in the vicinity. Our savior was a Special Forces captain with a radio and he called our operations for help. We were completely out of hydraulic fluid which may have explained the roughness of the controls. Our operations officer arrived with #8589, now flyable. I thanked the captain and we headed back for the patients. I would see that SF captain again, next time with our roles reversed.

Finally we spotted white smoke and landed. The American adviser on the ground told us he had no patients but there was a fire fight 400 meters to the east and they had casualties. Once in the air, we were able to establish contact with the casualty site and they popped smoke. The pickup was in a rice paddy on the east edge of the Bao Trung River which ran north and south. The terrain along the edge of the paddy and to the west was heavy jungle. The area was reported to be secure and I began a straight in approach from the south parallel to the river. At about 50 feet, just as I was beginning my flare we came under fire. There was a splash of blood across the cockpit and Brian announced, quite calmly I thought, that he had been shot. One of the rounds entered the left side of the bird and hit him in the ankle. I pulled up and rushed him to the hospital as he took off his boot and treated the wound.

It was not a good day for #8589. It had taken several other hits and it went back into maintenance for battle damage work. But the patients were still in the field, one with a broken back, and another bird was ready. My atheist friend jumped in, I flashed my medals, he laughed, and we headed back for the patients, this time with gunship escorts. There was some talk that we were lured into the area but I had seen the friendlies standing near some patients when Brian was hit. We did know that many friendly units had VC mixed in but I was reasonably sure that there were legitimate patients at the site. I was not, however, thrilled at the prospect of going back in there. I was on my third chopper for this mission.

As we neared the site we were able to establish radio contact and were once again assured that the area was secure. You bet! I could hear gun fire when our contact keyed his mic. I was sure enemy troops were mixed in with the friendlies in the tree line west of the rice paddy. I knew the death spiral was not the way in, but I wasn't sure what was. As we approached I noticed that there were contour changes and berms in the paddies and the grass on the edge of the jungle was pretty high. I put my eyeballs in the sockets of the enemy and tried to imagine what I could see if I were him in those trees and high grass looking up. Perhaps if we got low enough we could find some cover in the terrain. I decided to fly well to the east and lose my altitude behind some trees in a secure area and come in low and fast. The key was to hit the spot where the patients were and get in and out as quick as possible. The gunships would circle nearby and react to enemy fire.

Navigation is a whole new challenge on the deck. I told the friendlies to hold the smoke until I gave the word and have the patients ready. I spotted some bench marks, went to the deck, and started to snake my way in. I asked for smoke at the last possible moment and brought it to a stop in a 180 degree turn and set down. From this mission on I would always turn my tail toward the direction of the enemy, or last received fire, not only to be set up for departure (assuming I came in correctly) but also because it was harder for a bullet to get to you if it had to go through the engine and transmission rather than only the windshield. And it is disquieting to sit and look out that windshield waiting for a bullet. The patients, including the one with the broken back, ran to our aircraft and were on in a few seconds. We went out the same way we came in. I knew that terrain was secure. We were well on our way when Charlie noticed us and cut lose. We did not get hit this time but both gunships did and one pilot was hit.

For Brian, it was the first Purple Heart for a Dust Off crewman and the end of his tour. (I think it was the first, but some say Bob Mock got one earlier.) I would miss him. He was cool under pressure and had the right attitude. And he was, of course, Irish. It was the medic's first mission and he must have wondered what was ahead. For me, I was excited. I had a new approach that would be invaluable for my patients in the future. I was learning that each PZ has a key, a safe route in, and a pilot only needed to find the key to open the area. The snake approach was perfect for much of the terrain in the delta and around Saigon. I could not wait to get to the Delta where the real action was and I could fly many such missions. The bad news came the next day.

The day after Brian was wounded, while on his way to see him, Major Kelly was diverted to Cai Cai an outpost near the Cambodian border on Rach Cu Cai, River. The VC had slipped across the border and massacred everyone in the outpost to include women and children before retreating back into Cambodia. Kelly landed to search for possible survivors in the surrounding area. He found five dozen and with the help of his other bird, evacuated all of them. He resumed his flight to Saigon and was again diverted to a major operation near Tan Hiey. A U.S. helicopter was shot down and Kelly went in to get the crew. Once on the ground they came under heavy enemy fire from all directions. Kelly jumped out and provided suppressive fire while the downed crew was loaded. (In the early days, the pilot would on occasion get out and lay down suppressive fire while the crew loaded the patients. I never did this and did not think it was necessary.)

We were happy he made it to Saigon alive but I was not happy with his message to me. Brian had some Irish luck. It turned out the round that hit him was armor piercing and went right through the ankle or the damage would have been ugly. All my luck was bad. Kelly called me in: "Brady, you got my supply officer shot. You are now the supply officer." Words cannot describe my hatred for that job. But worse, I feared that Kelly was looking for an excuse to stay at Detachment A. He was burning up the Delta. They loved him down there. Entire villages were turning out for his pickups. The patient load had doubled and night missions quadrupled. Kelly was averaging over 120 hours a month, 36 of it at night. American advisers stayed up to hear his comforting southern drawl and visit with him during his nocturnal trips. He raised their morale, lowered their loneliness, and instilled a new sense of security. Jim Lucas, a Pulitzer Prize-winning writer, heard of Kelly. He was astonished at the ability of Kelly and his pilots to fly at night and moved to Soc Trang to cover him. I feared that I would never get to command Detachment A.

· 16 ·

WHEN I HAVE
YOUR WOUNDED

KELLY spent little time in the officers' club, or town, and never missed church on Sunday. He was a deeply spiritual man, having become a Christian in World War II; but he was not flamboyant about his faith or anything else. Ernie once wrote an inspirational quote on the bulletin board. Kelly liked it and asked Ernie to do it every day. Kelly, for all his rough demeanor, was a romantic. He spent much of his time writing, lovingly to Jessie certainly, but also just writing—some of it actually poetry. For these letters, indeed all his writings, he insisted on paper water marked with an eagle. What he wrote no one knew. He kept a can nearby and burned most of it. Maybe it was his way of getting things off his chest. He was in the battle of his life and no one in the Medical Department seemed willing or able to help.

He worked at a small desk dominated by a picture of an angel. He wanted to replace our unit patch, a rather drab thing, with something more exciting, something that, of course, included an angel. His request started the creative juices flowing in some of us.

There were some beautiful unit patches being created at the time and I knew one of the artists, a gunship pilot. Ignoring the angel bit, I asked the artist to design a patch that included a kangaroo in flight regalia with a wounded baby in its pouch. I got the idea from the Aussies who worked with us on occasion. The result was a 3x4-foot painting, truly a thing of beauty. I liked it so much I copied it on my flight helmet. I could not wait for Kelly to come to Saigon so I could show it to him. But he seldom came to Saigon. That would mean meetings at HQ with the brass, which he hated.

His legend continued to grow. On one mission, Kelly responded to a call for help from Song Trau, a small compound under attack. He was told that there had been no shooting for quite awhile. Despite coming under heavy fire on his approach, Kelly landed just outside the compound. The fire was so intense no one on the ground would move to help load the patients. Kelly and Ernie got out and put down suppressive fire while the medic and crew chief crawled under the barbed wire to pull the wounded through and load them on the Dust Off. During the loading they discovered that an enemy round had severed a fuel line causing a severe fuel leak. Another round had jammed the main fuel drain valve in the open position. They could not stop the leak. A simple spark from any of the multiple electrical wires and systems on the ship would have destroyed it and all aboard. The patients needed care and Kelly decided to risk the flight. Once airborne, he called Soc Trang and alerted them of his situation and patients. The commander scrambled every available ship in case Kelly went down in enemy territory. The commander asked if there was anything else he could do. Kelly thought a minute and replied, "How about some ice cream?" The engine quit as Kelly hovered down the runway and there to meet him was the commander with a fire truck, an ambulance, and—a quart of ice cream.

In June the commanders were called to Saigon to say farewell to General Stilwell. Kelly could not miss that. Before he got in, I placed the kangaroo painting on his chair as a surprise and hung around for what I was sure would be a moment of great praise when he saw it. He came in, slipped between the chair and the desk, never sat down, gave some orders, and on the way out asked, "Brady, are you still working on my patch? I think it should include an angel, don't you?"

That evening he and I, and a recently arrived chaplain, were sitting together listening to the Stilwell farewells. I had never seen Kelly so animated. He was by nature a quiet, private man, but this night he was cheerful. He read between the lines of the speeches, and his remarks were colorful and his language rather earthy. The chaplain winced on more than one occasion. At an earlier meeting, Kelly presented Stilwell with a plaque decorated with five red crosses and the tail numbers of our aircraft. He told Stilwell, "General, you wanted my aircraft so bad, here they are." I have a picture of that encounter, and Stilwell is smiling. I don't think the Dust Off issue was completely settled by then, but Kelly had his antagonist at bay. For all their differences, I always felt there was something rather special between Kelly and Stilwell. After Stilwell's farewell I bugged Kelly on his promise to let me have Detachment A. I was shocked when he said I could take over on 1 July. I think he was concerned about the fight for Dust Off and decided he should be in Saigon to battle Stilwell's replacement.

Kelly came to Saigon one more time, on the last day of June. He brought bad news. I would not replace him the next day as he promised. He still had things to finish in the Delta. I was deeply disappointed and feared I would never get to command Detachment A. At lunch that day, we got word that a ship had gone down up north. A 2LT pilot was killed. Kelly had more access to operational information and I asked him if he knew the pilot's name. Kelly wondered why I wanted to know that. I told him I had some flight school friends up there, including a close friend, a 2LT, who was my stick buddy in flight school. He remarked that no, he didn't know, and no he didn't want to know. He said it is better not to ask for names in this business. I worried about the coldness of his remark but figured two wars might do that to you. I flew him back to Soc Trang that night. It was the only time I ever flew with him and the last time I would see him.

I still remember the cold chill in my belly when we got word that Kelly was down. We all raced for our birds and headed for the Delta. I never waited for a co-pilot and was the first to launch. On the way down I monitored the operation. A slick picked up the Kelly crew and we heard they were safe at Vinh Long. We all breathed a sigh of relief, and I remember smiling to myself as I thought about Kelly's reaction to being picked up by a slick. I saw a lone Dust Off on the ramp at Vinh Long and parked behind it. Ernie was sitting in the cargo door. I was in a cheerful mood until I noticed he was crying. Then I saw the body bag behind him. Before I could say anything, he nodded at the bag and said it was Kelly. All the air went out of my body and I sank down beside him. He had escaped so many tight spots, so close so many times, that it never occurred to me that they could kill him. The reality just shook me.

Kelly and Dick Anderson with PFC Earl Pickstone as crew chief and Doctor (Captain) Henry W. Giles as medic (in the early days, we carried a physician as medic if the wounded was U.S. We abandoned this practice later when we found our enlisted were better in the field) had gone into a supposedly secure area 10 miles SW of Vinh Long for some allegedly urgent wounded—one of them a U.S. soldier. While landing they noticed the "urgent" U.S. adviser standing in the LZ guiding them in. Andy quietly cursed him, "urgent my eye!"

While on the ground, they began drawing fire—once again coming out of friendly lines. The ground forces call sign Dragonfly Bravo, screamed at Kelly to get out. He replied stubbornly: "When I have your wounded." His next words were, "my God," and he curled up from a single bullet shot right through his heart. The ship curled with him, and the rotors beat it to pieces. He would not let anyone on the controls with him or Andy might have saved the bird. Andy cut off the fuel for fear of a fire and noticed blood on his visor. It was from Kelly who was on top of him. They were still under fire but Andy got the crew out safely and dragged Kelly behind a berm. Doctor Giles, who broke his leg in the crash, tried to administer an IV but it was too late. He declared Kelly dead on the spot. Then they were rescued by a slick.

Kelly's crew had only been at Long Binh a few minutes before I got there and the same people were yelling for a Dust Off to come back for the urgent patients Kelly was killed trying to rescue. I recall my atheist friend, now our new commander, rushing over to us as we sat there in silent numbness. He began to shout and wave and give orders and question why we sat while there were patients in the field. I can remember rousing from my stupor and becoming outraged at his insensitivity to what had happened to Kelly. They had been friends for years. He saw my anger and said simply and quietly, "It's over; it's done; and we've got work to do." He was right. Kelly was probably smiling in the body bag behind us.

Ernie and I cranked up and went back for Kelly's patients. As we came over the area I spotted Kelly's ship in a mangled heap. The area was still called secure and the patients still classified urgent. I was not thinking clearly after Kelly's death and made the mistake of taking them at their word. I did not come in tactically; I came straight in beside Kelly's ship. I noticed the tail number—63-8591, one of the ships Brian and I flew the day he was shot. Just as I was sitting down, all hell broke loose. Bullets blasted through our ship, probably from the same folks who shot Kelly. They were in the same tree line with the friendlies. We jumped over some foliage into an adjacent rice paddy and checked to see if our bird was flyable. It was. Amazingly, they were calling us back to the same area! "We are now secure Dust Off." Right! I went back to altitude and took a closer look at the area.

Since Viet Nam, I have been able to visualize most of the hot areas I landed in. For many years they were burned into my being. Some are getting dim but that area will forever be clear. There was a heavily vegetated river west of Kelly's ship with canals running off on the north and south to form a U. I noticed a perfect square of banana trees east of Kelly's ship. They were a bit thin but I could find no other place to hide. We then asked that they get the patients in the banana square and hold the smoke. I was sure there were enemy mixed in with the friendlies and did not want smoke to give them any notice of our arrival. Since it is easy to get lost low level without a signal, I memorized the terrain as I flew east. I got as low as possible, snaked up to the banana trees, jumped over, slid into a 180, and sat down. We didn't get out before the shooting started but we did get out with the patients. The "urgent" U.S. patient walked to the aircraft carrying a bag. I was told later that he was coming out of the field to go on R&R. All the patients were ambulatory. None was urgent. Kelly had died for a routine patient. That bothered many but it would not have bothered Kelly.

We finished our missions well after dark and I stayed in Kelly's room that night and slept in the bed he had slept in his last night on earth. As I sat at his desk and wrote up the missions of that day, I noticed it was the first of July and I was finally the commander of Detachment A, just as Kelly had promised. He couldn't break a promise even though he tried. His room was now my room. I cried myself to sleep that night.

He was the 149th hostile American death in Viet Nam, and the outcry was overwhelming. I think it was then that we all truly realized how beloved he was in the Delta. I was told that Stilwell broke down when told of Kelly's death. He was given the highest awards of the Vietnamese government, and all their brass were there. It was the biggest funeral service I had ever seen. General Westmoreland would later write a eulogy for Kelly in which he called him a living legend, and described him as an example of the ideal GI, men who have given America more than they have taken from her. For Westmoreland, Kelly epitomized the greatness of the human spirit. I was a pallbearer along with Andy, Jeff Grider, Charles Allen, and Billy Mitchell, Ernie flew Detachment A up from Soc Trang in weather that would have grounded most other aircraft. Nothing would keep him from Kelly's memorial.

There were two coffins in the chapel that day. One was my stick buddy and dear friend, Bill Cawthorne, the one Kelly told me not to inquire about. Bill had died heroically. He was shot and crashed near a remote village called Hiep Duc an area that would become familiar to me later. Although fatally wounded, he managed to get his crew out of the burning bird. He then sat down and died. They were now side by side. The chaplain was the same one who had winced at Kelly's war stories earlier. He never mentioned the names of the dead on his altar that day and I have often wondered if he knew who it was he was praying over. It was an emotionally tough time for all of us as we grieved for our commander and especially for me as I also grieved for my stick buddy. I never really had a father and often thought of Kelly in those terms. His death hurt me deeply. I looked on him as an advocate in all my troubles; he wished me well and had prolonged my career. Grief is a part of death but with Kelly I also felt a loneliness I could not describe or even explain. I wondered who would protect Dust Off now that he was gone. He was such a force.

Shortly after I took over Detachment A, the local commander called me in. I listened while he said that he was not at all surprised that someone had been killed. He didn't think it would be Kelly. He thought it would be one of the young pilots. He expected Kelly's death would teach us a lesson, and we would modify our ways. As I listened, it was clear that some really did think Kelly was crazy and that much of the flying we did routinely was believed by others to demonstrate poor judgment. To this day, there are those who call Kelly a fool who is a hero only because he was killed. We can talk forever about the difference between a brave man and a fool. Death is often the decider and a dead fool, or a genuine jerk, becomes a hero. I think caring is the answer; it is founded in goodness, will overcome fear, and with courage, define a hero. Kelly was a good man with courage and therefore a hero.

When he had finished, I told him nothing would change. We

would continue to fly as Major Kelly had taught us and try to learn as much as possible from the only battlefield we had for use on the battlefields of the future. We would be wasting our time to do otherwise. Besides, we were in a battle to win the hearts and minds of the people, and there was no one doing it better than Dust Off. To his credit, he never tried to change or restrict us despite his personal convictions.

As I was leaving, perhaps as a warning, he gave me the bullet that killed Kelly. It had entered the open rear door, passed through Kelly's heart, and lodged in the door to his right. No other round had hit the aircraft. I have often wondered if Kelly could have been deliberately targeted by a VC sniper. He was doing good representing the Saigon government and the people loved him; all of which the communists hated, much like Doc Smith's hospital. Kelly would not wear a flak vest and he had been criticized for that. It was uncomfortable and really didn't stop much. But some said that if Kelly had had one on, he might have lived. I guess his mortician is the only one who knows.

17

THE KELLY WAY

AFTER my visit with the local commander, I sat down to analyze what he meant by "modify our ways." I knew only one way—the Kelly way. He was driven by his goal to save Dust Off but his way was simple: The patient came first, then the rest. If you focus on the patient, everything else fell in place. All the rest, the enemy, night and weather, the terrain, communications, friendly fire, were nuisances, mere annoyances to be dealt with on the way to the patient. For some, the rest came first. Not Kelly. We were to go for the patient as if it was you yourself, or a loved one, down there in pain, bleeding to death. If you were stopped by the weather or enemy action, you came back again and again until you got the patient. Under no circumstances did you sit on the ground and use the weather reports or anything else as an excuse not to launch. You got your ass in the air and took a look. Some Dust Off pilots tried to eliminate the obstacles before they left the ground. Kelly did that en route. And "preventive medicine" missions could be medical missions.

The dead may be classified as a quartermaster mission, but

there was no reason for Dust Off not to carry them if the situation allowed. They were, after all, angels and who would not want an angel in their aircraft? What pilot, in combat, would not want to be on the side of the angels? Amazingly some Dust Off pilots did not. I had co-pilots question me for transporting the dead. And a least one crew refused the dead who had died while they were en route. They accused the troops of lying. On another occasion, the grunts threatened to shoot the Dust Off if it did not carry their dead. The Vietnamese were superstitious about their dead and would not fight until they were evacuated. Americans would risk their lives before they would abandon their dead. I believed that removing the dead was an operational necessity; another "preventive medicine" mission, and I would never refuse them. Of course, in some instances, it may have been impossible; I just never faced such an instance. Later I would define specific criteria but I could not bring myself to leave them, regardless of the rules.

I think that much of the Kelly combat psyche was developed in his time as an infantry man in the mud and blood of World War II. If you were given a mission to take a hill, you took it using the tools at hand, a rifle, a grenade, a tank. Excuses were not allowed. The same should apply in missions to rescue the wounded. A pilot and his helicopter were not more precious than a soldier and his rifle. Of course, safety and the prospect of success were considered, but they paled before mission accomplishment—patient rescue. If necessity is the mother of invention, then caring is the mother of flying Dust Off. A caring pilot would find a way.

Shortly before his death, Kelly had written to Jessie: "It is a known fact that if you bend a twig a certain way and keep pressure on it, it will grow that way." He had bent Dust Off a certain way, the Kelly way, and it would be my way as long as I flew Dust Off. I was a Kelly twig and always would be.

Now that Kelly was dead, we remembered his angel and made a metal crest of an angel in a flight suit and called it Doctor Dust Off. We wore them on our hats and holsters. I lost my last one during my second tour when my hat flew out the door on a night mission. I still grieve over that loss. (Amazingly, a flesh and blood beautiful angel, Cheryl, read of my loss and had an exact replica made for me. It is one of my most prized possessions.) Thanks to Kelly, Dust Off would be known as battlefield angels by many. The only change to the 57th patch was made some time after I left when they added the words, "The Originals." I flew with the true originals but never got to wear that patch. I can tell you that members of the 57th wore that patch with pride to the day the unit was disbanded. But I must confess I feel a strange emotion when I see others wearing it. I don't really know why. Perhaps it is because the real originals were the young inexperienced pilots and crewmen who flew with Kelly in Detachment A; who risked their lives with him daily to help establish a system that was unsurpassed in the history of warfare as a Battlefield Operating System. Someone someday in the medical community should erect a large bronze plaque to the real originals. And on it should be engraved names like Grubbs, Succop, Bender, Sevilla, Spurril, Pickstone, Sylvester, Mock, Shaw, Giles, Anderson, and Simmons.

Charles Kelly was one of the most remarkable soldiers we have ever produced. He had a tough youth, as did many of his era. His dad deserted his family when he was a child. He was a junior but would later change his name to show contempt for such a father. He fibbed his way into the Army at the tender age of 15 serving for over four years in World War II where he earned the Combat Infantry Badge, Jump Wings, and the Combat Medics Badge as an enlisted man. He would later add flight wings to become the only soldier ever to wear all four of these badges. He was shot by the Germans at Aachen and almost lost his leg. As a young soldier, Kelly was a bit rowdy and got court-martialed three times. After the war he returned home to Sylvania, Georgia, finished high school and college, and was a high school principal for a time. But he missed the Army, his first love since the first grade. That love cost him his life. If Army aviation had aces, he would be the ace of aces.

Kelly left a letter for his wife to be opened only if he was killed.

He said all he ever wanted to be was a soldier and that it was a soldier's duty to sacrifice himself for his country. He said he hoped to die alone, if he was to die, as he had flown alone most of his career. It was rather remarkable that in a crew of five, he was the only one killed. He got his wish. And he did not want to die at night. He knew that would provide fodder for those who feared night flight. His words reveal a man of extraordinary faith and compassion, with a passion for his flag, his family, his dog Major, and the Army. (Actually Major was Jessie's dog who was fed by Kelly's mother and liked Kelly—Major may have brought them together.) In the letter, he noted his fondness for a Robert Service poem, "The Song of the Soldier Born." One passage is all Kelly: "For I hold as a simple faith there's no denying: The trade of a soldier's the only trade worth plying; the death of a soldier's the only death worth dying."

Ernie's daily saying for 1 July was, "He that looks for a star puts out his candle." The author was unknown but I guessed his comment had something to do with ambition. Ambition can be ugly but not Kelly's. His ambition was simple: do what's right. His candle was out but the light from it would shine for a long time. Perhaps no other combat death was ever more productive. We never heard another word about portable red crosses. I am sure Westy's admiration of Kelly weighed on this. Kelly's death saved Dust Off, the greatest life saver in the history of combat. "When I have your wounded," what a great way to die and for a true Dust Off pilot, after Kelly, the only way to fly.

Through the years, some have compared me to Kelly and I consider such comparisons a compliment. Certainly I flew as he taught us but in later years, I would discover that our personal lives and careers, our skeletons, were also comparable (as was our mutual love of ice cream); it then became more evident to me why he had given me another chance. Both Kelly and I had begun our career in service to the grunts. Our time with them in the field, in the privation, misery, and hardship that is their lot fostered empathy, an understanding, even love, for them. Too many aviators never had that experience.

Even negative comments in our Officer Efficiency Reports (OER) were similar in terms of being outspoken and headstrong. Robert Service was also my favorite poet and I grew up without a father. And the Army tried to boot him out as it had me. When he came back in the Army after World War II, he failed to note in his application his three court martials. His omission was discovered and a board convened to determine his fitness to remain on active duty. I had also failed to note some problems I had with the law when I was commissioned—also three incidents. The Kelly board recommended that he be discharged from the Army as Stilwell's G2 had recommended on me. A higher board reversed the ruling on Kelly and he was allowed to continue serving. Kelly was my higher Board in the Stilwell/G2 affair and because of him I was allowed to continue serving. Salvaging my career would be a continuing challenge but for now, my challenge was to succeed Kelly in Detachment A and meet his standards, standards set long before Viet Nam.

For all his outward gruffness, Kelly was internally a romantic as revealed in his letters and his poetry. His poetry also reveals that his concept of Dust Off was formed in World War II and at a remote outpost in Korea. He arrived in Korea in 1960 with his career under a cloud, after the Board action, to find drunkenness, debauchery, and no flag. He ran off the whores, outlawed booze, and put up a flag pole. His methods were old Army as his poetry notes:

> "An officer of old army principle
> Stern discipline and rigid order
> Were his beliefs, pure and simple.
> A proud unit could be built with this mortar."
> Then he set the standard.
> "Now this will be the order of the day,
> As long as I command this hill.
> We will always fly, no matter what the rules say."
> As always, he set the example, *"missions were flown day and night."*

And in any weather:
"On a mountain ledge an injured soldier lay. Rain fell and the clouds were low,
And slowly the chopper pilot made his way, But he knew that onward he must go."
And he understood the importance of reaction time.
"Word had gone around.
The mission will be flown at all cost. The evacuation time must be cut down. No more time is to be lost."

I have always believed that we experience our greatest triumphs and failures through our children; and no one is a failure if his children succeed. Kelly was far from a failure but even without Viet Nam, he would have been a success because of his family—they are remarkable. I have come to know and love them, and lovely Jessie, down through the years and would be proud to be their parent. His daughter Carol is a poet and artist. She wrote a wonderful poem, as a child, when he was killed named "Why?" In Vietnam, a cold war rages / soldiers fight, for very small wages / Men fight, women cry / and day and night, more people die / Why?, Why?, I don't know why/I never will know why/men have to die on the battlefield. One of the proudest moments of my life was when my portrait was hung beside his in the Medical Museum at Fort Sam Houston, Texas—both painted by Carol.

Kelly's brother Mike was a great Marine and I still proudly wear a tie he gave me as we shared a drink from the same bottle of bourbon he and Charles sipped from before each of their many separations. Mike has never fully recovered from the death of his brother.

Finally, I think Kelly and I shared another characteristic: We did not like to have someone tell us we couldn't do something we thought was right, or that we knew we could do. This particular trait got me in a lot of trouble as it did Kelly. It took some time for me to realize I was not always right and there were things I couldn't do, and shouldn't do, if I was to be a good soldier. But I did do some things that many thought could not be done, and soldiers are alive because I tried. I always believed, and I think Kelly did also, that if we died doing what we were doing, so what! There could be no better way to die than saving the lives of the greatest citizens of our country.

18

KELLY'S KRAZIES

SOC Trang featured a 3,000-foot runway posted at two feet above sea level in the dry season and two feet below in the wet season. It was built by the Japanese but much improved by the GIs. The camp stood out like a bulls-eye among the rice paddies just south of the town. It was a good target for the VC, many of whom worked in the compound. Mortar attacks were not uncommon. It was a colorful place and so were the Soc Trang Tigers, the 121st Aviation Company, based there. The name came from a real live tiger, Tuffy, who succeeded the pooch, Drunken Sam as mascot. Drunken Sam died tragically an alcoholic. Tuffy, in his youth, once roamed freely about the compound as playful as a kitten romping and wrestling with the troops. But Tuffy grew up, 300 pounds up, and made the mistake of romping on the back of the half-naked commander as he emerged from the showers. The fact that Tuffy was a vegetarian did nothing to quell the COs terror cum anger. He was not an animal person and Tuffy spent his remaining days in a stateside Zoo. Tuffy was replaced by a nine foot no-name python.

The python was game for wrestling and romping and photo ops as long as it was not hungry. A hungry python is not a romper. A weekly ration of one live chicken restored its playful ways.

The troops will have their pets. They take minds off the war and provide and outlet for affection and boost morale in the absence of loved ones. I had grown up around animals and loved them. Dogs have always been a favorite of the GI but the dogs of Viet Nam were amazingly similar—and ugly. They shared the same DNA common in canines found near the equator worldwide: nondescript, broad shouldered, square-jawed, terrain-colored, and short-legged. Our beloved mongrel was appropriately named "Nothing." Unfortunately puppy chow was a favorite culinary treat for some Vietnamese and we carefully guarded our precious Nothing. Some costly, poorly guarded, sentry dogs became expensive repasts for the Vietnamese.

As much as we loved dogs, Viet Nam had more exotic choices for pets, pets we could only dream of owning in the states. I bought a Myna bird and named it Napoleon. I was determined to teach it to talk, cleanly: which would be difficult as my buddies were constantly trying to teach it dirty words. My beautiful Myna bird later disappeared under circumstances that remain a mystery to this day. I did make a mistake in its diet. One would assume that such a bird would eat bananas and that is what I fed it. How could I know that it would relieve itself of those very bananas, and then some, while flying over my roommate's pillow? In any event, that was not an excuse for its demise (for which my roommate denies responsibility to this day). One of our pilots had a pet monkey which he once, and only once, took on a mission. The monkey did to the helicopter what Napoleon did to my roommate's bed. The crew chief was as unforgiving as my roommate and that ended monkey missions. I also bought an ocelot kitten, a beautiful creature, but even then ferocious and proved impossible to tame. Others bought "ocelots" which lost their spots after a bath.

When not releasing steam with the pets, the troops found solace in their clubs. The Soc Trang WETSU club was of course known as the Tiger's Den. Steam letting consisted of running palm trees through the ceiling fans I guess to create a jungle ambiance or simulate rotor blades chopping their way into LZs; and playing baseball with tree branches and beer cans. A poker game ran continuously while others bet on Battling Betas, ferocious fish that fought to the death. War stories were allowed but only in a Huey flight seat mounted at the bar. We ate many of our meals in the club since we were often gone during mess hall hours. A specialty was hamburger steak, Ernie's favorite. I favored peanut butter and jam sandwiches. We also ate a lot of C-rats in field standbys. C-rats were surely designed by some deranged bulimic. You had a choice of five entrees, some caked with enough lard to gag a maggot. Each entree came with a portion of fruit, cheese, and peanut butter with crackers, and a canned desert. They also included cigarettes but no snuff, which offended me. (I had my first taste of Copenhagen in the second grade while skinning logs for a lumber jack; I still love the filthy stuff.) Thankfully, in the midst of this culinary catastrophe were the exquisite beanie weenies, which with some hot sauce or peppers is still a gourmet meal for me. Hunger makes for some strange culinary combinations.

The Tiger's Den was an unlikely setting for gunship pioneering but a lot of it went on there. It was alarming to find a group of gunship pilots huddled around a bomb at the bar. They were seeking ways to arm and detonate it so they could drop it on VC shelters. It was at the bar they solved the technology of dropping hand grenades from a chopper. Timing was a problem, how to keep it from exploding before it hit the ground. They tried rubber bands but finally settled on peanut butter jars, many of which I had emptied. We have been taught that when you pull the pin, Mr. Grenade is not our friend, yet they would pull the pin and carefully place it in the jar thus keeping the detonator intact. When the jar hit the ground and broke, the detonator would arm and—boom. This was not rocket science but could be effective and was in fact a precursor for the mighty Apache. I tried not to spend a lot of time in the Tiger

Den. I had visions of it flying through a rice paddy. I had heard of a GI attempting to disarm a bomb in a Saigon bar while showing off to his girlfriend. They picked him up with an ink blotter.

Our hooch was only a few feet from our birds which provided great reaction time. We were fortunate to have a flight surgeon in the compound, a pilot's best friend. His extra duties included sanitary inspections of the local brothels in an effort to protect wayward GIs. The inspection consisted of vaccinating the ladies with penicillin, at the time the only known killer for some of the exotic diseases popular in the area. I could understand that the vaccine might kill what they had but wondered what it would do for what they caught from their next customer. Timing was as important for the naughty GI as it was for the gunship pilot and his grenade.

The damp weather in the Delta had a bad effect on everything, especially our weapons. The first things I did was check the weapons. One of my enlisted men spoke with a bit of a Spanish accent. When I got to him, he indignantly held up his rifle. "You see theese weapon? Eet will never fail me. Do you see a speck of dust on eet? No! There eese none. Look down theese barrel. Eet gleams like a diamond. Theese weapon, eet weel never fail me." He had a weapon fail him on a mission; it would never happen again.

At this time, we all carried a weapon of our choice. The country was full of caches of weapons from the French and Japanese occupations. We could pick and choose guns from all over the world; the Thompson sub machine gun made famous during the Capone era, Swedish Ks, German Smizers, Grease guns, even the communist AK 47, a favorite. The new army rifle, the M-16, was not a favorite because of jamming problems. I settled on a shotgun which, with the plug removed, held five rounds of double ought buck each containing nine .30 caliber balls of death. I could think of nothing better for close action in dense terrain. And I wore a machete under my arm which I felt would be more effective than the survival knife if I ever had to escape and evade in the jungle.

We were issued survival kits but I could not imagine ever using the stuff they put in it. (We actually had pot-bellied stoves in our assigned equipment [TOE]. It was designed for another war in another place, as is our wont.) Fishing hooks? Like there would be time to fish with the VC on your tail. The only item that may have been useful was the bug repellant—if it worked. The bugs loved the stuff. But I had my snuff. In Alaska, the mosquitoes were big enough to stand flat footed and f*** a turkey. We searched for repellants that worked. Nothing did—except snuff spit. We rubbed it in our hair and on our arms and nary a mosquito came near. A downed crew gets rescued, gets dead, or ends up in bamboo cages. In the meantime, you better be able to fight. My greatest horror was facing the enemy without ammo. I emptied my survival kit and filled the container with double ought buckshot cartridges.

We all had our own ideas of survival. Ordinarily it is wise to stay near the downed bird but doing so could be deadly if no other aircraft were in the area. The VC were sure to swarm toward the downed chopper. One guy said he would crawl in a deep murky hole and all that would be above ground would be two white eyeballs looking for help; and when the sun came up they would go down. Others would head out across country. My plan was to crawl in a canal and stay there, following it only at night until I found a safe exit.

Pilots carried revolvers as opposed to the .45 caliber semi-automatic universal to the grunts. Because of the humidity, the revolver was less inclined to jam than the .45, or any automatic or semi-automatic weapon. I carried a .357 Magnum, used by bear hunters in Alaska, as a last hope. But, of course, the revolver was used more fruitfully on missions, as noted, for a protector of the family jewels than as protection in a fire fight.

Westy would later standardize crew weapons. It made sense. One crew might have four different weapons all using different ammo. After Westy's edict, I policed up all our stray weapons, including my beloved shot gun, and took them to Father Hoa, a personal hero. Father Augustine Nguyen Lac Hoa was a Chinese Catholic priest who had earlier fought the Japanese and the Chinese Communists. He had organized the Vietnamese peasants at Binh Hung into a formidable fighting force against the VC. Binh Hung was near the mangrove swamps of Cau Mau deep in VC country but, thanks to Father Hoa, one of the few Delta areas relatively free from communist atrocities. His elite troops were famed as the "Sea Swallows" a title adopted after a swarm of sea swallows mysteriously arrived to rescue his precious rice crop from a plague of locusts. Several of our pilots wore a swallow emblem on their hats in tribute to this heroic priest. Father Hoa was grateful for the weapons and gave me a box of Springfield '03s, still in Cosmoline. They were of no combat use to him but were great souvenirs for my men and to some extent alleviated their vexation for giving up their pet weapons.

Three of the original Kelly pilots were gone within a month of his death; one began bleeding from the ears and nose and another had a serious medical problem with his child. Detachment A now consisted of Ernie, Si Simmons, Bruce Zenk, and me. I never flew with a more willing co-pilot than Ernie. A former Pride of Mississippi drum major at Southern Mississippi University, he defined conscientiousness and professionalism. Although I outranked Ernie by several years, he would beat me, and most of his contemporaries, to Colonel. Ernie was in the habit of being number one at whatever he did. Bruce and I were in flight school together where, unlike me, he excelled.

Bruce was all man, an all-state football and basketball player from South Dakota and an Eagle Scout. He started in the infantry and understood the grunts as only one of them can. Bruce flew both slicks and gunships before transferring to MSC and joining us at Soc Trang. I never heard him say an unkind word about anyone or anything, nor was he ever without a smile. His son, Patrick would follow in his steps as an outstanding Dust Off pilot.

Si was one of a kind, like me a solid conservative but of the redneck take-no-prisoners variety; and perhaps the smoothest pilot I ever flew with. Si took the old saw: there are old pilots and there are bold pilots but there are no old bold pilots—there are bold pilots and there are bold grunts, and there are old pilots and there are old grunts but without old bold pilots (Dust Off) there wouldn't be as many old bold grunts. Si would later lose his brother Bill, an Air Force flight surgeon, in this war. Despite the fact that the rules governing his brother's death allowed Si to forgo another tour in Viet Nam, he volunteered to return and command the 82nd. Under his command, the 82nd set records that rivaled any Dust Off unit to ever serve in combat to include the awarding of the MOH to one of his pilots.

Major Kelly had hardened these pilots and I was proud to lead them. I had never served with such dedicated and capable enlisted men. They matched and exceeded the elite troops I commanded in Berlin where America deliberately showcased the Army's finest. Two superb NCOs led the unit, Charles Allen the chief medic, and Billy Mitchell, the first sergeant and maintenance supervisor. Three of Kelly's enlisted men would end up in the Dust Off Hall of Fame. My favorite was Wayne "Tiny" Simmons. He epitomized these men. He would be seriously wounded yet refuse to leave; and then be tragically killed two months later.

They asked no quarter, gave their all, and contrary to the image of GIs, seldom complained. Think how difficult it must be to sit in the back of that machine with no control, completely dependent on the pilot, and listen to the chaos that is part of every mission; then without warning, to be able to react to and suppress enemy fire and care for the patients. Yet, I never had a disciplinary problem with these men. Our medics actually carried morphine syrettes controlled only by the honor system. There was never a hint of drug abuse as the media over-hyped later. Saving lives will change a person.

But a few could not deal with the stress. There were commanders who would not fly at night and some pilots turned in their wings to keep from flying. In one case, a pilot wanted to turn in his wings. He had enough. He was sure if he kept flying he would die. He was talked out of quitting, went back to flying and was killed. In most cases, we let them go immediately, no questions asked, no adverse inserts on records. Kelly insisted on this. There were plenty of volunteers to replace them. There was an incident of possible sabotage on one bird. During a mission I noticed looseness in the controls. I knew nothing about maintenance but could pick one up and pretty much tell if it was whole. We found a bolt missing off one of our controls, thankfully not the Jesus Nut (which secured the main rotor). There was another bolt to hold it together, but maintenance said it was a minor miracle we never crashed. We could not tolerate slack, deliberate or otherwise, especially in the maintenance of our aircraft.

To this point in my career, I had never taken over a unit that I didn't believe I could improve. Detachment A was an exception. Not only the flying. The organization and discipline of the area and the men were by the numbers. Unlike most of the hooches, our area was immaculate. A pilot may fly all night, but he cleaned his area every morning. I wonder who the fool was who said no combat ready unit ever passed an inspection. The old saw about "I am a warrior" and "appearance doesn't make the man" may be colorful but it is irrelevant. Appearance may not make the man—but it does announce him! And so does the appearance of the area where he lives and works. There is a tendency to let down in the field. Discipline and appearance often go together and sloth may be deadly. Kelly knew this and insisted on the area excellence I found.

But my greatest challenge as commander of Detachment A was the Kelly legacy—patients, lots of them, day and night, in weather and on hot battlefields. The Delta expected the same service he provided and would be hard on me if I failed to perform. I probably should have been intimidated, but I couldn't wait to get going. I was determined not to embarrass him. Another beauty of Detachment A was our remoteness from higher HQs. We were free to do things our way, Kelly's way, with no one to challenge us. Such a deal, but it would only last a few months.

July, the month after Kelly's death and my first as commander of Detachment A, was the most productive month ever for the 57th—768 patients rescued. We flew almost as many night missions in July 1964 as were flown in all of 1963. The 57th would not match that number for a long time. In that first month, I increased my flight time by 50 percent and doubled my night time. I flew the first three weeks without a day off. I was now flying over 100 hours a month with one third of that at night, about the norm for Kelly and his pilots. Those numbers were, however, much above the norm at the time, especially the night time. No one was challenging our ownership of the patients or the night.

Saigon was hotter than Pleiku and the Delta was hotter than Saigon. Ten days after Kelly died, Detachment A flew some 20 hours (Ernie and I got 15) and carried more patients than had ever before been evacuated from the battlefield in one day. The VC had actually hid under water with breathing reeds, their weapons floating beside them, and came up out of the rice paddies to ambush a detail of ARVN. Bodies and wounded were scattered all over the paddies. One hundred and eleven patients were floated up to Ernie and I while we hovered above the water from san pan to san pan. Si and Bruce got another 41. Mixed in with the wounded in the muddy water were the dead, many with only their face visible, staring eerily up at the sky with that puzzled look I saw on so many of the casualties.

In the middle of the mass casualties as we recovered, treated and backhauled them, some religious leader with a minor wound demanded that we stop everything and fly him to a hospital. We refused and for a moment I thought we might have a shootout with his body guards. He was not unlike the Vietnamese medics who cared nothing for the Montagnards. I would find other leaders who showed little concern for their wounded, even the lives of their men, a rare but disturbing reality.

On occasion we would land among unfriendlies, once in the middle of a VC village, and we were taking a lot of hits, but Kelly's remnants, to be known as Kelly's Krazies, were staying alive and providing a service worthy of the man himself. In fact, staying alive was becoming more than luck, indeed, it became something of a science for us.

· 19 ·

BETWEEN HIS ANKLES

BECAUSE of Kelly, we were very popular with the peasants and, accordingly, hated by the communists. Each helicopter crewman had a $486 price tag on his head, a sizeable sum at the time. The VC mission was to control or kill the peasants and their families, not help them. Brave doesn't stop bullets, nothing does. But good tactical flying helps to avoid them. Before Viet Nam tactical flying had been the realm of the fighter pilot. He was a romantic figure, silk scarf flying, maneuvering at the speed of sound, choreographing the sun into the eyes of the enemy, and contemplating the face of God. The helicopter pilot was not a romantic figure. He never saw the face of God. He was down in the mud and mangroves between God's ankles. And, worst of all, the Dust Off pilot had to land—and sit there during the fire fight—naked, surrounded by the enemy and JP4. And therein lays the difference between Dust Off and the fighter pilot, in fact, all other pilots.

Dust Off under Kelly became the first aviation unit ever to knowingly and repetitively land on the battle field—during the battle. A well known aviation aphorism proclaimed that flying was the second greatest thrill, a safe landing was first. For Dust Off there were few safe landings; escaping from the landing, getting out alive, was the greatest thrill. Thirty and more landings per day was not unusual, 42 was my high. Once on the ground, Dust Off became the biggest target around! Let me give an illustration of one pilot's reaction to being a sitting duck.

The PZ was hot and as was often the case, there was a lot of confusion; the usual shouting and shooting while we tried to get the friendlies off their bellies to help us load the wounded. On this occasion, I noticed my co-pilot going through some extraordinary, snake-like gyrations with his head darting to and fro, side to side, all over the cockpit. Back to the patients, get them on, let's get out of here, and then to my buddy whose head I feared would depart his shoulders as his gyrations became faster and faster the longer we sat there. Finally, in the midst of the chaos, I could bear it no longer and I broke down and began to laugh almost convulsively. He did not miss a stroke as he eyed me coldly between gyrations and said, "Laugh you son of a bitch, but it's harder to hit a moving target."

Sitting there is a lonely time characterized by bulging veins, beating heart, and total pucker (the feeling that the cheeks surrounding your pelvis are slowly moving up to envelop your ears). For me there was added my burning ears. Few pilots know pucker like a Dust Off pilot. Perhaps those pilots who have bailed out and slowly floated to earth during a dog fight will understand that feeling.

Each mission presented a new challenge and a new learning experience as we searched for ways to beat the sitting duck quandary, to become a moving target. There was no book on tactical helicopter flying; in fact, there was no book on anything we did. The Dust Off pilot was a combat entrepreneur deciding when to fly and how to fly; and most importantly, how to land. Each Dust Off pilot wrote his own book as he went along—unique books based on individual capabilities, imagination, and experience. The approach was life and death and as varied as the terrain, the friendly situation, the enemy situation, his weapons, and the capabilities and imagination of the crew. Everything in this equation is pretty well fixed except the imagination; an imperative that varied wildly among pilots.

George Bernard Shaw wrote, "An Irishman's heart is his imagination." For this Irishman, imagination was life. Imagination is the ability to create something new by combining current knowledge and previous experience. It is the image forming power of the mind. Through it we discover, we create, it illuminates and enlightens, and we see things we've never known in reality—a safe path into the PZ. Of course, it includes visualization. I found it useful to put my eyes in the enemy sockets and visualize what I could see if I were him, where he was. If you properly exercised your imagination, visualized the terrain, the enemy situation and weaponry and the friendly location, a highway would spring up from the area marking a safe route into the PZ. Eventually I developed a great confidence in what I saw; I did not second-guess myself during the approach. Confidence is not always a good thing, and one can get a distorted situation if the friendlies give inaccurate information, and that can kill you, but I would die comfortable and confident and so totally focused on what I was doing I might not notice it.

I already had several chapters in my tactical approach book including the death spiral and snake approach. But now I could come in on the deck at a pretty good clip, following the highway, slip into a 180-degree turn, keep flat, and by cross controlling the pedals and cyclic, stop on a dime avoiding the dreaded flare and its deadly float. And it is easier to get away if you are low and fast and receive fire. Low and slow was death and had to be minimized. Some pilots would try to stop with a flare, either straight in or on the side. They even extolled the virtues of the side flare—left pedal at high speed, blades 90 degrees to the ground, max pitch and mush to a halt. I hated the flare. If you were too close to the ground, there was a danger of a tail rotor or main rotor strike. If you were a little high, you would go into a float, a period during which the controls were useless and you were a nice waffling target just above the terrain. If the approach was successful, you departed along the same highway, airspeed first then altitude. At night it was the opposite—altitude then airspeed.

Communications can be life and death in a Dust Off operation; not only in determining patient information and PZ disposition but also enemy location and weaponry. Since we always used the same frequency or push, Charlie could monitor our missions. (We did, on occasion, deviate from our frequency by using an up or down from Jack Benny's famous age [39].) Some pilots were actually threatened by the VC on the air ("we kill you, Dust Off") and they put out contracts on us, at least $486 per head as mentioned. We frequently had no radio contact with our pickup site, or if we did, the voice was Vietnamese. Since we could not speak Vietnamese, we had to devise other means of communication. We tried using two letters of the phonetic alphabet to be pronounced by friendlies. For example, we would say, "alpha, bravo" and the ground was supposed to answer, "charlie, delta." It never worked. Even with radio contact with an adviser who spoke English, it was not uncommon to have the friendlies announce they were popping green smoke and then see several green smoke bombs from numerous locations. We solved this by training the troops not to identify their smoke, just pop it and we would identify the color. If there were a number of colors, we could verify the correct one. This worked. I studied Vietnamese, but the only words I remembered translated into "pop your smoke." As a last resort we simply made a low fast approach and, if we spotted friendlies, landed.

Because of the perceived danger, many units avoided night flying except for the most urgent missions. I thought that was foolish. It does no good to avoid something that you must do. The key is to get good at it. The units I flew with flew night and day missions the same. We had a lot of practice and got good at them. The result was that, although we had more exposure at night than most units, we never had an accident. I preferred night missions. You have different challenges but the enemy is not as much of a worry—nor are his bullets as accurate. Many areas which may be too hot in the daytime are readily accessible at night. Most of the pilots at Detachment A agreed with me that night flying was the safest time for patient evacuation. A blacked out helicopter, on a dark night, could land on top of you and not be seen. It could be heard, of course, but the enemy needed more than that. It is never comforting to be shot at but to see Charlie firing wildly at our sounds in the darkness was not all bad.

A few of us flew night missions completely blacked out. No more flying Christmas trees. This violated flight safety rules but was perfectly safe since there were seldom other aircraft in the air at night. Rules are mostly a good thing, but they can establish patterns which can get you killed. Rules are manmade and often made for man to hide behind. We broke man's rules but not Mother Nature's, that would get you killed for sure. I also dimmed the instrument lights, and turned out the console lights which are visible in a bank near the ground. Unless absolutely necessary I never used the search light on night approaches. On most nights this is not difficult. I shot the approach with my head well out of my window, circling to the right while carefully ensuring that nothing came between me and my signal. The troops appreciated this since a light could give them up to the enemy. But the visibility at night is not predictable. You have to get airborne to find out. It may be a beautiful moonlight night and there is nothing but ink down below. On other nights, I have gone out under low clouds with excellent visibility.

The pilot shooting the night approach should always be in the right seat. The Huey was designed for this. The landing light and search light were both controlled from the right seat. The landing light was two dimensional and of limited use on night approaches best set for autorotation. If lights were necessary, you had to use the search light which was multidimensional and controlled from the right seat where all instrumentation was better. Some pilots liked the left seat, the seat of their role models, their IPs, in flight school. And some just felt good there. That could be fatal. If they needed a light, they had to direct the right seat pilot where to shine it. Some famous last words were: Why is it doing that? Where are we? And the ubiquitous—oh shit! That list should include, "shine it over here." Most pilots seldom flew at night, let alone landed in the field. They never much concerned themselves with lights or seats. Their major emergency was a lost engine to which they joked, turn on the light and if you don't like what you see, turn it off. Every night landing was a bit of an emergency and we needed to do it right.

I always flew the right seat, not only for night missions but because it allowed me to lead with my right foot on takeoff which reduced power demands. This was important with the big loads we carried. We often took off at 6,000 RPM, 600 below normal. I found that by taking off sideways and leading with the right foot I could get to translational quicker than by following the nose. The fact that the fuel lines are on the left side of the engine certainly made that side more dangerous but had nothing to do with my decision to fly the right seat—contrary to what some of my co-pilots would claim. You did not, however, want to crash on the left side if at all possible.

Two classes which interested me in flight school were weather and night vision; not for any expected utility, they just interested me. I found the classes about off center vision, the importance of looking at all quadrants of the flight helmet and moving the head and eyes together, interesting. These lessons bore fruit. We were also taught about the importance of dark adaption, the need to avoid light and wear red goggles for 30 to 45 minutes before a flight, less we bleach the rhodopsin needed for night vision. We had no time for dark adaption in Viet Nam, certainly not 30 to 45 minutes. We often went from a lighted room into the darkness in seconds and regardless of the medical dictates, I never noticed any noteworthy visual shortfalls going immediately from light to night. Others may have, which could have accounted for some of the fears associated with night flying. Perhaps the fear of not having adapted may have added to those fears also. In any event, I do not remember any problems with any of our pilots. Alcohol damages night vision, and so does smoking, and being on the wagon may have helped but I felt very good about my ability to adapt quickly to the darkness and, given a choice, would always prefer a night mission.

Each crewman is indispensable; as necessary as each finger to a functioning hand. One sloppy eyeball can ruin your whole night. Every crew member had to be engaged, the co-pilot on the instruments and the crew with their head out the door searching for obstacles, clearing the tail rotor and helping the pilot set the bird down. Any light at night is sufficient for LZ identification (some pickups have been made to cigarette lighters, in one case, Ed Taylor landed to a flickering lighter that would not ignite), but there should not be any flares on approach. They will blind you. My crew saved us on one mission when a flare was ignited as we neared the ground and I was blinded. The crew guided me to a safe set down. I worried that on occasion the crew placed too much trust in the pilot and would relax en route. Again (and again and again...) there can be no slack eyeballs at any time and I would pique their interest with devious questions: is that gun fire ahead? Is that a mountain in front of us? Are those thunder clouds yonder? Alertness should not be something requiring a wakeup call at a critical time.

As important as the crew alertness and eyeballs are, their psyche is priceless. Once the mission began, the crew was not allowed to speculate on whether or not it was a good idea. They had to buy into the mission and be enthusiastic participants. No matter how sure you are of what you are doing and how confident you are that you can do it, dissent or unease in the aircraft can cause uncertainty and may break your concentration. It cannot be allowed. There have been situations where I was a bit uncertain and a word of confidence from a willing co-pilot restored my confidence. Although there were no unwilling co-pilots or crewmen in Detachment A, some borrowed pilots never understood our ways and were challenging. Most of these pilots were used to following the leader with multiple aircraft around and a command and control bird at altitude. Solo missions scared them. Solo night missions terrified them.

It has been said that you should not fly with someone who is braver than you. I would prefer someone who is braver as long as they knew what was going on. There are people you do not like to fly with and others who you would certainly not want to die with. Most issues are solved by strict chain of command, the same guy commands in the air as on the ground. As I said, Kelly bought into this and I seldom flew as other than the pilot in command for which I am ever grateful. It would have been easy to tell a borrowed pilot to get in, strap in, shut the f*** up, and don't touch nothing, but you might need him again.

The demeanor in the chopper was half the battle, the demeanor in the PZ, the other half. Nothing was more disturbing than a confused panicked voice. Patients will do that to the troops, especially if it is a buddy. And so will the enemy. But you had to calm them down and get good information if the pickup was to succeed. It was a joy to hear a calm professional tone in the midst of the chaos. After a while you became familiar with those voices, they became your friend. One such voice I dearly admired. I wanted to meet him. One night I asked him to come over and say hello.

He said he wanted to meet me but was too damned tired to walk the short distance to my bird. I did catch a glimpse of him on another mission, short, wiry with a pencil mustache seemingly all over the place but never rushed. Later I was called into his AO for some wounded. It was night. I smelled the rubber tire odor of a body bag and looked back. There was a circle of troops around the bag all at attention. And there was a flag over the bag. I had never seen that before. They saluted as the body was lifted into our helicopter. I had never seen that before either. I asked the crew to check who he was. He was my pencil mustached voice. He had been shot in the back of the head by an enemy in friendly lines. They had to shoot him in the back; he was more than a match for anything in front of him.

We were learning. Because the skies in daytime were often filled with choppers and most flew at even numbered hundreds in altitudes, i.e., 2000, 2500, I flew at odd hundreds 1900 etc. Pilots refer to each thousand feet as an angel, i.e., angels two, two thousand feet. It seemed that the angels would protect you from small arms at 2,000 feet and 12.7s at 3,000 feet, although I had a friend hit by small arms at night at 2,000 feet; an amazing shot.

I tried not to fly in a straight line but rather gently moving from side to side with the pedals. We had some data on the VC training for shooting down helicopters. A straight line made it easier for them. I was involved in a mass casualty crash which resulted from one of the many one-shot Charlies, snipers who set up at the end of runways. They took a shot at departing and approaching aircraft and then bugged out. One sniper destroyed a Caribou and the 16 souls on board. He took out one engine. One good engine on a two engine aircraft is just enough to get to the scene of the crash. To make matters worse, the pilot turned into the dead engine. It was the worst mess I had seen to this point.

As I walked through the wreckage of man and materiel, both in pieces, I noticed many of the personal effects. One guy was reading *Donovan's Brain*, a book I had read long before. There was an unbroken record of the comedy, "The First Family," and a newspaper clipping with the headlines announcing Kennedy's death. Another soldier had a bunch of silk panties. And there was the guitar, such a treasure in the field. Music is like pets for the deployed grunt. No professional, not Elvis Presley or Frank Sinatra, was as soothing as a GI that could sing and play on, a quiet evening after dinner or around a camp fire. From that moment on I never again approached straight down a runway in combat; I always came in perpendicular to it. I did not want someone looking down on my religious icons and wondering why they failed me.

Eventually we would shoot approaches with one pilot on the controls and the other close (in case the pilot was shot) but focused on the instruments. Our visors were down for the tad of protection they afforded our eyes. Nothing we wore was fire retardant. That came later, but gloves were worn and sleeves down, despite the heat, to mitigate burns.

We were in the foul weather season and this presented new challenges. None of us were fully instrument qualified. We had gotten some instrument orientation in flight school and came away with a tactical instrument ticket which authorized a particular approach nonexistent in Viet Nam. But our paltry ability to fly on instruments was invaluable for some of the situations we blundered into. There was no instrument approach in the Delta but we did have a radar flight following service from the Air Force call sign Paddy Control. They could track our transponders. They were life savers.

The flatness of the Delta as well as the absence of wires enabled us to fly low in bad weather. We could stay under the clouds and follow the many canals, much like a road system, right into the PZ. If you got above the clouds there was no way to get back down to the patients. On occasion we would get right down on a canal, turn on the search light and successfully fly the mission. During this time, I began flying sideward taking advantage of the improved visibility out the open side window. This technique would prove useful later. If the mission was in the Plain of Reeds or mangrove swamps on the Cam Au Peninsula, difficult areas to navigate, Paddy Control would vector us to the site. If we got caught in the weather, we could climb into the clouds and they would guide us home or to a safe spot to let down.

This flying was not legal but it was necessary. As always in Army Aviation, if you break the rules, you better not break anything else. If the mission was successful you might get a medal; if not, you might get a court martial. But the weather, later to be a prime killer of Dust Off pilots, indeed all pilots, was not the show stopper in the Delta that it was in the mountains, thanks to the terrain and our guardian angels, Paddy Control.

My experience with weather in the Delta was enlightening and would be invaluable my second tour. I noticed that no matter how bad it looked a click to the front, it looked just as bad a click to the front—after you flew the first click. Weather was capricious but often localized. It might be devastating at the forecast site but manageable at the PZ. I developed a technique in which I would keep a light in sight to the front and the crew would keep a light in sight to the rear. I was careful not to lose sight of either light. Whoever said a forecast is nothing more than a horoscope with numbers was right; an educated guess perhaps, but a guess none-the-less.

On one mission, a crew encountered some rough weather and called for the weather at their destination to determine if they should abort. The forecaster declared no ceiling and unlimited visibility. The crew proceeded and the weather got worse. Again they called and got the same report. In frustration they asked the forecaster where he was getting his data. He replied it was direct from a weather report. "Where are you?" "I'm in a bunker." "Would you mind getting off your ass and looking outside?" He did and responded, "Holy shit, I can't see a thing out here!" Weather is awesome, and deserves reverential respect, but there was no substitute for getting off your ass, launching, and taking a look. This applied at night also.

But even with all that we had going for us, fear could mess everything up. Fear can produce terror which will cause to happen that which caused it. Fear has the eyes of an eagle, it does horrible things to our senses, it sees things that don't exist and wont unless the fear is unchecked. As I have said, imagination is vital but it must be controlled. Fear is the product of an unchecked imagination. Fear is not an option in the business of Dust Off. Some pilots dwelled on every conceivable form of the unexpected. If you have properly prepared, you will have already vicariously experienced the unexpected and are ready for it. My faith took care of fear for me. My faith was for me a substitute for fear. It was a source of comfort, calm, and it gave me the confidence to do things that for me would have been otherwise impossible. I never experienced fear in combat, apprehension, yes, but not the incapacitation brought on by fear. Many a soldier, in the incredible loneliness of death and near death experiences, also find comfort in their faith. I always felt sorry for those for whom death was the beginning of nothingness. If these folks enjoyed life, they had a problem risking their life. For those of us for whom death was the beginning; no problem—especially if you died saving lives.

We often heard rumors about American POWs being tortured and herded through the villages. Some were executed. One such POW, who at the time, caught my attention was Rocky Versace, born Humbert Roque Versace. I have no idea how the stories got out but he was reputed to be a belligerent in-their-face double tough guy who mocked his captors. He captured my everlasting admiration because I heard he was dedicated to becoming a Catholic monk when he got out and it was clear it was his faith that gave him the courage to act as he did. Eventually he was executed by the communists who could not control him or the courage and inspiration he provided his fellow captives. He had perhaps the greatest death rattle ever. He was last heard singing "God Bless America." I never forgot his name and many years later would hear it again, when he was awarded the Medal of Honor.

One of the most exciting, though frustrating, missions we flew was surprise rescue missions of American POWs like Versace. Based on "intelligence" reports, we would launch an armada of guns and slicks in an effort to swoop down on the POW camp, surprise the communists, and rescue our guys. Dust Off fell in behind the flight as it low leveled into the target area. On one of these missions, we were approaching at about 10 feet or so when suddenly a man in black pajamas darted out from cover into the rice paddy waving his hands in front of us. Black pajamas often spelled VC and I instinctively took evasive action. As we passed him I noticed he had no gun but more astonishing, his face was white, his eyes round. Good Lord, he was one of us. By the time I could process all this, and because of our high speed, it took a bit to get turned around but I jerked it into a 180 and headed back. I was not sure of the exact spot and we searched the area but without luck. Meanwhile the slicks had landed in the village with the usual results, bamboo cages, warm food, but no POWs. The VC intel was just better than ours and no wonder—a multitude of them worked for us. Saving lives was a daily occurrence for us, certainly never routine, always thrilling, but to rescue a POW! Wow! Every POW mission failed, but they never failed to get my adrenaline flowing. That would be a highlight of any life. In my fantasies I did rescue him, but his face and his fate haunt me to this day.

As the UTT developed so did our ability to work missions with them. They were absolutely fearless and could be very helpful. The gunships would flank us as we flew into the PZ and then set up a daisy chain on each side suppressing enemy fire. Sometimes they would follow us right to the ground and hover on each side of our bird, physically protecting us and covering the terrain in 180-degree turns. In the absence of gunships, some crewmen liked to play door gunners on approach. In fact I found that a lot of crewmen liked to shoot target or no, it seemed to give them comfort. My first experience in crew fire resulted in a bunch of hot shell casings going down my bare back—without warning! I was sure I was shot. The problem with all this was that the enemy was seldom seen and the friendlies were often all over the place. Enemy and friendly gunfire all sounded the same to me, each equally disturbing. I have heard that enemy tracer fire was different but I did not notice that either. And shooting out of a moving helicopter requires special skill and training. We found some secure lanes for training often using racing peacocks as targets (not to worry, they were never in any danger). You actually had to *shoot behind the target*, tough to teach. I had serious doubts that the door gunners ever hit the enemy; there was simply no way to tell. I was not a fan of all that shooting but had not yet sorted out what to do about it.

Throughout this learning period, I fell in love with repetition. If cleanliness is next to Godliness, then repetition is next to cleanliness. We did the same thing over and over again day in and day out, deviation could be deadly. A trained soldier is measured by his alertness. An alert soldier sees things no one else sees and he sees them first. Repetition fostered alertness and alert thoughtful repetition was vital in survival. And it was this repetition that developed the skills unique to Dust Off, not only in confronting and overcoming battlefield challenges, but in regulating the medical resources to care for patients in those conditions. The cockpit was often the operations center. No other kind of flying prepared a pilot for Dust Off. You had to do it—day in and day out.

We hear of pilots flying by the seat of their pants. Dust Off pilots flew by the seat of their hearts. You knew that you would be almost dead on many missions and you hoped that it would be almost—and you got used to it. The great military analyst Carl von Clausewitz wrote that you can get soldiers to go into battle but once they see a buddy get shot, getting them to go back is a problem. Clausewitz was wrong about Dust Off. Kelly's twigs saw their fellow soldiers, and their helicopters, shot over and over and went back again and again.

· 20 ·

LESSER NOBLES
AND BUTTERFLY BALLS

THINGS were going well—or so we thought. We were maturing
as combat pilots becoming harder and harder to kill. Nothing,
not the enemy, the night or weather stopped us from getting to
the patients.

We never left a patient in the field. Our casualty load was double
the previous year, despite a more difficult combat environment and
the weather. We flew more night missions in two months than the
57th had flown the previous year. Our maintenance was superb and
our mission reaction time and communications were improving.
We used the fire truck system. We ran to the bird and it was mission ready when we got there. No one was getting killed, although
we had many close calls. Even though he wouldn't have said so, I
was sure Kelly would have been pleased. But our headquarters in
Saigon was not.

Shortly after Kelly's death, new leadership began to arrive in the
57th. One of the FNGs said he had been instrumental in the development of aeromedical evacuation doctrine—a thing of mystery to

the rest of us. He claimed to be an expert and if anyone wanted to challenge his methods they would have to get in line. I wondered about his cockiness and the source of his expertise since he had never flown in combat and neither had the other FNGs. They visited us in Soc Trang and we discussed at length the Kelly school of thought and our flying techniques. For the first time, I heard another school of thought. This new school was more cautious in terms of types of patients flown at night, single ship night missions, landing without communications, pilot rest, hot areas, carrying corpses, not to mention ammo, and even running to the bird. One pilot may have spoke for many when he said, "night air has no lift." Some of them believed you should use two ships on night missions, even if there was only one patient. Our foul weather missions really upset them since in their eyes they were illegal.

A few of the FNGs were high-time fixed-wing pilots with low helicopter time. I noticed that some pilots who had grown up in fixed wings were uncomfortable in helicopters. These folks were especially reluctant to fly with us in the clouds. A fixed-wing actual instrument (AI or IFR, Instrument Flight Rules) flight was a kind of "on your ass let the airplane do its thing." In a helicopter, you not only had to coordinate all your limbs, you had to coordinate all the instruments—everything in the green, needle and ball, altitude, trim, airspeed, heading—with all your limbs. A sneeze could turn everything to shit. And there were those who had spent their whole career flying, not a minute in the dirt with the grunts.

During a mission with one of the FNGs, it was clear that he was uncomfortable. Although he had much more time than I, he said he had never made an approach that fast. He wondered if it was necessary. He also wondered why I had gone in low level (I would meet pilots who would never use the snake approach preferring to come in from altitude, regardless of the situation). When he asked why I went out the same way I came in, I knew there would be a considerable learning curve for the high time "experienced" FNGs. It was becoming clear to me that combat flying excellence often had little to do with flying time.

Soon after their arrival, for first time since Kelly's death, we started getting bugged about our flying time, *from our own headquarters*, not some Aviation safety weenie at higher headquarters. Kelly flew 147 combat hours in the month before he was killed, probably more combat hours in a shorter period than any previous aviator. He averaged 122 hours per month during his stay at Soc Trang—well beyond the limit. And he flew 171 night hours, probably more than any unit in Vietnam at the time. We thought we were over the excessive time harassment bit. The day after Kelly was killed, Ernie and Si took 21 bullets the length of their aircraft, one just missing Ernie's head (for which he thanked God for his shortness). They were not upset because of the rounds, only because one round killed a patient. Saigon was upset about the rounds as they bugged us about our time.

Challenges to both our number of hits and flying times were cloaked in safety and maintenance but I detected some envy. Time is important to pilots, especially combat time, and the pilots at Saigon were not flying the hours we were. But time and hits were not the only issues. The pilots of Detachment A were getting a lot of recognition and awards. At times it was embarrassing. Still, it was clear that some FNGs did not agree with the Kelly philosophy, and believed that we were crazy to fly as he did. One FNG said Kelly had influenced us to fly recklessly, i.e., irresponsibly, and we heard rumors that the "wild and wooly" days were over. What did that mean? We were evacuating more wounded than ever!

But the FNGs pretended outwardly to agree with Kelly and were careful to praise him. Surprisingly, some of the criticism was coming from pilots who were there with Kelly. They had been quiet during the aftermath of his death but now wanted change. It would not have been wise to try and change anything too soon after his death. I was grateful that it was Kelly and not one of our FNGs that confronted me on the ammunition mission. In any event, we ignored them and flew the hours, and took the hits, the patient load required, just as Kelly had done. I was sure we could turn them to our way but had an uneasy feeling some of the FNGs were morphing into REMFs (Rear Echelon Mother F*****s) the scourge of any efficiently operating field unit.

About a month after arriving, the new leadership in Saigon put out a directive called Team Unification. We were ordered to come to Saigon and read it, and sign that we had, along with a bunch of other documents that backed it up. The operations officer notified me of the directive and sounded grave but would give no details. Team Unification? I could not imagine what in the hell that meant but it made me and some of my pilots uneasy.

The evening we heard about the directive, Ernie and I were called out for an Air Force A-1E shot down east of Rach Gia. It had been downed by quad .51s, the enemy weapon we feared most. It was a clear night and as we lifted off we could see tracer fire miles to our front in the vicinity of the burning A-1E. Another A-1E was in the area desperately trying to protect his downed comrade. Within minutes, the second A-1E screamed that he was going down. Ernie and I hopelessly watched the bird crash but I was sure I saw a parachute. Then I heard a voice: "come get me I'm down." Elated, we continued into the first crash site.

We were blacked out and I went to the deck thinking that would be the safest route in since the .51s had been focused on the sky. As we came up over the burning aircraft, the night lit up. I had not seen quad .51s at night before. It was like four flame throwers, in a square, blasting fire at the same time. What was disturbing about tracers was that there were five rounds between each one. The A-1E pilot must have crashed right on top of the 50s. Talk about a bad location for him—and for us. As the burning A-1E lit up our bird—so did Charlie. We were right over the guns. The .51 caliber rounds hit our helicopter like a sledge hammer. I had been hit by .51s before but nothing like this. Some rounds came up through the floor between Ernie's legs. A tracer lit his pants on fire and blew out a chunk of the roof. Ernie later said at that moment he realized he was about to die. Other rounds came in through the windshield and filled our faces with Plexiglas. Our choppers shuddered violently from the rounds and my convulsions on the controls. I was astonished, and grateful, that we were still able to fly.

I yanked us away from the fire and headed across the ground as fast as I could while Ernie put out the fire on his legs. I was not sure how long we would stay up and called for help. Thanks to Ernie's knowledge of the area, we found a small strip with friendlies and set down. Si and Bruce launched from Soc Trang and so did the gunships. Our operation officer from Saigon also launched. No notice night combat flight was a new experience for some of the gunnies and when they joined us at the strip, some were in various stages of dress, underwear, shorts, shower shoes, and some reeked of alcohol. They were a comical sight but it was clear that they were coming after us no matter what. We were happy to see them. But our operations officer was not happy to see us and began to rant about us trying to get killed and messing up his aircraft. We were always short flyable helicopters. I was certain there was someone alive and alone out there in those dark paddies. We asked if we could borrow his bird and go back. He threw up his arms, cursed us, and stomped away. He would not even take us back to Soc Trang. We had to bum a ride.

Meanwhile Si and Bruce continued searching the rice paddies for the survivors we had assured them were there. Over head another A-1E watched in amazement at the courage of the gunship pilots as they low leveled the area, fully lit up, doing all they could to draw hostile fire so they could destroy the enemy and protect the downed pilot. That A-1E pilot's words: "My strongest memory of that morning was watching [those] choppers just taxiing along the canal—taking tracers from both banks—and yet continuing to slowly search every possible hiding place that George [George Edward Flynn, III, the downed pilot] may have picked. I have teared up telling that story. What guts and determination. What a poignant example of man's care for his fellow man. I have said, regarding that moving scene, those 19-year-old warrant officers are fearless." (Such comments gave rise to the fabled fighter pilot's prayer, "Lord, I pray for the eyes of an eagle, the quickness of a hummingbird, the reflexes of a cat, the radar of a cave bat, the heart of a lion, and the balls of a helicopter pilot.")

After hours of flying, Si spotted a pencil flare flickering near one of the wrecks. It could be the downed pilot—or a VC with a pencil flare. Si told the gunships he was going in. The downed pilot of this A-1E, Bill May, had escaped his plane just before it exploded. A piece of his ship landed near him and he hid under it as the VC searched for him. They got his back seat Vietnamese observer but he survived their search—and the gunships who he was sure were trying to kill him. He could hear Dust Off coming in but could not see the blacked out bird until it landed and he saw a flicker of the rotor blade. He came up out of the rice paddy from under the piece of fuselage right next to the Dust Off and Si's crew chief almost shot him. When Si asked about his Vietnamese observer, the pilot said he had left the area and they should do the same. This pilot, May, from one A-1E and an observer from the other were rescued. The other pilot, George E. Flynn III, was captured as was May's Vietnamese observer. We heard that Flynn was brutally beaten by the communists and paraded through villages. He was later killed trying to escape and may have killed one of his guards in the attempt. The other Vietnamese observer would later be released from captivity but in dreadful condition.

That night, as I said my prayers of thanks, I marveled at the indifference of bullets, their amazing trajectory, and the coincidences of combat. I recalled the mission we actually took three rounds through the leading edge of the tail rotor! What were the odds that the A-1E pilot would land right on top of those 50s? How did all those bullets miss our bodies and not knock us out of the sky? A fraction of an inch in any direction and we would have been dead and our bird blown to pieces. But no one in our crew was killed and Si and Bruce had made a miraculous rescue. God was good.

But I was worried about the new directive and the attitude of the operations officer.

The next day Si and I flew up to Saigon to read the new directive and sign that we had. Two weeks before he died, Kelly changed Ernie's daily passage to: "no man knows his friends." Kelly was a bit paranoid and he must have been anxious about the support he had for what he was doing and the future of Dust Off. His death settled that issue. We never heard another word about portable red crosses and his request for more Dust Off units was being honored. Detachment A did not change his system. But things seemed to be changing in Saigon and I knew how Kelly felt—I was getting paranoid. Some in the unit had joined local clubs and I heard the new commander had been taken off the night duty roster. There were other commanders who actually took themselves off night duty. Some called this cowardice, but many of them were old fixed-wing pilots and it was actually the safe thing to do. One night we called Saigon for help with a high casualty situation. We were refused. That would have been unimaginable in Kelly's time.

The team unification directive was the most baffling decree I have ever read, and the most disingenuous. Based on rumors of disloyalty and some unidentified pilots deliberately misconstruing the commander's policies, we were threatened with relief of key position (read commander of Detachment A, me), disciplinary action, adverse efficiency reports, revoked awards, and cancelled AC orders. The directive highlighted that I was not a commander but merely an officer in charge and Detachment A was not a separate team. Amazingly, the directive emphasized that there had been no, repeat, no operational changes in the manner in which the 57th functioned.

Loyalty is the essence of military service and any question of loyalty was a death sentence for an officer's career. It ranked right there with security violations. I wondered where the questions of loyalty originated.

I could not believe any of my pilots at Soc Trang were guilty.

Clearly there was no split in the pilots in Saigon. The commander was there. It had to be Detachment A. I feared it was written for me. But I was convinced it was not our loyalty to the new leadership that was the problem. It was our loyalty to Kelly. Under the guise of disloyalty, our loyalty to the Kelly system could ruin our career.

The team unification (really a Brady loyalty) directive was not to unify under the Kelly legacy, it was to unify under the new leadership. As I pondered the shocking directive on the trip back to Soc Trang, I choked up. Si saw how upset I was and did his best to comfort me. This would be the final nail in my coffin. Along with my other problems, if my perceived disloyalty was reflected in my OER, my career was over. They were trying to straighten out Kelly's twigs. But I was determined that as long as I was in charge, there would be no change in the way we flew at Detachment A. There was no way they could change me; but they could change who was in charge. And they did. I would not be in charge much longer.

Despite "no, repeat no," operational changes promised in the loyalty directive, many things did change. All of which made it easier to refuse a mission. Kelly carried his balls in a deuce and a half; some of those who came behind had the balls of a butterfly. From the date of the loyalty directive, patient load and flying time went down in the 57th, especially at night. The true purpose of the directive, camouflaged under disloyalty, was to reeducate Kelly's Krazies to the changes that the new leadership wanted. It forbade the Kelly round robins, even though I never flew one—ever. I don't think Kelly flew any after he established Dust Off in the Delta.

Other changes would follow. No landing in hot areas, period. No take offs during weather. No landing without radio contact. Only urgent patients were to be flown at night and then two ships would be used if possible as was the case with other units. Dust Off had been through the two-ship business before Kelly and abandoned it because of the drain on pilots and maintenance. Some FNGs even challenged our fire truck approach to missions. Better they said to take time to prepare; the haste makes waste type excuse. One pilot said time spent on the ground before takeoff pays big dividends. I had never heard such nonsense. Time spent doing what? True waste was in not being prepared before the mission—then waste was a lack of haste.

Within two weeks of the directive, pilots began arriving to form a new Dust Off unit, the 82nd. It would replace Detachment A. Kelly had requested help months earlier and Soc Trang would now have five helicopters to do the work we had been doing with two. I had no desire to return to Saigon and neither did any of my pilots. We all volunteered to remain at Soc Trang and transfer to the 82nd to help break them in. As commander of Detachment A, I would have been the logical person to help break in the 82nd. My request was denied. I was the only pilot ordered back to Saigon. I would not be allowed to influence the new pilots in the 82nd. But Si and Ernie and Bruce did. They made it clear to the new pilots that the Kelly way was the right way. Many of the new pilots agreed. They ignored the changes and flew as Kelly's Krazies did.

The new commander was no Kelly and would struggle to keep operational control of his own unit. He insisted on approving all missions. Si found himself in the embarrassing position of begging to be allowed to rescue a great number of patients one night in marginal weather. The commander refused to allow the mission. Si convinced him to allow a launch into the flight pattern to check the weather. Si then pleaded by radio (hoping no one heard the conversation which he found embarrassing) that the weather was OK. It was not but Si knew he could fly the mission; and he did. Si noted that the new commander did fly at least one night mission—into the flight pattern—to heroically rescue local nurses from a mortar attack on Soc Trang.

We had a debate over what the call sign of the 82nd would be. Some suggested that they adopt Dust Off and just use their tail numbers. I was opposed. I did not want to see the tradition of Dust Off diminished by some who disagreed with the origin of that tradition. I was overruled and every subsequent helicopter ambulance unit also kept Dust Off as their call (and do to this day) sign except for those organic to the 1st Cavalry Division. They would be known as MEDEVAC and rightly so for they were different from Dust Off. Many of the pilots were thrilled to use Kelly's call sign and wanted to add to the Kelly legacy. And they did. I am thankful I lost this battle.

21

I GOTTA GET OUT
OF THIS PLACE

ALTHOUGH I had three months left, my tour was essentially over. The new commander said he wanted to see me go home alive. I flew very little and neither did anyone else. Yet despite the lack of missions, they would not let me leave two weeks early to spend Christmas with my family. They really did not like me. In three months in Saigon, I flew the equivalent of one month in Soc Trang. And my night missions were one sixth of what they were in the Delta. I covered the monotonous Ranch Hand missions which dispersed the notorious Agent Orange (actually it was pink and purple in 1964, named after the color of the bands on the storage drums). We flew in trail behind the Air Force C-123s as they dispersed the agent. (Years later I would develop and be treated for a form of cancer possibly caused by Agent Orange. I have no idea if there is a relation but they track me to this day.)

In the midst of all the down time, I did have one payback mission. I was able to return the favor to the SF captain that helped Brian and me at Trung Lap. He was in the midst of mass casualties soaked in blood from his belt to his boots but refused to be evacuated before his wounded ARVNs. When I finally got him on board he rejected treatment pointing to the other wounded. He feared we would neglect them because he was American. All he wanted was a cigarette. For a lot of reasons I never allowed anyone to smoke on my chopper. The crew chief looked at me and I nodded. For this soldier I would make an exception.

Perhaps because I was diligent in recommending awards for Detachment A, and few officers in Saigon had the interest or writing skills to do the job, I was assigned an additional duty as awards officer. It was a time-consuming tedious job if done correctly. In this capacity I learned much about the inequity of the military awards system. For example, I heard that the pilots of the A-1E who were shot down received Silver Stars; Si and Bruce who risked their lives in the rescue got nothing. Such examples were not rare.

My tour in Berlin resulted in two medals, both for service, earned simply by being there, but I was still proud of them. Viet Nam was not even called a war and for a long time combat medals were restricted for that very reason. There was even confusion over whether or not a wounded soldier could get a Purple Heart, awarded for wounds incurred in war. But as our involvement increased, perhaps influenced by politics and the awarding of the Medal of Honor to Roger Donlon for actions the week after Kelly's death, combat awards to include Purple Hearts were being awarded. At an awards ceremony in Saigon I received four combat awards ,some that I previously thought were only for the great warriors of our great wars. I was certainly proud of these medals but at the time not sure I deserved them.

It became clear to me that two things were necessary for success in an award for valor: Someone had to be aware of the heroic action and take the time to document it; and the document had to be well written. The action itself often was less important than how well it was written and who supported it. For this reason, it should be evident that we do not own our awards. They result from the care and effort of our fellow troops. This fact, we do not own our awards, make the actions of those who use their awards for political purposes especially despicable. Such conduct is an insult to their fellow soldiers who in good faith, and hard work, were responsible for the awards.

But given solid documentation, the commander had to be knowledgeable and truly care about rewarding his troops. Some commanders would not take the time and did not care about awards. To them, all actions, no matter the heroics, were simply one's duty. Others did care about awards, but only for themselves. It was rumored that some ranking officers in Saigon were putting themselves in for awards. (I noticed that most of the awards for rescue included the word "volunteer." I could never understand how those pilots volunteered any more than a grunt volunteered to take a hill. But such language gives insight into the psyche of some, not Dust Off, who flew these flights.)

Since the "war," such as it was, was now more open to hero awards and they could be invaluable for future promotion, I took my duties as award officer seriously. Early on I noticed that our medical HQ seemed to spend a lot of time downgrading our awards. The officers there were mostly MSCs as were we, but few would ever be shot at. And some resented the fact that they would have to compete against MSCs who were shot at and, accordingly, highly decorated. Rescue missions were very conducive to awards and one officer actually said that if they took the time to write awards for all the deserving Dust Off crews, they would have no time for anything else. (I have heard that some commanders outlawed medals for Dust Off crews.)

For this reason I found that awards to non-Dust Off pilots for rescue missions were often higher than ours. I also noticed that in some cases, the AC was the only one put in for an award, or was put in for a higher award than the others in the crew. I did not think that was fair, although there were exceptions. They were all essential to the mission and should be treated equally. I promoted a policy that did just that. Since I had to write them, no one disagreed. I actually flew a mission in which a non pilot crew member got a higher award than I did. I must say that I am rarely impressed with hero awards for ranking officers. (In later years, I was often asked what emotion I felt when I received the Medal of Honor. I was certainly honored, but the only true emotion I felt was embarrassment.)

There is no accurate way to measure the heroism of the Dust Off crews because their heroism came to be taken for granted. Still, we received our share of awards from grateful grunts. But I am amazed to this day to read medal citations, to include some for the Medal of Honor (mine included), that describe actions that were the daily fare of Dust Off crews. I am convinced that the heroism of the military in Viet Nam matched that of any war. In fact, I believe that the most under-rewarded troops of any war were the helicopter pilots in Viet Nam, probably because what they did was novel in warfare. And the army seems to be less interested than the other services, especially the Marines, in highlighting heroism. (I am always amused at the fighter jocks et al, who boast of missions flown in the hundreds. I never fail to remind them that the helicopter pilots counted their missions in the thousands.) And many of us had a hard time, initially, comparing ourselves with the great warriors of our past wars, our fathers and grandfathers who were the heroes of our youth.

The changes depressed me. The patient was no longer the center of our universe. The new center was weather, enemy action, terrain, and darkness. Almost immediately after the arrival of the FNGs, the 57th patient loads, and night missions, were cut in half. There still was no doctrine, no set system for patient information or evacuation except that U.S. Soldiers and civilians came first. Dust Off was essentially a free enterprise system and its future effectiveness rested in the hearts of the individual pilots. And some of those pilots really thought Kelly was a madman. And some of the pilots were simply afraid. I feared he had died for naught.

I went in search of my beautiful little flower girl who I knew would lift my spirits. I couldn't find her and when another girl persisted, I decided to buy her flowers. Just as I was paying her, my flower girl appeared. When she saw I had bought flowers from someone else she jumped in my face and began to curse me with language more vile than that of the foulest-mouthed GI I ever heard. I left in tears as she continued her ugly tirade. The final straw fell on a standby mission in the field.

Some FNG ate my beanie weenies. I could not wait to get out of that place.

But I did have one pleasant experience during this period, actually two. I won a tidy sum in a poker game and was able to go on R&R to Hong Kong. My plan was to buy some presents for the family and some civilian clothes for future employment. The GIs (diarrhea), also known as Ho Chi Minh's revenge, was not uncommon among GIs, including me. Joyously, while in Hong Kong I had for the first time in 10 months, a solid bowel movement. I did not want to get off the toilet and actually wrote my wife during that memorable event that as much as I missed her, this was a close second. The other good experience, Bob Hope came for Christmas and I got to see him.

Bob joked about the Brinks Hotel passing by his aircraft on his way in. The VC had bombed the Hotel, which housed U.S. officers, the day before. (That bombing may have influenced the introduction of U.S. combat troops in Viet Nam.) Surely there is a special place in Heaven for this great man. Years later, I would meet Bob on several occasions. He was exactly what he appeared to be; unlike so many other celebrities. There is no way to measure what he has done for the morale of our troops over the years. It always amazed me that a country which produced a man so in tune with the importance of troop morale could have produced a media which cared so little for it.

One of our enlisted men drew duty on Christmas Day and missed Bob's show and the pretty girls. He also had duty on Thanksgiving and he was very bitter. A duty rooster has no heart.

He was savoring his bitterness as his chopper passed over the show en route to the Navy Hospital with a load of dead and wounded. Then a blanket blew off the face of one of the dead who seemed to be looking at him. He was overcome by shame as he realized that he did not have it so bad after all. One day he would be among the wounded.

At my farewell party, where I fell off the wagon to the tune of a fifth of scotch, my atheist friend took me to one side and asked for my spare .357 ammo (we both carried .357 Magnums) and snuff (no smoking on my birds but dipping was OK even though the crew swore my emissions took the paint off their helicopters). I said OK and then he asked almost in a whisper if he could have my .50 caliber medal. He allowed that all of my close calls could not have been luck, especially our dead buffalo mission during which we were hit by numerous .30 and .51 caliber rounds. (The mission I was sure he had tried to kill me.) I guess he had thought about that mission and decided it was not so funny. I almost fell over. I told him not no, but hell no. He looked hurt; I later relented and gave it to him. At the time his eyes were a bit misty—and so were mine. I would later try to get it back.

My atheist friend went on to become a famous army aviator. *Time Magazine* wrote of his exploits and he was the Army Aviator of the Year one year. There was a barracks named after him in Germany. He survived several tours in Viet Nam, which I told him was due to my medal. Unfortunately, he was killed later by terrorists in Germany, terrorists trained by the same communists who had tried to kill him so often in Viet Nam. I have often wondered if he had my medal at the time. But of course it was not the medal it, was his faith that was important. The fact that he wanted my holy medal told me that he came to believe. Maybe there are no atheists in foxholes—or cockpits.

Once again Andy and I were on a plane, this time going home. We were off to the land of round eyes and the "Big PX." Andy was at Kelly's side and had heard his dying words, words that would never die: "When I have your wounded." It was Andy, not Kelly, who really gave those words to Dust Off, words that would inspire pilots forever. Yet, I never heard much about those words from Kelly's successors.

The medics gave me a sleeping pill, my first, but I never slept a wink. I sat there thinking about the year that began with great hope and ended so dismally. In a way, I hated to leave. I would have liked to prove I was not disloyal, nor was I a security threat. But there are no do-overs and too many minds were made up. In the end, the G2 was probably right; I had no future in the Army. I was going home on a low with a poor Efficiency Report. The OER is the single greatest determinant of an officer's career potential. Very few reports will openly damn an officer. Rather, the damning is done by faint praise. My report was a classic in damning by faint praise a killer in a combat report; but my lowest grade was on loyalty, a killer in any report. No matter how poor a report may be, an officer's loyalty is seldom challenged. Mine was. I got the lowest grade I ever saw on loyalty. My OER removed any doubt about the subject of the loyalty memo. I now had a dismal record in the two biggest career killers an officer can have—loyalty and security. My hopes that a combat tour would rejuvenate my career were trashed. My end of tour award was one usually reserved for lower enlisted—more damning by faint praise.

Yet despite my bitterness, the year had some highs. I had learned much about the use of a helicopter in saving lives in combat and there is no way to measure the joy of saving lives. I would always have that. I had been awarded numerous medals including six for valor. The one award that impressed me most was a Vietnamese Cross of Gallantry with Silver Star, rather common and not really noteworthy. But whoever wrote the citation said that I was well known for my compassion and caring for the wounded. I know the writer never had a clue about what I had done—but I enjoyed those words none the less.

An aviation magazine did a story on my awards. My aircraft

had been hit by enemy fire many times but, as far as I knew, only one patient had died in our care. By now magnet ass had been replaced with Bullets Brady. I had been wounded, although very slightly, and three of my co-pilots had been wounded beside me but no crew member was killed. I was involved in 21 percent of all unit night hours flown, and I was told that I held the unit record for patients evacuated up to that time, even with several wasted months. The 82nd adopted my kangaroo patch for their unit. I was delighted. It brought a smile to my heart when I thought of Kelly's reaction; although he might not have objected now that he was surrounded by angels.

But, of course, the tour highlight was meeting Charles Kelly, a man who defined honor. That was a life-changing experience and would serve me well no matter the future. He had tried to save my career but my refusal to betray him, I feared, would finish my career.

Despite all my efforts, I had been unable to be assigned to Fort Lewis, near my home, where I could best look for a job. Both Andy and I were going to Fort Benning to be a part of the 11th Air Assault Division (Test), now two years in the making. Fort Benning was not a garden spot and seemed to me to be another hardship tour. But I had no choice. I owed the army two more years for flight school. I knew my record would precede me and did not look forward to another "Buck up Letter" which was sure to come. And with my record, they could still board me out.

But knowing I would soon see my family trumped all the depression over my failed tour. Separation from loved ones is difficult even though that love is much of the reason for the separation. I knew everything that had happened to each of my children as we had kept in contact with tape recordings, but I knew they had changed and wondered how they would react to me. In their last letter my oldest son wanted a yellow lion. My daughter just wanted. The number two son kidded his mother that he could not remember what I looked like: "Does he have a mustache?" "No," she said, "just freckles. Daddy can't grow a mustache." "Oh, now I remember."

And then he winked at her.

As I sat there with Andy, immune to the sleeping pill, I remembered my last flight with the 57th. They say all pilots will one day walk to the flight line knowing it is their last flight...or one day they will walk to their bird not knowing it is their last flight. Dust Off pilots often ran to the flight line not knowing whether or not it was their last flight. In fact, we often feared it was our last flight—during a flight.

On 6 January 1965, I walked to the flight line thinking it would be my last flight in Viet Nam. It was a year to the day that Kelly arrived in Viet Nam and he was on my mind as I strapped in for a routine 30-minute maintenance flight. I had the crew film some of it for posterity. But it wasn't my last flight and everything that happened in my first year of combat would pale before what was to come. I would fly in Viet Nam again, and on that same date, six January, the feast of the Epiphany, I would fly a series of missions that would change my life forever, missions that would surely make Charles Kelly proud of me.

· PART 2 ·

PREPARATIONS FOR WAR

22

THE FLYING RED A**HOLE

FORT Benning was known as Fort Beginning since every significant leader of the last century trained and matured in its red clay. It was also the school house of many of the CEOs who, post-World War II, built this country. Napoleon may not have known it but when he said hardship, misery, and privation are the school house of the soldier, he was talking about Benning. The military owns some of the most beautiful terrain in this country, mostly because they got there first. Benning was not one of those places. In addition to the sticky red clay and putrid heat, it was populated by every known creepy, crawling, buzzing creature imaginable, and all of them bit.

It was at Benning that Marshall schooled the likes of George Patton, Omar Bradley, and Dwight Eisenhower and earmarked the team that saved the world. He also established himself as the premier military leader of his time. He did not lead by his rank, but he scared the living hell out of people. General Patton, who was certainly no girly man, once said if he had to choose between being called on the carpet to face Marshall, or facing a whole Nazi Panzer division by himself, his choice would be easy—face the Panzers. Benning developed black and white either/or men dedicated to the principle of KISS—Keep It Simple Stupid. Marshall taught that if you truly understood an issue, you could explain it in less than five minutes. He would prove his point by explaining the entire Civil War from Fort Sumter to Appomattox including state's sovereignty and slavery in less than 5 minutes. Eisenhower began his development as a superb staff officer at Benning. He would later insist that his staff condense complicated action papers to one page. Our soldiers not only learned, they learned how to do, from concise staff work to shooting, moving, and communicating. It is training in places like Benning that insure America's security.

I had served with many Benning products in the Berlin Brigade. Their leadership spoiled me for what I found in the Medical Evacuation Platoon (MEDEVAC) of the 11th Medical Battalion and the aviation staff officers (ASO) who dominated my experience at Benning. Too many of them were not trained at Benning. The 11th Air Assault Division (Test) had 470 aircraft and the growing demand for aviation expertise jerked many aviators, who had spent much of their career ensconced in the cozy orderly confines of a cockpit, into the cold reality of enormous logistical as well as command and control challenges. The results were both humorous and horrifying. The patch for the 11th consisted of a shield including an 11 back dropped in red with wings. As you might expect, it was known as the "flying red asshole."

The assignment folks in the Surgeon General's office said my Viet Nam experience would be of great value in the training of the helicopter ambulance crews in the MEDEVAC platoon. It was an open secret that this Division was being groomed for Nam. On my initial visit to my new unit, near King's Pond, I was met with few aviators eager to tap my combat experience. Instead I found an indoor card game and an outdoor volley ball game. I was warned that only the early arrivers got in the card game. My love of sports did not include volleyball and they didn't play poker. To make matters worse, I hardly flew at all during my first month with the 11th. Slack was a virtue in this unit as in many stateside aviation units. I readied myself for some serious monotony.

Early into my check out in the D model Huey, it became obvious to me that this was not a good bird for Dust Off. They stretched the body of the B model over three feet, a good thing for patient load, but added little power, a very bad thing. The added length and reduced power made for tail low landings, reducing visibility at night, and increased the difficulty of high-speed flat approaches. I dearly missed the B model but the D model was fine for the 11th Med. Their pilots did little training in tactical approaches, let alone blacked-out night landings. Few pilots were interested in any approach other than what they learned in flight school—high recon, low recon, and 500 feet per minute. The 1st Cav. pilots understood the importance of fast low-level approaches but the MEDEVACs liked to come in from an altitude which often guaranteed a bull's eye around the red cross.

MEDEVAC's leadership was tied to the World War II evacuation system which moved the patient through various levels of medical capability from the front lines. The system was perfectly fitted to ground ambulances but outdated by the helicopter. And they were a direct support resource tied to a particular unit without responsibility for area casualties. Such a system mattered little at Benning but clearly was not suited for the battlefields of Viet Nam. This concept caused much confusion and inefficiency once they got in the country.

In addition to an underpowered bird, an antiquated evacuation system and closed minds, the crew work was appalling. I may have been overly obsessed with crew coordination but for good reason. Shortly after I left Viet Nam, Tiny Simmons, the ultimate Dust Off crewman, was left in a hot area for lack of crew coordination. He was killed in the ground battle before they could retrieve him; the first Dust Off enlisted crewman killed and second Dustoffer after

Kelly. During my check out I found to my horror that both crew members were sitting with their backs to the pilots in no position to see out either side of the aircraft, let alone clear the tail rotor. To make matters worse, they were reading comic books. It shook me to my core as did my co-pilot's indifference.

I immediately went to the commander, an older pilot who probably grew up in fixed wings. I explained that the crew was vital in combat missions and their seats had to be positioned perpendicular to the aircraft so they could see outside. The mission demanded four sets of functioning eyeballs. Comic books had no business in the bird. He quietly informed me that it was none of my business how they flew. This was not Dust Off. This was MEDEVAC, and it was not run by a madman. He had obviously heard of my tales about Kelly and the way we flew for him. (Some of the pilots had listened, were interested in the Kelly way, and would have been good Dust Off pilots if permitted.) It would do me no good to go up the chain since the commander was a physician who knew less about helicopter ambulance operations than this guy. I left with my tail between my legs, comforted by the hope I would never have to fly with this unit in combat and, most importantly, they would not besmirch the name of Dust Off. I then began an article on tactical flying in combat. Perhaps there were some aviators out there who were willing to learn.

They also worked us in gunships. Some of the Aviation weenies still hoped to take over the mission. I gained a new respect for the challenges to accuracy in the gun systems they used and the gunship pilot who saved us in Laos that night. We carried few actual patients, most of the time sitting idly on the ground waiting for the frantic call that there had been an accident or a crash. In mid-June we got such a call. Two birds had a mid-air just across the road from us. The weather was marginal and they were flying formation. I was always thankful that Dust Off never had to fly formation. Rotor wings are not as compatible as fixed wings. I was on duty and we were first to the site. It was the usual mess with no hope of survivors at the crash.

We went into the surrounding woods hoping that some had been thrown out before the crash and survived. We found only bodies—18 of them. There were no survivors. Early in their husbands' career, army wives have little in material comforts; their greatest comfort being each other. On the day of the crash, the wives were enjoying each other's company at the Officer's Club when some were informed of their husbands' deaths. Such grief can never be quelled; it can only be shared. No one does that better than military wives.

I should add that I did make some good friends in the 11th. Chuck Kane, a real pro, whose wife looked exactly like Elizabeth Taylor; and Nick and Patsy Lynch. Patsy was a beauty and a very talented musician; but often out of control. She once came to a party dressed as a Nun. None of us recognized her as she bummed drinks—until she cussed the bartender for skimping on the booze and asked where my bitchin' wife was.

It was just after midnight and I was in the field training near Augusta, Georgia. It took some time for them to find me but they did. They had actually put my picture on local TV, so desperately did they need a supply officer for immediate deployment to the Dominican Republic (DOMREP). Ever since the assassination of Rafael Trujillo on 30 May 1961, the Dominican Republic had been in political turmoil. A military coup in September of 1961 was followed by a revolution in April of 1965. Fearing one side of the revolution was controlled by communists, President Lyndon Johnson deployed 20,000 U.S. troops to establish order. I was to be part of the medical support for that operation.

I quietly cursed Brian, and Kelly, for branding me as a supply weenie, went home grabbed my ever-ready deployment gear, kissed my sleepy wife goodbye, and without a word on where I was going, left. When I got to the unit I found a mountain of materiel scattered over a large area. I was met by a Division logistics officer hurrying me to sign for that mess. My signature, of course, meant owner-ship—as is. I may have hated the job but I did understand it. Ownership without inventory was not an option. I ignored his protest of the emergency of the moment and set about the inventory. As expected, much materiel was from units anxious to rid themselves of junk. Sometime during the process, we got word that the 54th Medical Detachment (Helicopter Ambulance) (54th) would take the mission in the DOMREP. We had jumped through loops for nothing. Another ASO staff action.

Not long after this, I got another call in the field. Nick Lynch was on the other end. I noted a giggle in his voice as he asked if I would like to volunteer to go back to Viet Nam with the Division. On 1 July 1965, the 11th had traded the flying red asshole for a horse blanket and reorganized into the 1st Cavalry Division (Airmobile) (1st Cav.). The 11th Medical Battalion became the 15th after the reorganization. The Division was ordered to Nam two weeks later and would begin deploying in August. Since the Gulf of Tonkin incident, U.S. forces had increased from 16,000 to over 70,000. Things were getting serious over there. I had been back less than a year and under current policy they could not force me to return. I could hear laughter in the background as I cut loose on Nick about what I thought about flying in combat with the Medical Battalion. Nick was holding the phone up in the air so all could hear what they knew would be my response. In six months with the 11th I flew less than a below average month in Viet Nam, and a measly 11 hours at night. There are two ways to learn: personal experience or from someone else's experience. They had none of the former and ignored the later. This unit would have some sticker shock when they got in combat.

And they did. Few of us followed national news in those days but we did read the local newspaper, the *Columbus Ledger-Inquirer* and the articles sent home by one of its journalists, Charlie Black, in my book one of the greatest wartime journalists ever. Black went over with the 1st Cav. which left many family members in Columbus, Georgia. The 1st Cav. landed in Viet Nam in mid-September and shortly thereafter was engaged with NVA regulars in the celebrated battles of Ia Drang in the central highlands. The 1st Cav. set a

"Road Kill" Viet Nam style.

Kelly "giving" Stillwell our air ambulances.

ABOVE: Awards ceremony,
end of first tour.

RIGHT: Our beloved Francis and Dusty.

OPPOSITE: Kelly portrait by daughter Carol.

LEFT: Gertrude abusing Super.
RIGHT: Francis consoling Super Oink.

Super enlisted men Jim Coleman, Brian Burwick, and Don Goody.

TOP: Our own Kennedy and Johnson –
Jim Kennedy and Johnny Johnson –
super everything.

ABOVE: Low valley.

Maintenance miracle workers, Don
Goody, John Hodgdon, and Jim
McDaniel.

An unusual "patient."

LEFT: Charlie Ramirez – first hit.
RIGHT: Charlie Ramirez – second hit.

Coconut Head, Lester Shadrick.

TOP: Schenck and Hall got everyone out alive.

ABOVE: Another blessing of our work.

Who could not love these people?

record for U.S. casualties in that engagement and the reports came back that it was a disaster. However, thanks to the power of the pen, a book and movie made it the most heroic battle of Viet Nam resulting in three awards of the Medal of Honor.

The introduction of the NVA was a signal that Hanoi did not trust the VC to do the job; and a sure indication we were headed to war. Chuck Kane was killed on 12 October, my wedding anniversary. I think Chuck's death had an influence on the operational philosophy of the 15th Medical Platoon. The leadership began to focus on area security and came up with ridiculous security standards such as insisting an area be "green", i.e., secure, for so many minutes before they would land. Two-ship missions were routine and only urgent patients could be evacuated after dark. These policies absolutely guaranteed over classification and misinformation on security. They also mounted machine guns on each side of their birds adding an extra crewman and reducing patient space, none of which enhanced security.

After one mission in which the MEDEVACs refused to land, the MEDEVAC commander (the same person who chewed my ass when I complained about the comic books) actually attacked (verbally) another commander for calling his birds into an insecure area. In the midst of his amazement, the soldier almost took the medic's head off. Where else would there be casualties? He had also tried to show two MEDEVAC pilots a low-level approach (as I had tried to do) into a PZ. They refused and came in from 1,500 feet in a normal approach! They took fire and aborted leaving the patients for pilots who could make a tactical approach. (There were other helicopter ambulance unit commanders who shunned the low-level approach coming in from altitude regardless of terrain and tactical situation. I could never understand this, although the snake approach does require some skill.) This commander lost all confidence in MEDEVAC and declared he would ignore them in future plans for casualty evacuation, instead using his own resources. The MEDEVAC leadership was of the same school as the guy who wrote the "book" and the other REMFs who followed Kelly.

Needless to say, none of this endeared MEDEVAC to the troops who lived in insecure areas and others who had been covered by Dust Off on past tours. One trooper was dismayed by the conduct of MEDEVAC and wondered where they got such a great reputation. MEDEVAC had not been in the country long enough to have a reputation; the trooper was obviously confusing them with Dust Off. I am not sure this unit ever found its identity but they did effect the reputation of helicopter ambulance operations. In what was one of the most embarrassing moments in my life, I sat in the White House listening to a Medal of Honor citation in which the recipient rescued casualties: "After medical evacuation helicopters refused to fly...." I wanted to hide under my chair. Still, I must add that many of the crew members of the 15th performed heroically despite confused and flawed leadership.

· 23 ·

THE GOLDEN-WINGED 54TH

I was assigned to the 54th after the 1st Cav. deployed and joined them in the DOMREP in August. DOMREP was a good war. I am not sure to this day who the good guys were. I remember going to mass one day and watching a leader of the revolution going to communion completely surrounded by machine gun toting guards. But no one was shooting at us. We watched the tracers at night over a beer in the safety of our hooches, later replaced by hotel rooms. The most dangerous mission was remembering the secret password to the challenge as we drove through a checkpoint on the way home from dining out. We actually ran a bar out of our hooch. The duty pilot served as the bartender. Since our birds were parked near the hospital and all hospitals have nurses, our bar was the most popular on the island. Even though all drinks were only a quarter (including water), our unit fund prospered. I made friends with some Air Force pilots and we would drive our jeep into their bird, fly to Puerto Rico, drive to the liquor store, fill up, and return. When the stress got too much for us we went on R&R in Puerto

Rico. As I said, this was a good war.

However, I did have some close calls not related to combat flying. As always, the troops need their pets and rumor had it that Trujillo had populated a nearby island with monkeys. I loaded up a local zoo attendant, equipped with a tranquilizer gun, and headed out over the Caribbean to the Island. We landed on some rocks overlooking the ocean where I spotted what appeared to be sharks circling below us. I took out my pistol and began to pepper the fins of the deadly creatures. Much to my dismay, the zookeeper went berserk. I could not understand a word he spoke but it was clear that I was in the sights of his gun. We were able to calm him and discovered that the fins belonged to dolphins, apparently much beloved by our zoo man. Things only got worse when we found the island totally vacant of any living thing, let alone monkeys. Little wonder that the people had built a monument on the spot Trujillo was killed. The man could not be trusted.

Later I was persuaded by some scientists to fly them to an inland body of saltwater said to contain a special species of crocodile. I rested in the shade as they searched in vain for the rare creature. Some of the scientists were entomologists and I discovered, after we were airborne, they had gathered some spiders, including the grotesque tarantula. Some of them got loose and were bouncing all over the passenger area. I pushed my neck into my shoulders imagining one of the hideous creatures crawling into my flight suit. At that moment I would have traded them for the hot shells of Viet Nam. The hairy creatures were eventually captured by the scientists who were much amused at my panic.

DOMREP was a beautiful place with an ideal climate seemingly without any flying biting bugs. The people were poor and I often sensed hatred in their glances. Trujillo was not a benevolent dictator and they may have feared we would be the same. It is hard for many to realize that America is not in the habit of confiscating all that its power would allow. We occasionally ask for a plot of land to bury our dead, but that's it. I noticed that when we flew along the Haitian border, the villages were devoid of people. We could see smoke and animals but not a living soul. I later learned that Trujillo's henchmen often shot at the peasants out of airplanes and may have killed 20,000 Haitians along that border. Little wonder they fled at the sound of our engines.

As I said, I never knew who the good guys were. But unlike our intervention in Viet Nam, it all seemed to work out. Yet as good as this "war" was, I was anxious to get home. Nancy was pregnant with number five. We were moving to a bigger house and the boys were getting rowdy. My number one son had spray painted a neighbor's house. In those days, they could kick you off post for such a prank. We could not afford that. He might have gotten away with it but part of his artwork included his name. Nancy needed help. And too much of the good life is not good for a soldier. We were losing our sense of urgency, a deadly sin in our business. Soldiers have to be fruitfully employed or they get fruity. Some guys started to drink too much. I was not on the wagon during this war and spent more time in my cups than I should have. One of our pilots actually flew to a party, got drunk, and lost his chopper. We found it, thankfully unharmed, the next day. Too much good war, too little soldiering. It was time to get back to soldiering.

Bill Bush and I stopped at Fort Bragg on the way home and were asked to ferry an H-19 back to Benning. Bill was a slow-moving, slow-talking southern boy but an excellent pilot. I had never been in an H-19 but assured Bill that I could fly it if he could start it. The H-19 was a beast to fly much like Hiller the Killer, the H-23, I learned to fly in. It took every limb, plus a powerful left wrist, an iron left leg and perfect coordination to keep it in the air. And it could kill you in many ways as I learned on the way to Benning. Once en route, Bill leaned it out, tightened the grips, turned it over to me, and settled down for a nap. We were a few hundred feet off the trees moving right along when I noticed that the bird was shuddering. "What the hell is that?" He never opened his eyes. "Ease off a bit; you are right on the edge of retreating blade stall." As I was wondering what the hell that was, the bird violently pitched up and began a vertical descent. I was looking straight down the tail boom at the trees, not far away. Bill was now fully awake, moving faster than I thought possible, scrambling for the controls. He recovered right on the trees. He was not amused and tightly guarding the controls when I asked if I could have them back to see if I could repeat that exciting maneuver.

But that ugly beast was not through with us yet. On the approach to Lawson Army Airfield, we popped a tire. Once again Bill was wide eyed and bushy tailed. He explained that uneven struts or a flat tire could put you into ground resonance, another characteristic of this multi-bladed bird—not a problem in the two-bladed Huey. Sure enough as he tried to set down, it began to vibrate violently. During ground resonance there is a rhythmic beat between the fuselage and the rotors that together cause the transmission to come through the cockpit, killing everything in sight, while the aircraft disintegrates. I vaguely remembered a film of a helicopter doing just that. After a couple tries, Bill said he was going to jam it into the ground, cut the throttle, and bottom the pitch. I should jump out the window as soon as we hit. I did and it was quite a drop. I rolled clear of the bird and we watched it rock and roll for a while, slowly coming to a halt right side up.

It is relevant that the 54th, the medics, were the only aviation unit at Benning that flew the antiquated H-19; other aviation units flew the state-of-the-art Huey. This was the opposite of my experiences in Viet Nam where the medics, thanks to Kelly, had the pick of aircraft. What did this say about the ASOs concern for patients?

The 54th had 11 of these monsters. Good Lord, must I fly them? Yes! The under-powered D model Huey would outlift this bird; and it flew faster and climbed over twice as fast. Even the Huey dwarf, the B model, would outlift the 19. This bird was properly named; Chickasaw means rebel—this helicopter rebelled against flying. We usually flew single-pilot missions and it was a challenge to fly, navigate and communicate alone; but I became an H-19 IP and after two years flying it, I was a better pilot. The sensitivity of the 19 to weight and density altitude, and learning to deal with it, would be invaluable to the loads I would carry my second tour in Nam.

As feared, I became the supply officer for the 54th. Charles Kelly, responsible for me getting that job, was a former commander of the 54th. He was one of three 54th commanders killed in Viet Nam. I loved this unit from the start. Many of its members are friends to this day. Most of them were Dust Off veterans from Viet Nam, several severely wounded. And they were good pilots who shared my enthusiasm for night flying. Ed Taylor (of the flickering lighter) was one of them. He flew over 50 hours of night combat in one month. I would later serve as commander, safety officer, unit IP, and maintenance officer. Maintaining 11 H-19s would be impossible without my maintenance sergeant, John Hodgdon, the finest helicopter maintenance person I ever knew—and among a handful of the greatest people I ever knew. He once took us through a command inspection without a major gig on any bird, an unheard of accomplishment for the H-19.

Our mission was to cover the training at Benning which included the airborne school and ranger training in the swamps near Eglin Air Force Base, Florida, and in the mountains of Dahlonega, Georgia. We also had some area responsibility for hunters etc. in the area. The terrain, except for Dahlonega, was flat and woody. Most of our patients were non-urgent training accidents. The main challenge was the H-19 itself with the reciprocating engine and motorcycle grip. A few hours in that monster would physically drain Superman. You could not jerk this beast off mother earth as with Huey; in fact, you had to finesse that separation; a separation the 19 was loath to allow. It was often impossible to come to a hover before setting down. Thankfully we usually had runways and could execute running landings or the landing could be bumpy. This bird was a challenge but, as noted, made me a better Huey pilot.

Ranger Airborne soldiers are, I believe, the toughest, best-trained troops in the world. I watched one Ranger instructor, teaching the culinary delights of snake meat, get bit by a water moccasin—and then refuse to be evacuated until he finished the class. He later went into convulsions on my helicopter. A four-star general said he became so exhausted during a swamp training exercise in Ranger school, he decided to let go and drown. Fortunately his feet hit bottom. Charlie Beckwith, later of Desert One fame, was in charge of the Ranger school at Eglin. I hung out with him during training. It was not unusual for Charlie to spot a cool body of water and begin to undress to buck nakedness on the spot. He never wore underwear and ridiculed me, who did, as a wimp. I guess you don't hump the boonies with undies. My father was with Darby's Rangers in World War II and I had volunteered unsuccessfully for both Ranger and Airborne school. Thank you Lord, for keeping me out of Ranger school!

But I still wanted to go to jump school. The 54th commander made a deal with the honchos at airborne school. He would go part time, make his jumps, and get the wings. He greased the way for me to be next after he finished. Unfortunately he broke a leg and the commandant of the school found out. He was outraged. What in the hell was a pilot on flight pay doing in his school getting jump pay? There was some envy over our extra pay (as they said; pilots have fat wallets, big cars, big watches, and teeny...well you know what) considering the perceived luxury of our work. We always slept between sheets while the grunts slept in the mud and got no special pay. The grunt commanders made their point in many ways. We were not allowed to wear our flight suits to some places on post and never off post. Mixed in with the great soldiers at Benning were a few who wore their gruntness a bit too blatantly for my blood. Not only did they look down on pilots, they considered medics to be wimps even though we consistently whipped them in intramural sports. I took special delight in kicking their butts on the handball court. No man ever beat me in the two and a half years I was the Benning handball champion.

In September, I went to instrument school at Fort Rucker. I had none of the problems from flight school and breezed through. The flying I did in Nam was a great benefit and I enjoyed instrument flying especially the few times we were able to go AI. Viet Nam was on my mind as more and more pilots were doing second tours and we got reports from the 1st Cav. It was only a matter of time before I went back, if the Army decided to keep me. In December of 1966, my three-year obligation for flight school was over. My time in grade as captain was also up and I watched the *Army Times* for the majors list as I worried about my future. At least I had a marketable skill. I could fly.

In the meantime, we made some friends for a life time. Nancy along with Ed Taylor's wife Rose and Barry FitzGerald's wife Marion joined Patsy Lynch to become known as the Fearsome Foursome. They were all drop-dead beautiful and took care of each other when we were gone and many other separated wives as well. However, Barry never forgave them for ruining his German bride Marion. Before joining this pack she thought every good wife shined her husband's shoes and caddied for him. I spent a lot of time in the field and the family was healthy and happy (there may have been a connection) and enjoying Benning.

My number two daughter was born one Easter Saturday. While at church for the baptism, I noticed one of the ushers wore a light-blue rosette on his suit. I asked what it was and was told it symbolized the Medal of Honor. He was a recipient. His name was Bob Nett, a great soldier who would later be a good friend. The priest who baptized my daughter was Father (Captain) Angelo Liteky. He would later be awarded the Medal of Honor and be guaranteed some celebrity by throwing it away. He left the priesthood, got married, and spent a lot of time denouncing the military. It always amazed me how many people, often generals, who were nobodies without their military experience, turned on the military often in hopes of material gain or celebrity.

Two bright young MSC aviators came by to visit me while I was on duty one weekend. Jack Lichte and Tom Chiminello, close friends, were finishing flight school and would soon be assigned to the 54th. They were a delight and picked my brain for several hours on Kelly and flying Dust Off. They had read the article I wrote for the *Aviation Digest* on single ship, or Dust Off, missions in combat. The editors of *Aviation Digest* called it *Solo Missions* and it was their monthly award winner. It was so refreshing to find young pilots more concerned with the mission than the risks. Tom was an all-round athlete who traveled mostly by bicycle not only for exercise but because he was a tightwad. He did not take to handball but we played golf together and we became close friends. He was tighter than I was and used his golf balls until they decomposed. He spent more time on the course looking for balls than he did hitting the ball. I am sure he never bought a golf ball. After all, they cost almost two bits.

Shortly after joining the unit he tested our friendship when he taxied one of my birds into another and I had to do the accident investigation. Tom was returning from a mission with his crew chief in the left seat. After he reached his parking spot, Tom was signaled to move back to allow another one of our birds to depart on an emergency. He then turned to the left, away from his field of vision, and hit the tail rotor of another one of our H-19 swith his main rotor. Unfortunately, he did not taxi through the entire fleet. Tom screwed up but no one was hurt. It should have been a simple one-page report; but nothing was simple when dealing with ASO. The area was always congested and we could agree that a cleanup was in order albeit nearly impossible because of the number of aircraft and the space available. But what about taxiing techniques, where do you look, ahead or up at the rotor disk, why didn't the crew chief warn Tom—and on and on. In the midst of my frustrations, I recommended that my technique of placing one ear on each rotor tip with the nose in the front be made mandatory in flight training. A key was to develop some ear hair growing lotion for added awareness. No one was amused and after a circle jerk of monumental proportions we finished the report. It was some time before I would talk to Tom again, let alone give him my old golf balls. This was the initial volley in the 54th experiences with the ASO at Benning.

In the spring of 1967, we were pretty certain that the 54th would be deploying to Nam. All that was unknown was where and when. Things started getting messy. The commander retired and Tom and Jack left for Nam as did other unit members. The new commander was in place only a short time when he deployed. On 16 May, we got official word that the 54th would deploy to Viet Nam probably in July. We then began to reorganize to a 40 man detachment with six D Model Hueys. Thank God this would later change to H Models. Almost immediately we lost our enlisted men, and before summer we lost all our pilots. All that was left was four enlisted men; thankfully Sgt. Hodgdon was one of them, and me. The next commander was ineligible for deployment and was reassigned. Although he recommended that I replace him, and I had been in the unit two years, the powers that be would only make me the interim commander. In this capacity, it was my task to prepare the unit for overseas movement (POM). The designated commander Major Bob McWilliam (Major Mac) would not be in until 1 July.

Before the end of May, our enlisted cohort was assigned although many were on leave. I got the names of the warrant officer pilots (known as WOPAs, for Warrant Officer Protective Association) who would be assigned: Charles Schenck, Peter Schuster, Greg Schwartz, Allan Scott, Don Sewell, Lester Shadrick, Norman Shannahan, and (what, no S?) Steve Hall. Every warrant officer was graduating on 6 June 1967, and would report by 10 July. Only Allen Scott had any pervious flying experience and that was in fixed wing aircraft. Major Bob McWilliam, Captain Al Flory, and Lieutenant Jerry Foust rounded out the new officers (RFOs for Real F****** Officers) of the 54th. Only Bob had previous experience in combat. He had flown with John Temperilli and the first contingent of the 57th in 1962. Al and Jerry were as raw as the WOPAs.

In the middle of POM and personnel replacements and leave

and reorganization we continued to cover Benning as before. All this was manageable until we were taken out from under medical command and control and assigned to an aviation unit. As if we did not have enough on our plate, they immediately decided to move us out of our hangar. We were to be gone within a week. I went berserk! I attacked the chain of command until I was ordered not to go farther. If I had been aware of the Inspector General function at the time, I would have taken the mess to him. The Major's list was imminent or I would have resigned on the spot.

Shortly thereafter the major's list was published in the *Army Times*. I looked in vain for my name. I was only vaguely disappointed since I knew my record really did not merit promotion and I dreaded but expected I would be passed over. I was pretty depressed but continued working on our POM as I pondered my future.

A few days later, I got a frantic call from my new boss, a LTC ASO. "Brady, you and I are to report immediately to the colonel. There has been a security violation." His voice reflected the panic appropriate for any breach of security. I had been thoroughly beat up on this issue and was getting sick of it. After all, what could they do to me that they hadn't already done? Cancel my orders to Nam? Kick me out? I was pretty sure all that was on the horizon. In any event, I was much more at ease than my LTC when we joined up and headed to the Colonel's office. He thought I was a bit too relaxed for what he warned could be a disaster.

Unlike most of those in my new aviation chain, I actually liked the Colonel. I had flown some missions for his command in the Delta and he always said hello when our paths crossed. As the door opened to his office, I could see that the room was full. My LTC snapped to attention in front of his desk and reported. The colonel ignored him and ordered, "Front and center Brady." Oh, Lord why me. As I centered on his desk he roared, "What in the hell do you mean reporting to me out of uniform?" With that he leaped out from behind his desk with a golden oak leaf in each hand. He then took off the captain's bars and replaced them with the oak leaves as the room broke out in applause. Much to my chagrin, certainly of my LTC's, this was one of the ways of promotion in those days.

I called the MSC branch and told the officer what had happened. He had seen the list. "Are you wearing them?" "Yes Sir, I am." "Better take them off until I check." (After the buck up letter, I had checked with this same officer on my prospects of making captain. At the time it was almost automatic. But not for me. I might make it, he said, but I was far from a shoo-in.) He got back to me and said I was good to go. As it turned out, the date of the promotion orders used by the colonel was some time after the date I should have been promoted had I been on the list. They would later adjust my date of rank. Someone must have noticed that I missed the list, that I was preparing a unit for Viet Nam, and that my obligation from flight school was up. I could get out any time. With the buildup and shortage of aviators, they decided they needed me. I was excited about the promotion and the chance to do some real life saving again despite the additional three years that came with the promotion. Maybe I would do better this time and be eligible for LTC. But promotion to major was special since we now got to wear the hat with scrambled eggs on it. It was my best promotion party ever to include those to General. I was re-energized and raring to go.

As I was learning, amateurs talk tactics, professionals talk logistics. There are no tactics without logistics and maintenance in an aviation unit is the life blood of effectiveness, but an absolute night mare. We needed to check very carefully every piece of equipment dumped on us. It was not unusual, as I have noted, for those units tasked to supply deploying units to use that as an opportunity to get rid of their junk. I had a great supply sergeant, Stan Tucker, who had good connections on post and we were doing well in equipment readiness. I was delighted to learn that we would be deploying with brand new H model Hueys. It was also important to have as many spare parts as possible. But some spare parts are not authorized, albeit vital. And you often don't know what they are until you need them.

We did our best to anticipate but even so, I was surprised to find a stack of rotor blades in our area one day. They were authorized only at some echelon above us. And I did not remember any problem with rotor strikes my first tour. Sgt. Hodgdon assured me we would need them and not to worry about getting them to Nam. Specialist Don Goody, Sgt Hodgdon's good right arm, then showed up with a forklift, also way above our authorization. I tried to get authorization for our crew to have both a pistol and a rifle. They were authorized only the rifle but needed both. I failed. Needless to say, my reputation as a scrounger suffered. The men were collecting major items of equipment and I couldn't get them a pistol. I needed to stay out of the equipment area. There was no telling what was going into those CONEXES or what the ASO would do if they found out.

In the midst of endless turmoil, I began to size up our new people. PFC Wayne Aurich was assigned as a crew chief but was gifted in many ways. I would be the operations officer and needed an assistant who could deal with me as well as the other pilots and crew men in high stress situations. And he had to be administratively sound with exceptional communications skills. Wayne was the perfect man to do this. I took him away from the flight line and made him my assistant. I also tasked him to keep a record of all that we did. My hope was to put together some sort of a yearbook for the men. They didn't know it then, but I was sure this would be the most significant year of their lives.

The medics were a mixture of experience and eagerness headed by James "Pappy" Coleman, a quiet man, humble beyond reason and totally without fear. My favorite was Steve Hook a tall gangly Iowan, barely out of his teens, newly married who mirrored Pappy and reminded me of Tiny Simmons. The crew chiefs were solid and, as a category, among the best trained soldiers I have ever known. I think the fact that their work was tested in dangerous situations, with them present, had something to do with their excellence.

The WOPAs were something else. By this time, Dust Off

was becoming legendary, well known as the most difficult and demanding type of combat flying. Initially, MSC officers were designed for the Dust Off mission. When it became known that the war would escalate and the Medics could not fill the cockpits with MSCs, they had to turn to WOPAs. Every one of our WOPAs was convinced that they were handpicked for this mission. Never mind that they were fresh out of flight school and their names, save one, all began with "S." Could it be that some mindless bureaucrat simply took a block of names and gave them to the 54th? These guys were barely out of high school, hardly the stuff of legends and I had no idea if they even had any stuff, let alone the right stuff.

I did notice some similarities among them and the guys I had flown with in the 57th. As in most tight knit units, these men would acquire nicknames. Norm Shannahan reminded me of Ernie the prototypical co-pilot. Norm would prove as good as Ernie. He would be known as the "Worm." Pete Schuster was a big raw-boned kid out of Brown University, an athlete like Bruce Zenc. Pete's demeanor reeked of mischief. He reminded me of a guy I knew as a youth who would give you a wry smile just before he would get off the teeter-totter when you were at the top. If he could be kept under control, Pete would be great for morale. Charlie Schenck, to be known as "Dust Off Schenck" was as dedicated to the mission as anyone I ever knew. Greg Schwartz was close to Pete when it came to mischief, but also a natural born leader. In fact, they were all pretty full of mischief—among other things. Lester Shadrick was an innocent teenager until he fell in with this bunch. Lester was balding early and kinda looked like a Buddha. He became "Buddha" Shadrick. Allen Scott, later known as "Batman" and "Speedy" was the best pilot going in and Don Sewell was a tall Texan, much admired by the fairer sex, who I never saw without a smile. One of the guys was known simply as KIA. He was found one evening so devoid of sobriety that they thought he was dead.

Major Mac was a slender soft-spoken gentleman. He was one of only a few soldiers I ever knew who could lead by their likeability.

He never raised his voice; in fact, I don't think I ever heard him give a direct order. He just asked. The men were eager to please him and they simply obeyed. He was a liberal, I was conservative and I would raise my voice on occasion, actually, quite often. The mix of the two of us would be interesting. Time would tell if we would be effective.

We were well into July and still did not know which area we would cover in Nam. And the aviation chain of command was of no help. It was important to know this for training. Hopefully it would be flat wet terrain and we would not be faced with weather in the mountains. I wrote to Barry FitzGerald, now in the country, and asked him to see if he could determine our destination. In the meantime, I was determined to do as much training as possible. It was an opportunity to teach all that I had learned in Viet Nam to uncluttered minds. They would know only one Way—the Kelly way. They would not fly like the MEDEVACs, nor would our crews be reading any comic books.

I began to plot training areas and got checked out as an IP in the Huey. I asked for extra hours and some other IPs to help me in training our 10 rookie pilots. The IPs were willing to help but had no idea what I meant by tactical approaches. And neither did our new pilots. I had recently been awarded a "Winged S" from Sikorsky Aircraft for a rescue in one of their helicopters. It was at night but would not have been noticed in any Dust Off unit in Nam. Flying Dust Off was a whole new world and getting help to teach it was a challenge.

The new pilots were eager and positive but lacking in alertness— the key to a well-trained soldier. All told I had about 22 hours to prepare 10 pilots for the most demanding air work they would ever encounter. They would often fly more than 22 hours in two days in combat. Most of their check-out would be on actual missions as was mine; but they would have an edge on me—they could all start the bird. Ultimately it would be combat that developed their alertness, if they lasted long enough.

When I could not get them in the air, I talked about the mission and combat flying and reaction time and the thrill of saving lives. I told them that nothing must ever come before the mission and that the patient drove the mission. I assured them that, unlike too many in the aviation community, I would stick by them no matter what they did, even if they raped a nun (as vile an act as I could imagine), as long as it did not affect our ability to do our job.

I also emphasized the importance of maintenance and taking care of our birds. Vibrations in a chopper are maintenance multipliers. They must be reported and fixed; no slack in blade tracking. And set the damn thing down gently. I found too many of them slammed the poor bird into the ground if there was any wind at all. I had developed a tip-toe touchdown technique. The anti-torque pedals increased and decreased the demand for power and by gently moving them back and forth, I could set it down on an egg. I am not sure any of them ever understood this one.

July had passed and we were into August when we got our departure date. We took care of as many personal issues as possible. Both Major Mac's and Shannahan's wives were pregnant. Ready or not it was time to go. We would deploy in four groups: I would take the advance party; Don Sewell would escort our equipment out of San Francisco; Al Flory would accompany our aircraft by sea, and Major Mac would take the main body over by air.

· PART 3 ·

WAR

· 24 ·

WHERE THE HELL IS CHU LAI?

A T last we were escaping the clutches of the ASO at Benning. I would actually miss Benning and our friends there but not the ASO. Viet Nam would be a relief. In a final tribute to their efficiency, they could not tell us where in Viet Nam we were going! All I had was a rumor from Barry that we were going to Chu Lai, wherever that was. I had covered Viet Nam from Pleiku to the mangrove swaps of Cau Mau my first tour and never heard of Chu Lai. I took some of our best men on the advanced party. Norm Shannahan, Wayne Aurich, Stan Tucker, and I left Fort Benning at 09:00 on 18 August 1967 departing Muscogee County airport via Atlanta (yes, going to or from Viet Nam, or to heaven or hell, in those days, you had to go through Atlanta) landing in San Francisco at 13:30. Don Sewell met us and, after a three and a half hour wait for our luggage, we left for Travis Air Force Base. En route to Travis, Don regaled us with stories of the weird happenings in San Francisco; the flower children, druggies, demonstrators, etc. He said that the women actually stripped naked to the waist in the bars! We were amazed. Don, of course, never frequented such places and was passing on only what he had heard.

We left Travis at 02:00 on 19 August and landed at Bien Hoa, Viet Nam at 13:30, 20 August. My old buddy Captain Barry FitzGerald picked us up. While at Bien Hoa I had a chance to visit with Jake, another friend and former member of the 54th. He introduced me to a nurse who had just returned from Hong Kong where she had purchased a wedding dress. She was ecstatic over the dress which she bought for her marriage to Jake. I was a bit shocked since he was already married! His wife and mine were good friends. There were other such stories in that war. This tragedy would play out when she later discovered his marriage and committed suicide. Her death wish was that she be buried in the wedding dress, that her parents forgive Jake, and that he attend her funeral so he could see her in the wedding dress. He did. There were other such stories in that war. Another friend had the incredible misfortune to have his wife and mistress sitting next to each other under hair dryers, one talking about her husband, the other the boyfriend; and discover they were talking about the same person.

We left Bien Hoa at 04:00 on 21 August for the 498th Helicopter Ambulance Company at Qui Nhon. They confirmed our final destination as Chu Lai. My old friend, the Atheist, was the operations officer of the 498th. He told me the 54th was to replace two 498th aircraft supporting what was then known as Task Force Oregon (TFO) at Chu Lai, which was transitioning from Marine country and was, in fact, named after a Marine general. We were briefed on our chain of command which included the 55th Medical Group and the 498th. Billeting and rations would come from the 2nd Surgical Hospital (2nd Surg) based at Chu Lai. We could expect 12-hour days, seven days a week. None of our pilots would be singing in night clubs this tour.

I told the Atheist I wanted my .50 caliber medal back. He refused despite my harangue about its uselessness for a faithless wretch such as himself. I thought for a moment about beating up on his Godless body and taking it away. He was a big burly guy and I was sure I could whip him; well, pretty sure, but I was moved by charity. He would need it more than I did. I let him keep it—unfortunately for him, the medal only covered Viet Nam.

The 498th flew us to the Ky Ha heliport at Chu Lai where we landed at 11:30 on 21 August. As a herald of things to come, our first vision as we stepped out of the chopper at Ky Ha was of a 498th Dust Off aircraft dripping blood onto the ramp. The aircraft was full of bullet holes. My initial thought was that the blood resulted from a load of patients. Not so, a 498th crew chief had been shot moments earlier. The 2nd Surg had no idea we were coming but did feed us lunch and found a place for us to sleep. I was later directed to an open space near the Ky Ha heliport which was to be our new home.

I got an update on Dust Off the next day. The changes from my first tour were both monumental and frightening. U.S. troop strength had gone from 16,000 to half a million. And the 4,000 patients we carried my first tour paled before the 7,000 being evacuated by Dust Off *each* month. Dust Off had evacuated over 90,000 patients since I had left! Charles Kelly was the 149th American killed in the entire war. There were now 16,000 dead and counting at well over 149 each week.

25

AN AO FROM HELL

OUR AO ranged from Da Nang to Duc Pho, about 165 kilometers north and south, and to the Laotian border some 70 clicks to the west. Chu Lai was perfectly located, 88 kilometers from Da Nangand 75 clicks from Duc Pho. We had three of the five provinces of I Corps: Quang Nam, Quang Tin, and Quang Ngai, which had a history of revolution and radicalism. Uncle Ho had roots there and his finger prints were all over. It was the center of the first peasant revolt against the French and neither the French nor Saigon government were ever able to fully quench the revolutionary fire that burned in the breasts of its peasants. Quang Nam alone would suffer more causalities than most other provinces by double. The soon-to-be infamous My Lai complex, in Quang Ngai, was less than 10 minutes and six months away. Gone for the most part were the great flat, wet, and wonderful forced landing areas I loved in the Mekong Delta. Chu Lai had some rice paddies in flat terrain along the coast but most of the fighting was in the boonies to the west in jagged, jungle covered mountains rising up to nearly 6,000 feet. Some of the jungle consisted of triple canopy, three layers of growth some trees over 250 feet tall. We would make pickups in those canopies by zigzagging down, often losing sight of the sky on the way.

Our AO was marked by numerous valleys, notably Hiep Duc a.k.a. Antenna Valley, and Que Son. The weather throughout was vicious. Afternoon thunder storms covered the mountaintop locations of U.S. outposts with clouds. In the morning, the valleys below the mountains, where the troops maneuvered, were blanketed by a low valley fog that rose hundreds of feet up the sides of the mountains. It was not a wispy fog; it was dense and solid resembling a 500-foot snow bank. Flying conditions were zero zero with no letdown facilities or navigation aids in those mountains. To make matters worse, we were in the monsoon season. It rained 26 inches in September!

Charlie often worked the graveyard shift and used the terrain and weather very well. There would be casualties at night, and at night and day in weather. We had to fly in those conditions or troops would die. Our pilots would push themselves for a wounded soldier increasing the risks, almost certainty, of death and accidents. I knew what accidents and death do to the effectiveness of an aviation unit. You can break all the rules, and we had to break the rules to be effective, as long as the mission is successful; but break an aircraft, or kill someone, and there is hell to pay. And that hell will corral your capabilities, surround you with restriction, and could end your career. But worst of all, the REMFS will make you less effective in your support of the grunts—the only reason you exist. Sooner or later we would have to face the night and day weather pickup and I had no idea how to do it.

During my first tour, Dust Off totaled only one helicopter, Kelly's. By September 1967, Dust Off had lost 11 helicopters with 36 crew members killed, half at night and/or in weather. Three pilots from the 54th who preceded us to Viet Nam, one former commander, were, or would be, killed at night, two in weather, both hitting mountains. Dust Off still led the league in enemy hits but Mother Nature was killing more of us than Charlie. By now most of the Aviation units realized that the bird flew as well at night as in the daytime—a good thing but one which would add to the casualty flow.

Another former member of the 54th went down in weather shortly after we arrived. I would discover, to my shame, that he was in the 2nd Surg. I was walking by the hospital when one of our men yelled at me that there was someone there who wanted to see me. I went in and a heavily bandaged man waved at me. I thought he was waving me off and started to leave. "Don't you know me?" The poor man's face was a mess and I had no idea who he was. His eyes were full of tears as he told me his name. We had served together in the 54th for over a year. I was embarrassed to tears. In truth, I hated hospitals and visiting the wounded. It is an emotional killer. But one must do it and I do to this day. There is nowhere else more evidence of the quality of the American soldier.

The WO1 (a.k.a. Wobbly Ones) pilots were killed at a higher rate than any other pilots—and we had eight of them along with four commissioned pilots, only two with any flying experience much less combat experience. I was not locked into the experience factor, having seen many so-called inexperienced pilots perform magnificently. There was some truth in the caution about the ship building experience and skills of those who built the Ark and those who built the Titanic. I considered an inexperienced, but eager pilot, a blessing in our work. You did not have to retrain them since all they knew was what you taught them. But this was ridiculous. Maybe it was time to rethink the experience thing, especially considering the fact that TFO became the Americal Division, also known as the 23rd Infantry Division, and went operational the same time we did and began a massive operation the next day. The most experienced troops in our AO were on the other side and that spelled a bloody learning curve for our side.

We had only 40 men, including the 12 pilots, and six aircraft to support the largest, and most inexperienced, division in the country. We were also responsible for the 2nd ARVN Division, CIDG, Popular Forces, Regional Forces, Special Forces, Marines, Korean Forces, Scout Dogs, and all the civilians in an area advertised as the hottest in Viet Nam in terrain and weather conditions that gave great aid and comfort to the enemy—whose wounded we would also carry. Casualty numbers would be out of sight and I did not know if we had the resources or experience to handle them. We would have to be efficient as hell. I was scared to death and sorry I did not whip the Atheist and recover my .50 caliber medal. Good Lord, here we go again. I immediately went on the wagon and started a Novena.

So much for my orientation, there was work to do. I flew my first mission on Tuesday the 22nd. It was a night mission as on my first tour. The patient was a female Vietnamese having hard labor. As noted, I am superstitious about Tuesday and the number two but all went well (I inherited this phobia from my mother; but the fact that my baby was born on the 2nd and died on Tuesday reinforced it). That would not be true of my 2nd mission. The main body arrived at 07:00 hours the next day, 23 August. We set up tents in the open area and began to plan for permanent quarters. I requested the highest priority maintenance support from the 335th Transportation Company (DS) and they agreed. They were true to their word and would be a blessing for the rest of our tour. The Americal began maneuvering to gain control of us. Not a good thing. Our aircraft were still three weeks out and there would be little opportunity for pre-combat training. What we did at Fort Benning would have to suffice. Thankfully the 498th agreed to let us train with them as co-pilots and crewmen on combat missions. Not much different from my first tour except this time I could start the Huey.

I flew my first real combat mission, mission number two, my second tour, on the 24th. My first mission in '64 was at night and we were shot at but not hit. This time we were shot at and hit. It was a hoist mission. By 1967 Dust Off had hoists and hoist missions would surpass all other aviation missions as the most dangerous, in fact, seven times more dangerous. The pilot was required to come to a hover above the terrain and sit there while the crew lowered a Stokes Liter or Jungle Penetrator or Harness through jungle canopies to the wounded. It took more time than other missions and during that time the crew and aircraft were at a high hover and, depending on the terrain, could be sitting ducks.

We slipped up over the PZ and came to a hover. The crew seemed tense but our position provided excellent security. We were on the highest terrain and the jungle beneath us was thick, too thick for any enemy to see us, let alone hit us. I was back in the swing of things analyzing the terrain and enemy situation; we were not a sitting duck. We pulled the patients out of the jungle without incident, the crew relaxed and we flew over the trees down into a valley. We were now low and slow! Then I got tense. We were no longer on the highest terrain; it was on both sides of us. There is nothing worse than to be shot down at. We were now a sitting duck. Once again I was a FNG but this was not cool. Before I could communicate my alarm we were hit three times. We then hastened to altitude and returned to base without further incident. This was my first hoist mission in combat but it was clear to me that we would need to do some training before our guys used it. Crew coordination was more complicated than on a regular mission. The terrain, as always, determined the danger, but it was also clear that the hoist should be used only as a last resort.

Later in the day, I briefed our pilots on the mission and how we had erred. Unlike some briefings when my words fell like snowflakes on a mud puddle, I had their complete attention. I noticed that a senior medic, who also flew his first mission that day, was in a steel pot. He wore it until he left the unit a few weeks later. Within the first four days of our arrival Steve Hook, Don Goody, Jerry Foust, and Major Mac flew combat missions. The day after my bird was shot up, Goody, also on his first mission, had his aircraft shot down in the PZ and had to be rescued. One WOPA began sleeping with a loaded pistol next to his bed. This was war.

In between missions we finished plans for our area. The lumber would be provided but we had to do the work. We ended up with two area designs, a brilliant one that I did and one done by Major Mac. We had a vote. All but one voted for my design. Major Mac praised himself for allowing a democratic vote but lamented the fact that we had all voted wrong! We adopted his plan. The fact that there was a hill thwarting his plan did not bother him; he removed the hill. The lumber arrived on 30 August and we went to work.

There was no problem motivating our troops for this task. They were anxious to get into the new billets and away from the rat infested areas they occupied; especially Wayne who hunted and trapped the wretched rodents relentlessly. And the men were tired of shaving, brushing their teeth, and showering from a Water Buffalo (a trailer tank of water). The shower, which they called a "Whore's Bath" (not sure how they knew) consisted of a sponge down. After a short time, they radiated a strong unpleasant odor. Hygiene in the tropics is vital. Their first real shower, some said the best shower they ever had, came during the first monsoon when they all rushed outside, stark naked, and soaped and rinsed in the driving rain. And many nights we were warned of a pending enemy mortar attack. The attacks, more often than not, never happened, but were scary when they did and we were anxious to build a bunker.

The WOPAs were a work in progress but the enlisted were a finished product. Jim Kennedy and Johnny Johnson, our own Kennedy and Johnson, could do anything. They were electricians, carpenters, masons, and plumbers all rolled into two. There were some duds, and we weeded them out, but for the most part I have never been around such capable and talented men. They matched the military skills of the enlisted men my first tour but their other skills were amazing. And they were hard workers. They built a beautiful area, despite the design, nine buildings with the operations shack at one end and a two-story rock-faced enlisted club at the other. It was adjacent to the building housing our hot water showers and flushing toilet (the commanding general was still burning his shit). (I had all the men put their handprint and name in the wet cement of the enlisted club. I have been back and there were chunks of cement still in our area but I did not find the handprints. I hope to go back again and find it.)

The area was rectangular in shape with the enlisted on one side and the officers on the other. We built the enlisted billets first. Behind the operations shack was the bunker equipped with a bar in case we had to spend much time there. The enlisted club contained a bar, pool table, sauna, music room, and an attached 5,000-volume library (it took some creative writing on my part to justify the books as well as some bicycles). Outside was a pond lined with palm trees crossed by a bridge. I tried to get some water lilies for the pond but Ron Tweed, clumsy as he is, fell out of my hovering chopper and almost drowned among the lilies he was trying to capture. The men did this monumental work between missions without a day off for the first six months. As I watched them go about their business, many new to the Army, it was clear to me we had a truly remarkable bunch of guys. Among those 28 enlisted men was the talent to match any challenge we could possibly face.

Now, honesty dictates that I mention that the officers did help, albeit feebly. Hammers and nails have never been my forte (or any tool for that matter, they blamed every leaky roof on me). But I could scrounge and if I may be allowed a boast, I was a pretty damn good at it. My tenure as a supply officer under Kelly, at Benning and in DOMREP, had been invaluable. Despite my hatred for the supply function, I learned a lot about getting stuff. My job was made easier by the fact that the chief engineer, the guy with the stuff, was named Brady, a common name today, but to this point in my career, he was the only other Brady I had ever met in the Army. I floated a rumor that we were related and we magically started getting stuff on a priority basis. All that was lacking was pets and I went to work on that.

Dusty, a dog not unlike Nothing from days past was our first pet. The second pet began as a pig to be roasted for Thanksgiving. I have a thing about succulent juicy piglets roasting, revolving, sweating, yum. I asked one of the hooch maids where I could get a suckling pig which I described as best I could with sign language and gestures. Not a problem, she promised and we drove to her village where we surprised two young men; studs really, in black shorts. They were as big as me, unusual in Viet Nam, and had a hell of a lot more muscles than I did. I had seen very few young men in my trips to the countryside. They were certainly VC. I was armed and could see no arms near them. They smiled pleasantly and eyed my watch, a Rolex I won in a poker game my first tour. The hooch maid came forth with a goose! I tried to explain that it was not a pig but gave up. I was ready to get the hell out of there, pig or no pig.

Needless to say, the WOPAs ridiculed my efforts and the goose became "Brady's feathered pig." She stayed on to become Gertrude (appropriately named after one of the men's mother-in-law) a mean spirited creature that dominated our area. I would have loved to eat that vile bird but the men would not allow it. We did get a suckling pig which the men also refused to eat. The poor creature lost its identity. It was named Super Oink (in those days super was a prefix for much) and adopted by Dusty. Having forgot that it was a pig and seeing none, Super Oink took on the characteristics of a dog barking and frolicking with Dusty and her pups. We added some ducks for our pond, two more dogs, a cat, a rooster, and two more geese. The rooster met a tragic death. One of the WOPAs was caught by an RFO trying to kill it with a 2x4 after its untimely crowing rousted him from much-needed slumber. Apparently it was not the first time. The RFO warned the WOPA not to harm the bird. Shortly thereafter the unfortunate creature was found nailed to the RFO's door. Like the murderer of Napoleon, my Myna bird from my first tour, the perp was never identified.

To complete our zoo, we added our marquis critter, Francis, a beautiful rhesus monkey dearly loved by all. She often dove off the bridge into the pond and swam with the ducks and geese. I don't remember if Super Oink could swim but they did throw him in the pond and scrub him down periodically. All our beautiful creatures got along except Gertrude who hated, and was hated by, everyone.

Our search for a male companion for Francis resulted in a loathsome beast with no redeeming qualities. This ugly brown monkey tried to turn everything into an object of sexual gratification. The depraved creature tried to fornicate anything or anyone who came close. We had to chain it up. Finally, it sealed its fated when it fell upon the partially bald head of Buddha Shadrick and tried to do unspeakable things to his ear. Shortly thereafter the troops decided to answer a question which bothered them for some time—could monkeys fly? They are still not sure but it was flailing its arms wildly, surely trying to fly, as it exited the chopper at 2,000 feet en route to join other perverted monkeys in the jungle below.

I renewed my quest for a talking Myna bird. The first two died of natural causes (apparently, I initially feared we might have another bird killer in the unit) unlike poor Napoleon who was surely assassinated by either my roommate or the Atheist. Wayne came into operations with a shovel when the chaplain, Father Don, brought me number three. He wanted to know where to dig the grave. I figured it must be something I was feeding them. I put number three on hot peppers and it did well.

Finally we got the word that our helicopters were due in Saigon on 13 September. By the time we got to Long Binh, the ship carrying our birds, the USS *Card*, had moved with our aircraft to Vung Tau. The *Card* probably did not want anything to do with the harbor in Saigon. This was the same ship that was mined in Saigon by the VC during my first tour. I hoped that was not a bad omen. I noticed some stores of deck paint and pipes on the *Card*. The paint was just what we needed to weatherproof our new hooches and the pipes would be invaluable for plumbing. I bartered a deal with the Captain and we made a clandestine aerial delivery of a palate of beer. Apparently booze was forbidden fruit on the *Card* but I got my paint and pipes.

Tom Chiminello dropped by to see us while we were at Vung Tau. Tom had matured a lot since he and Jack Lichte dropped in on me at Benning. He was animated and jovial and obviously enjoyed saving lives in the legendary 57th. I ribbed him about his accident in the H-19 and the beat up golf balls and tennis shoes. Jack was already dead and Tom would join his dear friend in a few weeks. Both of them were killed at night in weather and are buried side by side in San Antonio.

While unloading on the 16th, we got word on our first Purple Heart. Allan (Batman Scott) was hit by a 12.7 mm. Scotty was flying with the 498th on a routine pickup for two GIs who had fallen down a hill. While loading the patients, they were warned of an enemy 12.7-mm antiaircraft weapon east of them on a ridge. They departed to the north but got too close to the ridge and their aircraft was slammed as only a 12.7-mm can. The chopper began to shudder and the pilot took evasive action. Scotty came on the controls to help for fear the servos were gone. He noticed blood all over his instrument panel and checked with the crew to see who was hit. No one? It was his blood. Then he began to hurt.

The round went right through the armor plate, shattering it and taking a chunk out of his hip and filling his arm with shrapnel. The armor was effective for .30 calibers, but we had nothing to stop a 12.7 mm. But the plate did help and may have saved his life. The medic pulled the pins on his seat and leaned him back to stop the bleeding. After his bleeding was under control, Scotty had the medic tape his hands to the controls in case they had to make a servo off landing. The landing was smooth. Once in the hospital, a nurse from Scotty's hometown saw him naked which pained him more than his wounds. His plea to her that turnabout should be fair play fell on deaf ears. Thankfully, he would be hospitalized for a short time and returned to us. While in the hospital, he found time to play, quite well, the organ for chapel services.

As an aside, Scotty's mother kept a list of all the members of the

54th in her Bible with a note to pray for us every day. It was found after her death and I have no doubt that it worked not only for Scotty, but for all of us as, miraculously, no member of the 54th was killed.

Two birds were not ready and we finally finished unloading on the 17th and set out immediately for Ky Ha with our six brand new H model Hueys. They were all purchased in July 1967 with tail numbers: 66-16659, 660, 661, 662, 663, and 664. The numbers ran in sequence right off the assembly line, same as our WOPAs. These choppers would amass a history along with our crews. The pilots wanted to know their call sign for the flight home. I told them to just use Dust Off followed by their name. Charles Schenck used the radios a lot and became Dust Off Schenck ever after. We flew in trail. There was no way I was going to fly formation with this gaggle, a dangerous proposition with experienced pilots. We ran into some severe weather, a useful eye opener, and stopped at Duc Pho. After an aborted fly by (we couldn't get the smoke bombs to work), we arrived at Ky Ha at 18:30.

We began training as crews in our own aircraft on 18 and 19 September. I went to Quin Nhon on the 20th and got word we were to go operational on the 25th and would fly our new birds second up to the 498th in the meantime. The formation of the American Division out of TFO was also announced on 25 September. The American had a proud history dating back to World War II. It would consist of the 196th, 198th and 11th Light Infantry Brigades with the 198th arriving on 22 October and the 11th arriving on 20 December. Immediately, the 196th, and the 3rd Brigade of the 101st, temporarily under the American, began Operation Wheeler, an aggressive campaign against the communists.

Mr. Hall flew his first mission on the 21st and was shot down. It was supposed to be an orientation flight with a 498th pilot. They overheard a mission request close by and decided to take it. The area was reported to be under fire from six locations. They requested gunship escort, took fire, and were hit on the way in. The area was too rough to land and they were forced to hover while the patients were loaded. On climb out, the friendlies warned that Dust Off was leaking fluid. The crew checked the out side of the bird and reported heavy leakage on both sides. Loss of power and fuel pressure followed and they made an emergency landing. One gunship provided cover while the other took the patients to the hospital. Hall was in the field several hours until the downed Dust Off could be rigged and hoisted out by a Chinook. Not a good start for a Wobbly One. We were not yet operational and Hall, Goody, Scott ,and I had been hit on our first mission.

The new Division, and Operation Wheeler, guaranteed a significant patient load. Thankfully, the disposition of medical resources was excellent. Army, Navy, and Vietnamese hospitals were located within 15 minutes of most PZs, although we could use some Vietnamese hospitals only in daytime. The VC often treated their wounded in them at night even though (as we discovered later) they had a three story underground hospital minutes from Chu Lai and there were three clinics in Quang Ngai. As noted, our operation at Ky Ha was perfectly located to quickly respond to most battlefields. Unlike my first tour when many missions went through an intermediary, the 54th got most missions direct from the battlefield. Many rescues took less than a half hour from the time we got the call until the wounded were in the operating room.

We were working on our operational standards. A source of irritation my first tour was the lack of a standardized Mission Request Form (MRF) containing essential elements of information (EEI). By 1967, the patient evacuation request form was in place but needed work. It included all the information necessary, location, patient priority and numbers, and PZ information to include the most misused element—area security. But you had to go to the last paragraph to get the call sign and frequency. It was important for reaction time that the location, call sign, and radio frequency *at the patient location* be transmitted first. That information was readily available and sufficient to launch the mission. Too often time was wasted as the requestor struggled with the types of injury and priority of each patient. The pilot could get more detailed information en route. Frequently the truth would not be known accurately until the patients were actually on board.

Knowing the patient condition was important, but the categories of patient priority were unrealistic. My first tour there was no system then they decided on urgent, two hours; priority, 24 hours; and routine, 48 hours. Later they modified urgent to immediate to save life or limb, priority within four hours or the patient becomes urgent, and routine, several hours. For example, a patient with a temperature of 104 was routine, 105 was urgent. What grunt can sort this out? What grunt would even try? Actually, there were only two types of patient: Urgent, immediate; and non-urgent, OK for a time. And the time should be set by the tactical commander. There should be room for a tactical urgent patient, not medically urgent but needing immediate evacuation to help the grunts continue their mission. But the three categories were set in the field and we initially went with them even though they would eventually be irrelevant in our system.

We took the EEI, put the three critical elements first and designed a MRF around them. The EEI, the mission request, would be on the front with the back reserved for an after action report (AAR), i.e., what actually happened. Together they formed our unique MRF. This form was essential. It would help us fly the mission, keep vital records, determine trends, and address problem areas. On one occasion we were able to track down an Asian American mistakenly buried in a Vietnamese grave. The key was to get the pilots to fill out the back.

Reaction time, the time to get airborne, was, of course, the long pole in the evacuation tent. The fire truck method was a given. We checked and timed our reaction capability before we set the standard at two minutes. A jeep horn attached to a battery sounded the alarm. One blast was first up, two blasts second up and three was for the third ship which was also rigged with a hoist. Operations would get the mission and hit the horn. The co-pilot ran (anyone caught walking was severely chastised) for the bird. Needless to say the pilots had preflighted the bird with the crew chief first thing in the morning, at which time they set the seats and pre-positioned personal gear, weapons, and maps. (I would later hear of units that had a 15-minute reaction time! *And others who had no standard!* As noted, one commander praised time spent on the ground prior to launch as paying big dividends. I would not want these folks coming for me or a wounded loved one.)

The AC ran to operations, plotted a heading and distance on the map, grabbed the MRF, and ran to the aircraft. By the time he got there, the co-pilot had the bird running and ready for lift off usually in less than two minutes. The crew took up the heading and immediately contacted the PZ. It was very important that they call immediately because it relieved the stress on the troops with the wounded who then knew help was on the way. Finally, the AC coordinated the proper approach with the friendlies. Patient destination depended on patient condition and capacity and capabilities of the medical facilities. A patient regulator assisted the pilot in all this but the pilot made the final determination based on his first-hand knowledge of patient needs.

We were having trouble getting gear, maps, personal protective armor (chicken plates), and weapons. Pilots had some armor in their seats but not the crew. They needed armor for their chest and to sit on. We could not get enough. Our higher medical HQs was useless in this effort. Initially, we scrounged and shared to get operational. I corrected my failure at Benning and got each crewman both a rifle and a pistol. They were only authorized a rifle, but it is hard to carry a rifle and a patient and they needed to be armed if they moved any distance from the aircraft to recover a patient. Unhooking and moving away from the bird was not a good thing considering what happened to Tiny but may be necessary (although one Dust Off commander told his men if they got out in a hot area and the ship came under fire, he would leave them on the ground). To reduce the need to unhook and lose commo with the pilots, we got extra-long wires for their head sets.

Once in the area, the medic took over and began to triage the patients if time, need, and security permitted. If not, they were loaded as fast as possible. All patients were loaded through one door, the medic's, under his watchful eye. The other door was kept shut. We learned this the hard way. Once anyone got on board, wounded or not, it was nearly impossible to get them off. If too many got on, getting airborne could be impossible. Time was life and death in the PZ. Litters were seldom used and unnecessary except when there was time and the patient had a neck or back injury. Litters posed an additional hazard when untrained people stood them up to open them. During my first tour, I had heard that a litter was stuck in the rotors and put the crew down in the field. There was a suspicion that it was done on purpose. I watched liter use carefully and almost shot a Vietnamese who was in the process of standing up a liter when a crewman tackled him. After loading, the crew strapped in for takeoff and covered the flanks. Once clear of the area, they worked on the patients. There would be no riding the skids, a popular pastime by some. Dust Off had already lost a crewman to this insanity. A pilot was never to leave any area until he had an up from both the medic and crew chief.

It was time to determine chain of command. I sold Major Mac on the system we used with Kelly. The 54th cut AC orders on everyone (even the lowest-ranking man in case a pilot from another unit flew with us) and the ranking man in the aircraft would be the AC. But how do you determine date of rank with eight WOPAs who all graduated from flight school on the same day? We had to go to enlisted rank, time of service, and even dates of birth. Steve Hall turned out to be the ranking WOPA and became known forever as Sgt. Rock after some mythical comic book character. And he was the Rock upon which the WOPAs stood for grievances. The RFOs would fly as AC with the WOPAs as much as possible until we got some time under our belt. Then the WOPAs would fly together with the ranking WOPA as the AC.

As I mentioned, this system was criticized by many. One helicopter ambulance unit required that a pilot be in the country three months and have 200 hours minimum before he could become an AC; they preferred 500 hours and six months. An aircraft was the only place in our army where a warrant officer commanded a major. Overlap for commanders is a good thing, and an orientation is also good but command should be based on rank. Period.

Call signs are important to a Dust Off pilot, a kind of autograph to his work. We decided to designate them according to rank using the first digit of the unit rather than aircraft tail numbers. The commander was always the six. Thus Major Mac became Dust Off 56, I was 55 and so on down through the RFOs and ranking WOPAs then up to 57 etc. Thus for the original 54th: Major Mac, 56; Major Brady, 55; Cpt. Flory, 54; Lt. Foust, 53; Mr. Hall, 52; Mr. Schenck, 51; Mr. Schuster, 57; Mr. Schwartz, 58; Mr. Sewell, 59; Mr. Shannahan, 254; Mr. Shadrick 255 and Mr. Scott, 256.

Keeping our birds flyable would be a problem; not only because of the enemy, but also because of maintenance and the effects of sloppy flying. On the 22nd, we had our first non-hostile incident when 661 hit a tree and tore up a set of rotor blades. On the 23rd and 24th of September, the officers moved into our new buildings joining the enlisted and uniting us in our new area. The 498th, our comfort blanket, left and the original 54th was now on its own.

26

OPENING WEEK

MONDAY 25 September. Major Mac and Pete Schuster led off in 660 taking a round through the push-pull tubes and into the transmission. They made it back with the patients intact. Although this was our first hit in our own aircraft, I was more concerned with a visit from LTC Bill Augerson, the division surgeon. He was carrying the mail for the division folks who wanted us to pre-position our aircraft in the field in direct support of a specific unit or operation. This was not a good idea. We were an area support resource and to tie our aircraft up on a direct support mission was a poor use of resources. I managed to hold him off, knowing the issue would return. I logged my first daytime AI on this day although I had flown much of it my first tour.

Tuesday 26 September. We dug the cesspool and laid some concrete thanks to the Seabees. They are a wonder. We will have concrete walkway between all our buildings, a blessing when the rain churns up the rest of the area into sticky, slimy deep mud. The Seabees, the Navy's construction force, took a liking to us and would do anything for some booze. We broke a skid. The terrain will be as tough as Charlie. Thank God for John Hodgdon and his crew.

Thursday 28 September. Major Mac and Buddha Shadrick were shot down. Fortunately the patients were transferred to another ship and they got to the hospital in time. Greg Schwartz and I took some rounds and we broke a tail rotor on 662.

Black Friday, 29 September. Our AO exploded. Charlie may have been testing the infant American. Major Mac led off again, this time in 661 with Mr. Shadrick as co-pilot and Brian Burwick, Travis Kanida, and Jim Barfield (as gunner) in the back. Friendlies had been pinned down in a ditch in an open area near Hiep Duc. Two slicks had failed to get in. McWilliam came in low and fast but still took multiple rounds some through the windshield filling Buddha's face with Plexiglas, an experience I had my first tour. He did not have his visor down. Buddha jerked his head from the sting of the glass and pulled the mic cord out of his helmet. Major Mac could not communicate with him and thought he was dead. 661 was gushing fuel and Mac aborted. This was the 54th's second Purple Heart but not the last this day.

Ten minutes later, Greg and I took 662 and went back for the same patients. LTC Augerson was in our AO and asked if he could fly medic. Jim McDaniel was the crew chief. I never flew with a gunner. The area was full of 10-feet high elephant grass and although we saw the smoke, no one would stand up to help load or locate the patients. We were hovering around looking for the wounded when we were hit eight times. I was not sure how bad we were damaged but the fuel gauges were out and I was losing directional control. I feared the aircraft would be unsafe at altitude and took it to the ground just clear of the PZ. It was a good move. Amazingly, two rounds went through the 2-inch 42-degree sight glass on the tail rotor. If we had lost the tail rotor at altitude, we might not have recovered. The Hogs put up a protective shield until we could be evacuated. Bill Augerson thereafter became one of our staunchest supporters, an ally in the direct support hassle. He was an outstanding physician/soldier and would later become a two star General. Once on the ground, he took out a flask of brandy and offered it to Greg who was looking longingly at it when I reminded him that we needed to find another aircraft and get back to work. His protest that it was prescribed by his doctor fell on deaf ears. It took us until after dark to get these patients out.

After he had cleaned the blood off his face, Shadrick joined Major Mac again, this time in 659 with Jim Mc Daniel, Bob Gabaldon, and Gary Lowder in the back. The pickup was south of Tam Ky near Than Hai. On takeoff, with the patients safely on board, they were hit in the oil cooler and lost oil pressure. Major Mac made it to the ground before the engine froze. The patient was transferred to another Dust Off and Mac's crew waited in the field until the oil cooler was replaced and they could fly it home.

Meanwhile Jerry Foust and Chuck Schenck in 660 with Charley Ramirez, Jim "Pappy" (a.k.a. Combat) Coleman, and Jim Garza were landing in the midst of a heavy firefight to rescue two soldiers with sucking chest wounds. Initially the troops would not stand up to help load the patients laying some 30 yards from the chopper. Jim Coleman finally got a helper and began loading the patients. The helper was shot dead at his side as they loaded the last patient. They were in the area far too long and the enemy zeroed in on the Dust Off riddling it with over 50 bullets. All the instrument lights were shot out and so were the hydraulics. The two pilots now had to try to take off without hydraulics.

Pilots are trained to fly and land without hydraulics but hovering and take offs under those conditions are forbidden and nearly impossible. But they did it...only to have their fuel cell shattered as they departed. They were now flying without servos and with a rapid loss of fuel. Any errant electrical spark would have resulted in a severe blow up. In the back, Jim was working feverishly to resuscitate the two soldiers when he noticed that his crew chief, Jim Garza, had taken a round in his leg severing an artery which was squirting his blood all over. Coleman quickly set a tourniquet saving Garza's life. He then went back to the two soldiers who he was unable to save. In the front, Chuck and Jerry fought the controls hoping to make it to the hospital before they ran out of fuel. Miraculously, the ship did not blow up and they survived a servo off running landing at Ky Ha.

Shortly thereafter in a tragic bird, 664, I went back for the leftover wounded from this area with Steve Hook as medic and Henry Hyde as crew chief. The area was reported to finally be secure. They had 11 wounded Americans. The PZ was a confined area, shaped like a keyhole, in deep jungle terrain surrounded by tall trees. I relaxed as I studied the terrain. In order for us to be hit, the enemy would actually have to be in the trees with the friendlies. He was.

As I rounded out and started to set down, two communists uncovered from spider holes on each side of our bird. They shot both Hook and Hyde. Hyde was hanging in his harness and I was sure he was dead. Hook went down and disappeared. I jammed the bird into the end of the keyhole as the friendlies killed the communists and began firing wildly into the trees. Then I spotted Hook in the midst of the fire fight dragging the wounded to our chopper. He had little help from the friendlies who were pinned down and heavily engaged.

I noticed he was bleeding on one side of his body, but he crossed the battlefield time and again until he got all 11 loaded. Then he gave me an up. The friendlies threw all the gear of the wounded on board and we were well loaded. I had to go straight up because of the height of the trees and it was slow going. We would be an easy target for any remnant enemy until we cleared the trees and could get some airspeed. Whatever rounds 664 took failed to affect its performance; it did its job and we got out in good shape.

The back of the chopper was a tangled mass and mess of bodies and blood. Hook noticed a squirt of blood from a severed artery in our crew chief and knew immediately he was not dead. But Hyde feared he would be. "Am I going to die?" "Yes you are," Hook replied..."but not today." He then quickly applied a tourniquet which saved Hyde's life as Garza's life was saved earlier. Then he began to treat the rest of the wounded. I was shouting for him to stop and care for his own wound but he was not connected and could not hear. Finally, for fear he would bleed out, I grabbed a patient with one hand as I flew with the other (this was the first time my co-pilot had been shot at and he was dysfunctional) and pointed to Hook's bloody back and the man's first aid packet. He got the message and stuck the bandage in Hook's wound while Hook continued to treat the wounded. We got them all to the hospital including half of our crew, Hook and Hyde.

With five ships already hit, one a float, Greg and I made it six for six that evening. We were hit on short final but managed to slip in and get the patients. One round tore up the electrical compartment and one came up under Greg's seat destroying his map and weapon. He was upset over the map since they were hard to get and he said I never had one—and couldn't read it if I did. That was not the only time my expertise with a map was questioned. In truth, I could read a map but insisted my co-pilot do the map work in order for them to develop skills commensurate with my own. This was the first, and perhaps only, day I was hit on three different missions and the hits the night before made it four birds in 24 hours.

We were not the only unit hit hard on this day. The local aviation battalion suffered its worst day ever: 22 birds hit, four Hueys destroyed, eight pilots wounded and one crew chief killed. Twenty GIs would die in our AO on Black Friday and the 498th suffered its sixth KIA of the year also on that messy day. But there was good news. On another mission that night we made a pickup in the mountains using flares for the first time. I noted in my diary the visibility was zero but an experience I had on this mission would prove priceless.

Opening week we evacuated 206 patients and six KIAs and flew 109 missions in 96 hours! A lot of units did less in a full month; eventually we would do more in a day. Each mission was an hour flying time and netted only two patients. We would have to get more efficient. The commander of the 498th came up to fly with us the next day. He probably was wondering what the hell was going on. Nine ships shot up our first week; all six of ours plus floats, loaners from other units. And 12 percent of the unit was wounded. The enemy got nine ships and we got four, a skid and three sets of rotors. We were going through rotor blades like shit through Gertrude. I again thanked God for John Hodgdon and his foresight in scrounging extra blades. We survived on floats thanks to the 335th which was always there for us. Wayne worked long late days with the administrivia, about four pages of reports for every bullet hole. On a lighter note, the mess hall caught fire but unfortunately never burned down; and Michael Allen Shannahan was born in September. His daddy, known as the Worm, sprung with free cigars and Champagne for all. We closed out September on the 30th by destroying another set of rotors.

27

OCTOBER: MAN-MADE STARS AND AN EPIPHANY

ON 1 October, Hook and I celebrated our birthdays at his bedside in the hospital. Thankfully we would not lose him. But we did lose two great soldiers. Both Hyde and Garza were seriously wounded and would have to be evacuated out of country. Hook's request for a birthday present? A new shirt to replace the one that was shot up.

It often takes time to combat harden a unit. Fighting can be sporadic, as they say, with long periods of sheer boredom interrupted occasionally by short periods of stark terror. A lot of learning takes place during the stark terror. Without consistency, learning comes and goes. We had a week of stark terror. The concentration of action the first week hardened us immediately. And as a result, we would be harder to kill. And since no one was killed, there would be no dreaded REMF oversight. After Black Friday, it would take a lot to get us off our game. I thanked the good Lord no one was killed and we did not have to face the dreaded night weather pickup. That came the second week.

The call came on 2 October late at night in the middle of a violent tropical storm. Several units of the 1st Brigade of the 101st Division, the famed Screaming Eagles, had suffered numerous casualties and were surrounded deep in the mountains to our west. All Army aircraft had been grounded. I knew the wounded must have been extremely serious or they would not have called us in such conditions. We headed out into that blizzard using a method that worked my first tour. We flew as low and slow as possible sighting a light from Fat City past Hill 54 and then keeping in sight a village to our front and, with the crew in back leaning out the doors, keeping in sight some lights behind us. Working the mountains at night in weather is like running through a dark room with huge razors jutting down from the ceiling and up from the floor. The key was to always have a back door, an escape route; to never lose sight of either light as we hovered from light to light toward the mountains. It worked on the flat terrain on the coast but as we neared the mountains, no joy, the front blacked out. As was my routine, I began lamenting with God. OK Lord, what now? Here I am, send me, but I need to know how. Why are you doing this to me? Remember, Oh most gracious Virgin Mary....

Then I remembered a river to the north that circled into the valley. I was sure I could get down on the water and using my search light work my way in as we did in the Delta. But I had never encountered such rain or winds in the Delta. The rain was so fierce it blinded me as it reflected off my search light and the winds jerked us about. Still no joy. Then I had a vision, an epiphany really. Thank you, Lord.

On Black Friday, on a routine night mission into the valley, as dark figures darted back and forth loading the patients, I sat there absentmindedly enjoying the sights. In the security provided by the darkness I could actually relax and enjoy the bizarre beauty of night on the battlefield. The flares drifted lazily down through the mountains illuminating the charming landscape in multiple shades of green pierced with deadly but strangely beautiful green and golden streaks of tracer fire. In my reverie I noticed that one of the mountains, covered with clouds, was perfectly silhouetted by the flares—a stunning sight. That was the vision that came back to me and I now knew how I was going to get those soldiers out. It would be dicey but doable.

Since most of our birds were still down, I was in a float aircraft, an under-powered D model Huey without a transponder. I called back and told operations to get me a more powerful H model with good instruments. Then I called the troops and told them to hang on, I would be back. The voice on the other end sounded depressed. He clearly did not believe me.

My plan was to fly instruments (IFR) to the PZ, using a vector from Peacock, an Air Force radar station. I would then let down using flares to clear the mountains and use my FM homer to find the troops. My hope was that the flares would silhouette the mountains or at least enough area around my bird to keep us safe. In the original Epiphany, the wise men had followed a star to our Savior. My star was a flare and we would follow it to save many GIs.

I got a new co-pilot and we took the H model IFR to angels six, (as I prayed for angelic help) giving us good clearance from the highest mountain in the area. There was an Air Force flare ship at 9,000 feet over the fight. He would be my angel...he would provide the star. I explained to him what I wanted to do and asked for help. I got his roger and started down circling under the flares working to position them out my window. Some of the flares got directly over us and in my busyness I decided to let one hit me. After all, it could not be worse than a tree. Wrong! As it got closer I saw a steel canister full of holes big enough to knock us out of the sky. I almost turned us upside down dodging it.

With all that going on, I forgot to tell the Air Force to keep a flare lighted at all times. I discovered this omission at 1,500 feet in 3,000-foot mountains when the lights went out. I was surrounded by razors. (Three years later, a crew from the 498th would be killed when the flares went out while they were hovering up the side of a mountain.) You cannot crash into the sky and there was nothing to do but come to a hover, not difficult in the H model, and start a steep instrument take off (ITO) clear the mountains and start over. After a few tries we got it right, broke out on the side of a mountain, and homed in on the PZ. We took heavy fire on final approach and circled to the other end of the PZ where we landed without mishap. We loaded nine patients and were informed of other patients in nearby locations. The storm had intensified and we were being rocked about rather violently. But the visibility under the clouds in the valley, with the flares, was good and we were able to find the wounded at several other sites. Once loaded, I did a steep ITO clear of the mountains and flew instruments to the coast where I was able to descend to the lights of Chu Lai and deliver the patients to the 2nd Surg. On the way out, we got an urgent call for more patients from another unit of the 101st. It was Tuesday the 3rd when we went back.

My co-pilot was exhausted and Major Mac jumped in. On this trip we were able to get down more easily but could not locate the wounded. They were fearful that the enemy would see their signal and tried to guide us in by sound. The enemy could hear us also but, as we flew blacked out, they could not see us and were firing wildly all over the sky. And that turned out to be a good thing. It was from the location and fire of enemy quad 12.7 mm anti-aircraft guns that we were able to orient ourselves and find the patients.

But there were still more patients and we returned. On the third trip, Peacock vectored us right into the eye of a thunderstorm. I had stumbled inside one in daytime. No matter how fearsome they look on the outside, there is nothing in the air as bad as the inside of one of these monsters. Up to this point I felt pretty much in control but there was no control in that chaotic cloud. I have never been so violently abused in an aircraft before or since. We were gaining and losing thousands of feet, jerked back and forth with lightning flashing through the cockpit. When I brought this to Peacock's attention he asked what we were. When I told him we were a chopper, he moaned an expletive and vectored us out. We finished the evacuations, four trips in all, without further incident although the bird had to be grounded and checked for structural damage.

I flew over nine hours the night and morning of 2-3 October 1967, and landed 12 times finishing about 4 am. I had a standard instrument ticket this tour and logged six hours of night AI—the first such entry on my flight records although, as mentioned, I flew AI day and night in the Delta my first tour. I don't know how many casualties we carried that night but they were all, as suspected, very serious and many would have died before morning.

Although I used three co-pilots on these missions, I used only one medic, and two crew chiefs (we borrowed a ship and its crew chief, Sp4 Glen Peck, flew with it as they usually did). They volunteered to stick it out. Jimmy Johnson, soon to be known as Super Medic, did his magic on the patients and was surely the difference between life and death for some of them. In addition to treating the patients, he scrambled after a stray grenade rolling around in back as the wind blew us to and fro. He was able to capture it and get it safely out of the bird. Don Goody was the other crew chief, maintenance pro second only to Hodgdon. It was a comfort to have him along in case we started hearing strange sounds, as often happens, flying at night and in weather.

The new technique got quite a bit of media attention, one headline heralding a breakthrough in Air Evac methods. But much of it was ill informed. One book actually recorded that we flew the wounded back low level *under the stuff!* Others called it the first ever IFR pickup in the mountains. Still others said it was a blind letdown. It was none of those things. I believe that most of the pilots killed at night in weather were killed trying to fly contact without sufficient visibility. It was an IFR flight with a VFR (visual, not instrument flight) letdown and pickup. Three Dust Off aircraft and 13 crewmen were killed in similar conditions later in October. This technique could have saved them and their patients.

My atheist friend was critical of these missions and told me the crew of a close mutual friend was killed imitating my technique. That was not something I wanted to hear and I later published an explanation of the technique in a popular aviation magazine to prevent hapless imitation. But as usual, the troops were very appreciative. One of the great Screaming Eagles, Tom Courtney, said what I did "was the bravest thing I have ever seen in my four combat tours dating back to Korea." He added, in a tribute to the gonad/glory thing, "When I met Major Brady and thanked him I was amazed that he didn't walk straddle legged." I consider that one of the finest compliments I have ever received, but I am sure Tom never realized that what I did had more to do with the Good Lord than my bravery. Our pilots knew the dangers and were instructed to call me if they were challenged. You don't fly where you can't see unless you are well above the terrain. Again this technique used IFR en route flight with a VFR, not a blind, letdown. We never logged the letdown as AI. You have to be able to make the IFR/VFR transition quickly and must never guess to the front or below. I always ensured that I was clear of the terrain and I never descended one inch blindly.

Aviators talk about rules and laws. Rules are made by men, often by lessor nobles, as a place to hide or cover one's ass. Laws (nature) are from God. You can deviate from the rules—if you execute flawlessly. Never mess with a law, no performance will save you.

What I had done was clearly outside the rules and had I broke the aircraft or hurt someone, I would have been in serious trouble. Some things may sound stupid, or dangerous, but if they work all is forgiven. As it turned out, I was put in for an award, initially a Distinguished Flying Cross (DFC) which was later upgraded to a Distinguished Service Cross, second only to the Medal of Honor, when they discovered the mission was a first. But more important, we could now save the night weather patient. We refined the technique later using mortar and artillery flares and never, if called, left a patient in the field at night, no matter the weather. On subsequent flare missions, I was actually able to enjoy the sheer beauty of the experience, multiple lights in gorgeous multicolored terrain, despite the tracers, as I had in my first vision. The only problem was letting the grunts, some who were reluctant to call us in severe weather conditions, know we could safely make it. Later, some did not call because of the weather and troops died needlessly. In any event, thank you, Lord—so far; we still faced the day weather challenge. Flares don't work in daytime weather.

The weather stayed bad during the first part of October (more helicopter pilots were killed in October than any other month). Jerry and I made another instrument flare pickup on the 5th and on Sunday the 8th another typhoon passed through. The ceiling was less than 100 feet and the winds reached 63 knots. All Army aircraft, except the 54th, were again grounded. The communists had overrun a unit of the 101st Division. When the friendlies came back they found the communists had executed the wounded except for four who were still alive having found haven in the stack of dead bodies. Buddha and I went after them on the deck with pretty good visibility. I was happy to again have Super Medic in the back. He was getting skilled at flying with me in the weather. En route we surprised three VC in black pajamas crouching in the brush moving toward the friendlies. We were too low and they hit us several times before we could get away. The bird was flyable and we worked our way through the weather to the PZ landing next to the dead, 18 as I recall, laid out in a circle feet to the center like the spokes on a wheel. We evacuated the wounded which included the sons of two army generals, 1LT Robert Fergusson and Captain John Lawton. Each of these men would be awarded a DSC for their heroic actions that day.

Buddha and I got special thanks from Major General Robert G. Fergusson, then the Berlin Brigade Commander, who flew to Viet Nam to see his son. He seemed overjoyed that the boy recognized him. He told us he would mention us to LTG Lawton. Fergusson's boy died three weeks later, a month to the day of his rescue. (Years afterward as I absentmindedly read the DSC citation of a 1LT for whom the officers Club at Fort Ord, California was named, I realized it was 1LT Fergusson.) I heard that when the priest tried to give the last rites to Lawton he was told, "Get the hell away from me. I ain't dying." And he didn't.

On 9 October, Al Flory and Pete Schuster in Dust Off 54 flew a mission that was more than heroic; it gained the undying gratitude and respect of some we served, respect vital in our work. The PZ was near LZ Mary Lou (the GIs often named areas after wives and sweethearts, Mary Lou was the wife of a colonel later killed) which sat on top of a mountain in deep jungle overlooking the Que Son Valley, an area that would haunt U.S. Forces throughout the war. The weather was poor and support helicopters could not fly. The troops from the 4th Infantry Division, under control of the 1st Brigade of 101st Airborne Division, were out of food and wet and miserable. Eleven were dead, some executed by the communists after being wounded as they had done on my mission the day before.

Dust Off 54 had tried to get in earlier and been forced out by enemy fire. He promised to return, a promise the troops took lightly because of the weather and intense enemy activity. They were more than delighted when he did return just before midnight. The grunts were still engaged and the weather still marginal. The PZ was tight in heavily jungled terrain. The grunts had difficulty directing "54" into the LZ. The troops could not believe it when Al and Pete offered to turn on their landing lights and expose themselves to enemy fire if it would help. With the assistance of Air Force flares, Coleman spotted the grunts and they got into the confined area within a few meters of the last known enemy positions. They were blacked out which certainly saved the crew. Pappy and Brian Burwick, the crew chief, loaded all the wounded and had them in a hospital in 15 minutes.

This mission was not unlike thousands of others the 54th would fly, but the grunts described it as unbelievable. We had not yet established ourselves with the troops and their trust generated the honesty between us that was indispensable for success—not only in saving lives but in the security of our crews. Al and Pete had done a great deal to establish that trust as the word of their mission spread and the troops began to talk of the courage, tenacity, and ingenuity of the crews with the biggest balls of all—the Dust Off crews. And as a result of this mission and another in which he tried to call in artillery fire on some VC he spotted, Al became forever known as FAC (short for forward air controller) Flory the hero of LZ Mary Lou.

I would log some 18 hours of AI night flare missions, all of them satisfying but none more so than one on 15 October when I used the flare technique to rescue a soldier who would become a great American hero, Webster Anderson. Webster's unit, an artillery battery (A, 2nd/320) in the 101st Division, was overrun at night in severe weather on a 2,400-foot mountain. The CIDG turned on U.S. troops (this happened too frequently) and let the NVA into friendly lines. In the fight that followed, Webster initially was hit by two enemy grenades which pretty much took off both legs. He propped himself up and continued to direct fire on the enemy. When a grenade landed among his troops Webster grabbed it and attempted to throw it clear of his position. Unfortunately the grenade exploded and pretty much took off an arm. Still he fought on.

Scotty and I were called out about 02:00 for a reported 21 wounded and seven KIA. We were on instruments at 70 feet. Some gunships were called to help but turned back when I explained that we would have to go in IFR and land with flares. We coordinated the pickup directly with Webster's men using artillery flares to land. We were able to load all 21 of the wounded. Miraculously, Webster got to the hospital alive and although they could not save his legs or one arm, they did save his life. A male nurse friend tracked his progress through the medical chain and kept us apprised of his condition. He would later be awarded the Medal of Honor for his actions that night. He was very appreciative of our efforts and we became close friends right to his death. (As an aside, this may have been one of only two instances in the annals of war in which one

Medal of Honor recipient rescued another.)

Units of the 1st Cav. arrived in our AO in October bringing with them my old unit, the 15th Medical Battalion and its Air Ambulance Platoon, from Benning. Some of the Cav. pilots were in our club one evening on a stopover en route to LZ Baldy. I asked a pilot where their aircraft were. He said they were parked on an island just north of us. "Not Gilligan's Island? Charlie owns that place at night." The pilot was a bit cavalier in his response and blew off my concerns. Our AO contained the schoolhouse for sapper training. The next day, many of the ships were a pile of ashes as VC graduates of the sapper school had a blast with them.

The 15th Med not only had a different call sign than the rest of the helicopter ambulance units, preferring MEDEVAC to Dust Off as noted, they were still stubbornly tied to an antiquated evacuation system which did not allow bypassing their battalion aid stations. Very often a patient would be put in a tent awaiting further evacuation when he could have been in a hospital in the same time frame. It made sense in World War II, but not in Viet Nam. I am not sure they ever recovered from the Ia Drang debacle and were exceptionally cautious in their flying. I heard that they once sent three ships for 11 patients and they still would not land in an area unless it was "green" (secure) for a specified time! Needless to say, routine night missions were anathema.

Since they were a direct support unit tied specifically to the 1st Cav. with little or no flexibility for area patients, we were often called to evacuate urgent non-Cav. patients 20 minutes from us when they were only five minutes away. That was stupidity, as well as medical malfeasance, at the extreme. This was a system the GI would call FUBAR (F***** Up Beyond All Recognition). As bad, they continually called us for back haul of patients from their aid stations, urgent patients, when their ships sat next to the patient once again, five minutes from an operating room, and we were 20 minutes away.

This unit also added machine guns to their ships and an extra crew man as gunner. They would later mix brown paint with the red to camouflage the red crosses. They were taken by the myth of the Red Cross as a target and put in the position of hiding something, the Red Cross, which was there only to be seen. This was insanity in my mind as was the gunner, which reduced patient space. If the communists shot at the Red Cross while the bird was on the ground, bravo! They should have been shooting at people. If he shot at the Red Cross while the bird was in flight, again, bravo! You had to lead a helicopter several lengths to hit it.

My protests that policy should not come before patients fell on the deaf ears of the LTC physician who commanded the unit. My concerns about a physician commanding an aviation unit, born at Benning, were validated in our interface with the 15th. This man was particularly inept. Rumors had it that he tried to tell the pilots how to fly and that an errant grenade that exploded in a movie, was meant for him. The operations of the 15th also reinforced my belief in the area support concept. We had the flexibility, because the combat commander did not control us, to provide direct support in some instances, and for good reason. The commander would always opt for DS. Non-unit patients in his AO were not his concern but someone had to take care of them—usually us. DS can be an efficiency killer and should not be mandated. But I emphasize again that a number of the MEDEVAC crews, some former Dust Off crewmen, hung themselves out for the patient and were every bit as heroic as most Dust Off troops.

Because of the increased patient load in our AO, two hospital ships, the *Sanctuary* and *Repose*, rotated off our shore from October on. Unfortunately they never told me of their arrival. My first trip to the Sanctuary was at night in the poor weather that continued throughout October. I had 11 GIs on board and asked the patient regulator where to take them. "Take them to the *Sanctuary*, 55." "What the hell is that?" "It's a hospital ship, 55." Where the Hell is it?" "Somewhere off the coast between Chu Lai and Da Nang, 55, try this push." I called the ship. I am about 100 feet over rough waves, it's dark as hell, and I'm working hard to stay out of the clouds—and the ocean, and I get a jumble of Navy jargon...interrogatory, starboard, port, relative bearing, etc. "OK guys, I am an illiterate Army pilot and you are going to have to speak English if you want these patients."

We worked on our commo and I finally spotted a circle of light in the fog and headed for it. I had never landed on a ship and was surprised at the small size of the pad and the immediacy of the mast; but the real problem was that the pad kept moving away from me and simultaneously bobbing up and down. As I moved up over the pad and started to lower the bird, the damn thing moved away. When I finally figured out how to keep up with it I had to deal with the up and down gyrations of the deck. There was nothing for me to do but quickly become a part of that thing before I hit the mast or something else. I got close to the deck and bottomed the collective. We were down but now rocking and rolling all over the place. Initially I tried to compensate with my controls but finally gave up and went with the flow. The whole thing was too much for my co-pilot who immediately threw up all over the cockpit. Years later, a coast guard helicopter pilot told me that he trained for six months before being qualified to land on a ship like the *Sanctuary*. Army helicopter pilots learned on one mission. The hospital ships increased significantly the number of operating rooms in our AO and were a blessing for our patients although a lot of them added sea sickness to their wounds.

They were also a blessing for our food chain. Only the *Sanctuary* PX had cashmere sweaters. The man who ran our class A (food) supply point had a wife with a weakness for cashmere sweaters. By this time we had a 32-cubic-foot walk-in cooler and BBQs in our area to go with the flushing toilets and hot water showers. A few sweaters kept that cooler full. Our guys spent little time in the mess hall. Although we ate pretty well, we had nothing on the troops aboard the Sanctuary.

I was unloading some patients one day when a sailor ran up to my window and asked me to sign their log—I had just made the

2,000th landing. They invited me to lunch where I was presented with an engraved lighter. The lunch was served in a fancy room with waiters. We ate on a table cloth, off china, with silver ware. In a war zone? I could hardly wait to tell the guys. But it got better. My lunch companion was a pretty nurse who seemed bored with the whole exercise. Finally she excused herself saying almost in passing, "I think I will go take a nap, would you like to join me?" I swear to God. No, I did not, but now I really had something to tell the guys. I had gained a whole new appreciation of the Navy.

After Buddha and I were hit on the 8th, the unit went two weeks without being hit by enemy fire...but we kept hitting trees! We had gone through five sets of rotor blades in less than a month. The 23rd was our busiest day thus far; 29 missions, one of them another flare mission. We were up to 1,000 total flying hours and 882 patients by the 24th; but down to one flyable ship. The quiet time was soon over as we had all six ships hit, one mortared, the last week in October.

On 28 October, B Company, 2/502nd of the 101st was in the middle of an equipment extraction when the VC unleashed a mortar barrage on them killing one and wounding eight. Three of the wounded were close to death when Al Flory and Alan Scott arrived. Dust Off was advised that two previous slicks had been shot up trying to land and forced to abort. The wounded were dying and Al had no choice but to give it a try. As he was rounding out to land, his ship was raked with enemy fire which wounded his crew chief, Charlie Ramirez. Al aborted and took Charlie to the hospital. He advised Jerry Foust and Don Sewell of the situation and they headed for the PZ as Dust Off 53.

Again Dust Off was warned that enemy contact had intensified in every quadrant of the PZ. The friendlies were reluctant to risk another ship. The count was now three ships shot up trying to land. Jerry and Don studied the terrain. A river bed offered good cover right up to the PZ. Five Three advised the friendlies to get ready, he was coming in. They slipped down into the river bed, sped along under cover of its banks, jumped the tree line and landed. Charlie could now see Dust Off 53 and intensified their fire which riddled the chopper as Pappy Coleman made trip after trip under fire to load the wounded. The friendlies could not suppress the fire and the commander screamed for Dust Off to get out. His troops hit the horizontal and 53's medic and crew chief were left alone and exposed to load the wounded. Jerry did not have all the wounded and advised the ground commander he would not leave until they had ALL the wounded—and to get off their ass and help. They did and Dust Off got all eight wounded loaded and the ship made it to the hospital barely in time for the three who otherwise would surely have died. The friendlies were astonished at the skill and daring of this Dust Off crew which mirrored exactly the mission that killed Kelly. The rapport between the 54th and those we served continued to grow.

In addition to Hook's and my birthdays, we celebrated Foust's on the 12th, also my anniversary, and Herb Spann's on the 6th, also my daughter's birthday; both reminders of my family which I missed every day. The mice were back driving Wayne nuts. Jon Belding, his roommate had left some C rat scraps in his mess kit which the mice ate and promptly shit in his mess gear! Those mice had the makings of good Drill Instructors. A few of the guys took their sadistic tendencies out on the poor mice some of which ended up on dart boards. A box floated up on the beach with two heads inside and we had the usual mortar scares, one time with the VC reported inside our perimeter.

In the middle of the operational frenzy, we had the standard share of personal tribulations which are often as heartbreaking as the casualties. Major Mac's wife, Pat, tragically lost her child in October. One of the guys got a letter from his wife with her wedding ring in it and another got a letter his wife wrote to her lover. Absence often makes the heart grow fonder for someone else. We also had the ordeal of the club.

In October some of our men decided to turn the enlisted club into a bar replete with bar maids and paying customers. I was out-raged but Major Mac thought it might be good for morale. Needless to say, our beautiful area filled with drunks and fights. One of our guys got drunk and actually went and got a gun to shoot another one of our guys. I feared that if we didn't clean up this mess it could destroy us as an effective combat unit. Unfortunately there were some in Viet Nam who used that conflict for their own personal enrichment. On Halloween day we had a meeting to discuss the club. I wanted to get rid of it immediately. Major Mac was focused on morale and I could not turn him around. The decision to close it was deferred. In the meantime, the club was polluting our area.

Since we all came at the same time, the higher ups were planning an infusion of troops with differing dates of rotation for future unit integrity. Several of our men actually volunteered to extend in the 54th to escape the dreaded infusion. Apparently they were as com-fortable with the unit as I was (most of the time). I certainly did not want to retrain a bunch of FNGs, but some of our troops were starting to show troubling signs. There were rumors of marijuana use and one of our enlisted put an M-16 round in his .45 pistol and played Russian roulette with it three times. It went off the fourth time, unfortunately not aimed at his head this time but it sent a stray round through our area. I found this same guy walking around with a cocked pistol in his holster. A slight bump could have set it off; and he was later caught shooting off our hill into the ocean. He got drunk and began to scream at me; first that he hated me, then that he loved me! This man was an excellent candidate for infusion—or the stockade. We got rid of him.

But overall, we were coming together as a team. In October, we had seven ships hit, less than the first week, but only one man wounded, Charlie Ramirez. He would be out of the hospital soon but not for long. Eye-witness statements for the heroism of Dust Off from the grunts began to flood our operations. I looked in vain for someone who understood the awards system and could write our guys up. I got the usual "we are just doing our job" but the intensity of the action and tenacity of our crews went far beyond my experiences my first tour and needed to be documented. I knew that military medals can be important for a soldier and was determined that our men got their fair share. I fell back on my awards experience from my first tour and began to write.

The last week in September, we averaged an hour per mission and 1.8 patients per mission, or two patients per hour. In the month of October, we improved to 45 minutes per mission, two patients per mission or 2.7 patients per hour while flying 355 hours. Not much of an improvement but an improvement nonetheless. We evacuated 966 patients, of which 27 were communists. At the rate we were going through aircraft we had to be efficient if we were to be effective. We had our biggest day on the 23rd, 75 patients in 29 missions. Before long those numbers would be close to our daily average.

October provided enough action to keep us sharp. We solved the night weather problem and were not leaving patients in the field for any reason. Thankfully, we had not faced the day weather mission, zero zero on mountain tops and the miserable low valley fog. That came in November.

· 28 ·

NOVEMBER:
THE FOG IS LIFTED

AT the rate we were going, we would be over 1,000 missions soon. It was time to turn the WOPAs loose. I did not want them to get too dependent on the RFOs (I had one actually go to sleep on me during a night mission, I slammed the collective down not only to wake him up but as a reminder that sleeping co-pilots were a no-no regardless of their confidence in the pilot). They were getting their approaches down. On one mission, as Norm Shannahan snaked his way into an area, an overhead observer exclaimed: "Wow, look at Norm worm his way in there." To this day he is known as the Worm.

But some were having problems with weather missions and they often called me. They could fly weather; they just didn't know they could. They only had a few hours of instrument training in flight school, not unlike we had my first tour, but it should have made them safe. One of the pilots aborted a weather mission. He became disoriented on an earlier mission and panicked. He thought he had vertigo. He didn't. Vertigo is a disease; a problem for the flight surgeon. What he had, and others as well, was spatial disorientation. It is a problem of self-discipline and should never result in death or an aborted mission.

I went back with him for the patients. The weather was not that bad. I forced him to fly IFR on the way back. He did well. I put as many of our young pilots as possible in actual weather and forced them to concentrate, to discipline themselves to do what they had been trained to do. There was only one pilot I put in weather who was good to go initially, Scottie; and he had some flight training before he went to flight school. All the rest were a bit shaky at first but overcame it. We may have been the only Dust Off unit in Viet Nam that never lost a bird at night or in weather due to pilot error. And we were flying missions no one else flew. We also were the only unit that flew all categories of patients at night. Our guys got a lot of practice in night flying. On the 6th, the WOPAs began to fly without an RFO. There were some fights initially but things eventually smoothed out.

I also quit smoking on the 6th. I never really had the habit, at least not bad enough to actually buy cigarettes, but did on occasion bum one.

And that got to be a challenge. My reminder to reluctant lenders that cigarettes did not come like coffins—one to a box—was wearing thin. I heard that smoking was bad for night vision and noticed I was starting to inhale. I decided to quit completely much to the joy of my suppliers. Snuff was another matter. After all, one did not inhale it.

On the 11th, Veteran's Day, Foust and Shadrick with Pappy and Bob Cronan as medics, and Charlie Ramirez as crew chief, added to their veterans' status. They took 32 rounds and the entire crew was wounded. The area was a mess of scattered patients and the friendlies were unable to suppress enemy frre. There were so many dead and wounded in the PZ, Jerry actually landed one skid on a dead VC. Coleman then took a round between his lips. When Ramirez ran to help him, Jim replied through the blood: "I am good to go, I just kissed the bullet that had my name on it." He went back to work.

Ramirez was then shot in the butt. This time he would be in the hospital for some time until the 63 stitches healed. But thankfully this great soldier came back to us despite all the butt jokes he had to endure. Buddha took a round right through his helmet creasing his skull. He had one of the new ballistic helmets (that Jerry had recently stolen since our higher HQ failed to provide any) and it may have saved his life; or it may have been the hardness of his head. Apparently the bullet ricocheted off his skull since its path through the helmet would have put the bullet right through his brain. He liked to pose with the helmet and an arrow through the bullet holes. Jerry took Plexiglas in the face that would continue to surface for years to come. Bob Cronan, although wounded himself, worked with Pappy, who was bleeding from his lips, to get all the wounded on board and they managed to fly the badly damaged bird to the hospital.

When the enemy wasn't destroying our aircraft, we were. We got rotor set number seven in November, another set of tail rotors and another ship sat down on a stump. And it wasn't only Charlie that was taking down our troops. One unit was almost wiped out by food poisoning, another by bee stings, and on the 19th another unit suffered significant casualties when a troop dropped a grenade in the chow line. The 19th was a bad day for friendly fire. Near Kontum, the 173rd Light Infantry Brigade had 42 killed and another 45 wounded when our Air Force dropped a 500-pounder in their midst. Another unit reported destroying a VC tank. The VC had no tanks. They had attacked a friendly tank. These things happen in combat and always will.

So far we were able to handle everything thrown at us, enemy and friendly. And our work was appreciated. The troops of the 101st Brigade were so grateful the commanding general invited Major Mac and me to dinner in the general's mess, quite an experience for us. He gave Major Mac a plaque for the 54th in gratitude for our support. They also challenged us to drink a flaming meme, a drink aflame, which was no challenge really but a good excuse for me to have a drink. The Screaming Eagles would soon leave our area and we would miss them. They were the only unit to this point that was able to secure their LZs and were excellent on missions. Like the 1st Cav. they had an Air Ambulance platoon assigned which I would command nine years later. Unlike the 1st Cav. MEDEVAC, they kept the call sign Dust Off and flew accordingly.

About this time, I noticed from radio chatter that there was a focus on body count. I heard this was a Robert McNamara effort to quantify warfare as he did in business. I would later see his book of apology on Viet Nam in a place of honor in a communist museum which says all that need to be said about this pathetic person. Needless to say, the commies and media had a field day with body counting and I once said only in half jest to a troop boasting about body count, "a pregnant female is two, right?" This whole thing smacked to me of Wild West gun fighter stuff. But as it turns out, our count and that of the communists were pretty close. I was indifferent to this practice but one practice that did disturb me was to hear a commander shooting "VC" out of his command and control helicopters. It was almost impossible, for me at least, to separate a peasant in black pajamas from communists. This commander actually kept track, bragging about 11 notches on his gun. I hope this practice was not widespread, but fear there may have been others. I became aware that there were a few, not many, but some who really enjoyed killing. And they are hard to identify until you put a gun in their hands. We would see more of this later at My Lai. The pro never talked of killing people; when he talked about it at all, he talked of killing the enemy—which is a good thing.

· 29 ·

ANOTHER EPIPHANY

ON 28 November, another dreaded Tuesday but one that turned out to be lucky, we solved the day weather dilemma. The mission was a snakebite victim on top of a 2,400 foot mountain. It may have been the same mountain where I picked up Webster Anderson. As I approached the area I saw, to my horror, that the mountain top was engulfed in thick clouds. This was my first confrontation with zero zero pickup conditions in daytime. I was in serious dialogue with God; OK, Lord, now what? Initially I flew straight into the stuff and tried to hover up the mountain. I calculated that if I got into trouble I could simply fall off in any direction and I would break out in the valley. I did have trouble, I became disoriented and had to abort into the valley several times. My crew was very tense. To add to my woes, the ground troops were screaming that the bitten soldier was going into convulsions. I had no idea how we were going to get that kid out. On what I promised my crew would be my last try, I really got disoriented.

We were blown sideways and I was looking out my side window

praying for a clear place to go in when I discovered that I could see the tip of my rotor blade and the top of the trees under it! That wind was the breath of God; another epiphany. I now had two reference points; I was completely oriented and knew I was right side up. I then turned that baby sideways, thanked God and the powerful H model, hovered up the mountain, focused on the blade and the tree tops, right into the area. The troops were delighted and we got the patient to the hospital. As a bonus one of them shouted, "God Bless you, Double Nickel [from '55'], you guys are angels." God certainly had blessed us although I was a bit upset that He took so long to do it.

Again, no one challenged the illegality of this approach even though one crewman refused to fly again. He was the unit's new, very experienced, technical inspector and this was his first mission. As I noted, some experienced people cannot be re-taught. He left the unit. The rest of us were delighted. We now had a solution for the day weather missions—at least on the mountains. To this point, I believed that daytime weather rescues could be made only by remaining VFR under the weather. There was no way to descend down through the clouds or fog, to the terrain, in daytime. And those who tried paid a dear price. You had to stay VFR all the way, no guessing. All that was needed was two reference points.

What I had learned with the snake-bite mission was that you can see in zero zero conditions, not far but far enough. All that is needed is about 20 feet in a Huey, the distance from your window to the tip of the rotor blade. But you had to be able to see to the end of your rotor disc and you had to have another reference point, a tree, a bush or the ground; nothing could ever come between your eyes and the tip of the rotor blade. And this mission could not be flown nose first; it had to be flown sideways. Attitude changes and the reduced visibility through the windshield made normal flight impossible. I could do it safely only flying sideways with my window open. On both the flare and fog missions I flew with my head out the window. I was able to do this and move my head without following with my hands. The hands had to stay quiet until I told them to do something. I noticed some pilots' hands would follow the head. Not good. There was no descending through the stuff; this was a straight VFR pickup, albeit in IFR conditions. I have no idea how many of these missions I flew but I never logged them as AI. They were not, we were VFR. All that remained was to refine the technique from the mountain to low valley fog.

The low valley fog missions required a careful map recon all the way to the PZ. Radar vectors were of no use but the FM homer was. Step one was to find a path, a trail, or river or some other terrain feature, or series of terrain features, which you could follow into the PZ. Next was a VFR flight to a mountain that was visible above the fog near the path into the PZ. I would then come to a hover above the fog and follow the path down the mountain into the PZ. My hover speed was not much more than that of a walking or jogging soldier. Although it never happened, I knew that if I became disoriented, or went IFR, I could stop immediately, climb through the fog and start over. To repeat, I never flew an inch blindly. As an added bonus, we were almost completely invulnerable to enemy fire on these missions.

The weather missions, especially the night weather missions, were beyond the capability of some of our pilots and they were instructed never to push themselves on any mission let alone those involving flares and fog. But they were also never to leave a patient in the field because of weather or the night. They were to call me. (I would later learn that these missions were called "Brady Missions.") They failed to do this only once that I know of. On the 22nd, the WOPAs took all three ups and we had for the first time four pickups in which they did not get in. Some other ships picked up our patients. Weather was involved. That of course was unacceptable and they knew it. The next day we broke our record for patients. Enough said.

We saw another decrease in our flying time per patient, down from 45 minutes in October to 40 minutes. Every bit helps. We were carrying 31 patients per day and flying 11 hours, about the same as October. Thanksgiving day, the 23rd, a month to the day from our biggest day in October, we again broke the unit record: 47 missions and 102 patients.

All in all November was rather quiet, five guys hit, over 12 percent of unit strength, but no one killed and only two birds shot up. We got 957 patients in 518 missions and 348 flying hours. Our mission time was down to 40 minutes but still almost two patients per. The WOPAs were flying together, we had the weather thing in hand and best of all, Major Mac decided to close the club. I was ecstatic. Some NCOs threatened to set up across the road in the Morgue (they did but were run out when some of the drunks were found messing with the bodies). I could care less about the club as long as it wasn't in our area. Some of the local surgeons wanted to put our birds in the field in direct support role. They would eventually come around to our way of thinking and reject the 1st Cav. concept of putting a man in a tent when a hospital was closer. The American asked if we needed more aircraft. I told them we were OK as long as we continued to get superb maintenance support from the 335th. The 2nd Surg got a new commander, Major Kenneth Cass, who matched the professionalism of Bill Augerson. We were blessed with great soldier physicians in our AO which was not always the norm. By now our walk-in freezer was filled with all the steaks and lobster a few cashmere sweaters could buy. Life was good. I wrote my wife that the war might end before I went home.

· 30 ·

DECEMBER: DOLDRUMS

DECEMBER would reinforce my hope that Viet Nam would end soon. The communists asked for a cease fire (so they could reload) and we had no ships hit! Wayne had no reports to write on damaged ships and I put him to work building a pen for Gertrude. He was spending too much time chasing her down as she wandered the area on nocturnal trysts, terrorizing the troops. On the 1st we celebrated Major Mac's and Scotty's birthdays. The troops gave him a special plaque, made from the remnants of a damaged rotor blade. They dearly loved him—moreso since he was an RFO and was also hitting trees. In fact, he led the league in ravaging our supply of rotors. I recalled an early photo of the 57th in the time of Temperilli. Forty percent of their aircraft were sitting on the ramp without rotor blades; certainly not the norm unless you consider that Major Mac was part of that unit. Buddha Shadrick turned 20 on the 3rd and we no longer had a teenage pilot.

Despite our good fortune regarding enemy hits, we shattered our previous high for patients, 1,658, 193 in one day, also a record. We increased our efficiency by one patient per hour. We were now at four patients per flying hour. We were carrying more wounded than Dust Off companies that had four times as many aircraft; and twice as many as the nearest detachment. And our pilots flew twice the hours as the others. (As time went on, I became convinced of the inefficiency of the company. The increased logistical burden kept pilots out of the air. Some of our pilots would fly more nighttime than the total flown by some company commanders.) December's biggest increase in casualties was Vietnamese civilians, double the total in November and for the first time, more civilians than U.S. troops. Something was going on out there.

The 11th Light Infantry Brigade joined the Americal and set up operations at Duc Pho, about 30 minutes to our south, on Christmas Eve. Thankfully they arrived during a lull and would have time to train. They desperately needed it. Unfortunately they did not get enough. The 11th would suffer over 5,000 casualties in Viet Nam, among the worst being what they did to the reputation of the Army as a result of their involvement in the My Lai atrocity. Because of the actions of a few in the 11th, the once proud Americal Division, which suffered four times the casualties in Viet Nam as in World War II, would become known as the "Atrocical Division."

We were immediately confronted with exceptional incidents of unprofessionalism among their units. My first encounter with the 11th was at night in weather. I was working my way low level to the PZ having great difficulty with commo. Along with the usual confusion in any casualty situation, there were several units on our push mucking up the air. Their Six, the commander, came on the air to help. He ordered all those who were not involved with the casualties to get off the air. The response from one voice was, "F*** you, Six!" That was an unusual response to a commander's orders to say the least; something you would never hear from a strac unit. The 11th was far from a strac unit. We managed to get the patients but I knew this was a unit that would have some serious problems in combat. Accordingly, we sent a ship to Duc Pho to provide direct support. We hated to do this, and the ship could do some area support as well, but this unit needed all the help it could get.

We used the quiet time for training. LTC Augerson brought some stokes litters and we simulated hoist missions. The best way to bring a man on a litter up through the jungle is vertical, but then he is very difficult to swing into the bird. If you raise him horizontally, he is more likely to tangle in the trees. A jungle penetrator worked pretty well for ambulatory patients. We were unable to improve hoist operations. They remained dangerous and difficult. The troops understood this and in most instances they would blow a hole in the jungle for us to land.

Although there was reluctance from some crew chiefs, we encouraged our medics to cross-train them on emergency treatment, often on actual missions. This training could be priceless when we had a big load and the medic was busy. If the crew chief was able to simply stop a troop's bleeding or assist the medic in CPR when there was also an airway blockage, it could save a life. Hook was teaching Gary Lowder how to do mouth to mouth while he did the CPR. The patient threw up C rats fruit cocktail in Lowder's mouth. Hook made him go back and finish the job. Lowder would never eat another fruit cocktail, but his knowledge of this procedure would help save the life of a great soldier.

Bob Hope came on the 19th. I had seen him my first tour and I flew 1st up while the rest of the guys listened to Bob Hope's wise cracks and googled his honeys. I also flew all day on Christmas with Hook. Hook had been saving up boodle, goodies from home, especially his favorite, Jiffy Pops, for the boon doggies and he carried it with him on our Christmas missions. Late in the afternoon we got a call for some wounded deep in the boonies. A young sergeant helped Steve load the wounded. He was maybe 19 going on 90 covered with mud and other people's blood. His face was bleak and dirty and he hadn't shaved in days. He was hard core at an early age. "Do we have them all Sarge." "Roger that, Dust Off." As I brought the bird to a hover, Hook remembered the boodle and threw the bag at the young troop yelling, "Merry Christmas Sarge." The bag opened up and one of the Jiffy Pops fell out. The boy Sergeant bent over, and then looked up, his eyes filling with tears. He mouthed "Merry Christmas Dust Off," as the tears washed the dirt off his face furrowing lines to his jaw. Hook smiled, gave him a thumbs up and we headed for the hospital and a cold Christmas dinner.

It is true that the Dust Off crews got much glory in the life-saving business. But it was the doctors and nurses and their remarkable skills that really saved lives. And they were heroic. On at least two occasions, a surgical team from the 2nd Surg, led by their commander, removed an armed M 79, 40 mm grenade round lodged in a soldier. The M 79 is a vicious weapon. The round arms itself by rotation a few meters out of the barrel. From that moment it either explodes on impact or is coiled like a deadly snake to explode at the slightest movement. There was no way to know if the round was armed and needed only a slight movement to set it off. I had flown a soldier with an impacted M-79 round and was warned not to make a fast descent or spiral landing for fear of arming the round. Some choppers had mysteriously blown up in midair for no apparent reason, save perhaps an errant grenade. The operating rooms were specially prepared but certainly not bullet proof. In one case the commander operated with his left hand hoping to save his good hand if things went bad.

Up to this time we had only met the hospital staff on the helipad or when we visited our wounded in the hospital. They were a light and cheerful lot but dead serious when it came patient time. And patient time went on 24-hours a day in seven operating rooms and 400 beds. We decided to invite them to our Christmas party and many came. And so did the hospital chaplain, Father Don, who had become a friend through daily Mass. The nurses were enamored of our flushing toilets and we would set up a guard to keep a wayward GI from wandering in while they used them. Some of the guys offered to stand guard if they wished to use our hot water showers. No takers though. We got to know them and naturally gave them nicknames. The chief nurse, a wonderful person, was the Chief Broad; one especially well-endowed young lady was Super Boobs (they could not find a flack vest to fit her) and another was known as Super Bitch. She looked and deserved the name, sharp featured, with viper shaped horn-rimmed glasses and a biting tongue.

Super Bitch never had enough stuff for her patients, hated the bureaucracy, and wouldn't hesitate to hiss her complaints to anyone within earshot. But she was accompanied by a remarkably unbitch like scent, an extraordinary perfume. I told her I would get her anything her patients needed as long as our guys got special treatment. "What do you mean by that, she asked?"

"How about waking them up with a kiss?"

Words cannot describe the look she gave me. But she did agree to wear an extra dose of that perfume when caring for our men. I got her everything she asked for including special coffee pots from profits I confiscated (much to the chagrin of the proprietors) from the hated club. The 2nd Surg people appreciated and expressed amazement at our flying. One nurse whose mother was a teacher had her students write letters and pray for us, a priceless Christmas gift.

The 2nd Surg would later be augmented by another American hospital. Our initial visit with the leadership of that hospital would be disturbing. They believed their sole mission was GIs. They did not wish to care for our Vietnamese allies. I was reminded of my experiences with Vietnamese hospitals in the Highlands. We quickly disabused them of this notion. Unless they were prepared to watch the patients die on their helipad, they would be taken wherever their condition warranted; and all patients would be treated the same; including the VC and NVA. That was the end of the issue. The 2nd Surg and its personnel remain my all time favorite hospital.

As the party progressed we discovered unit talent aside from building and saving and maintaining. PFC Frank Zuber, a quiet almost reclusive troop, did a roast of Major Mac and me that had us in stitches. We all agreed he should replace Johnny Carson. I recorded a poem to the music of Don Sewell and the rhythm of Robert Service's "The Shooting of Dan McGrew" that we still play. Sgt. Rock got drunk and went into a tirade on his uvula. He claimed alcohol made it grow so big he could see it in the mirror; that it then flapped back and forth and gagged him. He wanted us to be ready to save him. We had a great party and looked forward to more in what we expected to be the quiet months ahead. In December, for the first and last time, we had no ships hit or men hurt. I take that back. The hot water heater in the shower developed a short and zapped a few unsuspecting bathers. I worried about another DOMREP.

FATHER DON'S AIR MEDAL

Nᴏɴᴇ of us really know how we affect others but I think most who knew me before Viet Nam would say I was a pretty happy go lucky Irishman with a good sense of humor. A few months into this tour, I noticed I was losing my sense of humor— rotor blades and stumps and a saloon may have had something to do with it. Very little was funny to me anymore. Dealing with adolescent WOPAs could do that to you. On duty they would fly down the tube of a .50 caliber machine gun to get a patient, but off duty they were part of the zoo. They never lost their sense of humor, indeed found humor in just about everything no matter how bizarre or gruesome. I accosted one WOPA with some violence one day when I saw him walking to the aircraft. He jumped and ran as I fumed. I later learned he was returning a body to its village, a mission not requiring two-minute reaction time. There were other examples. (Two of the WOPAs complained that I deliberately chose them for a mission knowing full well they were hung over. They spent their flight stomping on the outside pedal taking turns vomiting out their window.) I was clearly getting a bit fanatical about details. The troops had begun to avoid me and I feared I was affecting unit morale.

One of the unique blessings of the American military is the Chaplains Corps. There is no way to measure the value of chaplains in combat. In a hierarchical environment crawling with Type A personalities with an occasional wannabe dictator thrown in, it is comforting to find a compassionate clergyman. Most chaplains are given special access to commanders who allow them an iron fist to bypass the chain of command and beat up the bureaucracy on behalf of soldiers in appreciation of their velvet touch when dealing with countless personal tragedies especially the most horrifying— notifying the next of kin. The chaplaincy is also is a reflection of our roots as spelled out in the Declaration. It distinguishes our military from those of most of the world. Can you imagine Hitler or Stalin seeking the council of a man of God?

The word chaplain derives from the cloak, or "cappa" in Latin, of a pagan Roman soldier who tore his in half to warm a shivering beggar. That soldier, Martin of Tours, became the patron Saint of France and French Kings carried the remains of his cloak as a holy shield into battle.

The guardians of Martin's cloak were "cappellanus." In time, all military clergy became "capellani," in French "chapelains." In the 8th Century, the Catholic Council of Ratisbon authorized chaplains, unarmed, to go into battle. They have always been a part of our military. Their courage and ability to comfort matched that of the medic.

In my first memory of our Chaplain, Father Don, he was armed with holy oil wading through a stack of bodies dropped by a Chinook at the door of our morgue (which unhappily resided practically on our doorstep). He was anointing with the Sacrament of the Last Rites everybody and body part in the pile. I was surprised and, to my shame, a bit amused. I told him that the head he was anointing was surely dead and he was wasting his time. He never looked up but reminded me rather sharply that no one knows when the soul leaves the body. Earlier, a soldier declared dead and sent to that morgue breathed on the attendant when they opened his body bag. They managed to save him but he had been deprived of oxygen for too long and would never be normal. Father Don would not make that same mistake and deprive anybody of oxygen for the soul, the Last Rites, by assuming it was too late, regardless the condition of the body.

Father Don was my all-time favorite chaplain. The son of a police chief, he would give you his entire Cappa. I was especially fond of the Mass wine and asked him for an unblessed bottle for Saint Patrick's day when I went off the wagon. It took until St Patrick's Day but he delivered (and this St Patrick's day I drank it, unlike my first tour). I told him the tragic story of my Myna birds and he showed up one day with one to add to our zoo. But he had his ways. Most chaplains provided a shoulder to cry on. Father Don would give you a hanky. We shared the same faith and I queried him on the changes taking place in the Church after Vatican II. I seldom got a satisfactory answer. God is an issue in combat and some of us argued religion. We would try to get Father Don to referee. Such efforts were usually in vain resulting in neither side being able to declare victory.

He seldom concerned himself with military decorum, demeanor, or discipline. After all, he reported to a different chain of command than the rest of us. He flew with us as much as he could to help the clergy in the local villages and visit the troops in the jungle. The missions were certainly altruistic but he insisted that we keep track of his hours so he could earn an Air Medal. He made clear to me how embarrassing it was to sit naked (no Air Medal) around the rectory with fellow priests who proudly displayed their combat medals.

I mentioned my sense of humor problem to Father Don in confession. He said to meet him on the deck above the enlisted club next to the library that evening. I was surprised when he showed up with some kind of telescope. He set it up and started talking me through the stars. I could understand how a priest would be interested in God's home but wondered how the hell that would help my sense of humor. But I decided to give it a good faith effort hoping this exercise would somehow relate to my sense of humor.

Despite his careful instructions, I couldn't find a scorpion or see a bull in among the billions of lights up there. To me, the "Big Dipper" was Wilt Chamberlain. I was beginning to feel the whole drill was bull. After many long silences punctuated with this constellation or that, he became lost in space and my patience was wearing thin. Suddenly, he gathered his gear and went back to his hooch. I never brought up why I thought we were meeting that night and neither did he. Maybe the secrecy of the confessional made Father Don avoid the topic or maybe his avoidance of words and focus on the sky was his answer. Maybe I shouldn't let the crisis of the moment dictate my mood; maybe I should lose myself in something bigger than the moment to gain a little perspective, and patience. Maybe he was ignoring me again. But whatever the intended message was, I never got it. I don't know if my sense of humor improved but I worked on it after my space odyssey. In any event, the WOPAs would have to live with it and they did start talking to me again.

Father Don's hooch was a popular gathering place. Many an evening we would gather there to cover the latest news and listen to his stories. Occasionally he would entertain us with his ability to pluck cigarettes out of the air with chopsticks. Most of us were novices with them but he had advanced skills developed as a missionary in China and while cruelly imprisoned by the communists. I spent New Year's Eve in his hooch partying with a group including the Chief Broad and Helen, a young nurse Father was preparing for marriage. She had recently returned from Hong Kong with her wedding dress. The group also included Super Bitch. Two of our guys celebrated their birthday this evening and a grand time was had by all.

After the party I went to my hooch sober and in much better condition than most. Two or three hours into the new year I was awakened by higher headquarters and told to fly immediately to Pleiku and investigate a helicopter crash. A 498th Dust Off had gone down in the jungle near Dak To. I was never happier to be on the wagon. No doubt my sobriety was a factor in my selection.

We flew to Dak To and landed as close to the crash site as possible but still well over a mile away. A guide met us for the trek through the thick, dark, and heavily bambooed jungle to the crash. I had never been in such terrain; some spots were like a jail with bamboo bars every few inches. Our troops had already been into the site and cut something of a trail. The guide led us in. We hadn't gone far when, seemingly as an afterthought, he stopped to tell us we were going through an active mine field. To emphasize this fact, he pointed to a "Bouncing Betty" and its barely visible trip wire. He then took off almost at a run. I wondered if he thought his quick feet would clear him of the blast area of any mine he tripped. That thought was not comforting to those of us behind him. I had cleaned up many a mess from minefields and my strong inclination was to move very, very slowly. But I wanted to step exactly where he did and worked to keep up with our gazelle guide. It was a quiet but quick trip to the crash interrupted only when the guide stopped to point out another trip wire or mine.

The crash was the usual mess but also surreal. As we broke out of the dark jungle into a dimly lighted clearing we came face to face with a dead pilot sitting upright in the AC's seat, still strapped in. The totaled bird was some distance away. We could clearly see the path it took through the jungle and there was little doubt what happened. They were flying too near the trees at night, got disoriented and dove through the triple canopy jungle into the ground. The other pilot and the crew chief were dead in the bird. The impact was such that one pilot had gone through the window and landed upright, still strapped to his seat where we first saw him.

We took pictures, drew a diagram, and I had a heart to heart with the guide making it as clear as I could that we were to go back to our bird at a human pace. We then interviewed those knowledgeable of the crash and other witnesses, including the medic who survived the crash and was in the hospital. He had been thrown clear of the helicopter as it ricocheted through the trees and was found miraculously alive some distance from the wreckage. He was not strapped in, a flight violation in our unit, but it may have saved his life. The doctors told us he would live but on one leg. Then we flew home to Chu Lai.

Both pilots were around the deadly 500 hour stage (when accidents increase often because confidence outweighs competence), but worse, the AC was flying the left seat without control of the search light or landing light. That was pivotal to this tragedy in my mind and the only real lesson to be learned. I recommended in my report that this practice be stopped. Again, both the landing light and search light are controlled from the right seat, the seat clearly designed for night approaches. My recommendation was overridden by some REMF who had never flown let alone flown at night. I read one accident report where the AC, in the left seat, complained that he lost contact with the ground and was blinded when his *co-pilot turned on the landing light.* Then to make matters worse, *the co-pilot maneuvered the light up rather than down* increasing the blinding effect. The accident board, in spectacular stupidity, faulted the AC for not properly setting the landing light and searchlight prior to take off! If he had been in the right seat he would have complete control over the lights and there would have been no "blinding." Another "shine it over here" tragedy. God help any of our pilots I found shooting night approaches to a field site from the left seat.

New Year's Day evening the usual group gathered with Father Don. He asked where I had been all day. I told him about the accident. Nurse Helen asked if it was a Dust Off crew and I told her it was. I should have taken note of the change in her face, but I didn't. I thought she was just concerned for the dead and when she asked for the names of the pilots I told her. She gasped and collapsed. Super Bitch gave me the vilest look I have ever received. One of the pilots was Helen's fiancé. They carried her to the hospital. I never saw Nurse Helen again and for that I was ever grateful. Once they were gone I looked to Father Don helplessly. He looked back sadly I thought, but had no words that could comfort me. Before I left, perhaps to change my mood, he asked again about his Air Medal. Father Don outlasted me in Viet Nam and I left before he got his Air Medal. Years later we would serve together for a short time. At our first meeting, he reminded me of his humiliation in the rectory as he sat with his fellow priests who had Air Medals and him bare-chested. He assured me he had earned the medal but my troops had messed up his records. I ended up inviting him to dinner one night and pinning my own air medal to his chair in hopes of shutting him up. He picked it up, put it in his pocket, without a word of thanks, and ate dinner. But it worked, he never mentioned Air Medals again, to me that is, but I pitied the ears of his fellow priests.

Dust Off rescued over 97,000 patients in 1967 in 47,000 flying hours with only 61 birds for most of the year. We were now up to 182,000 total patients for the Viet Nam War. Those numbers were considered astounding at the time. By the beginning of 1968, there would be 110 Dust Off aircraft and all previous evacuations records would be shattered.

· 32 ·

JANUARY: NEW YEAR, NEW LIFE

I was born in a leap year and so was my wife. My first tour in Viet Nam was during a leap year and 1968 was a leap year. I am not sure how I can work all that into my superstitions but as with the other Leap Years, 1968 would be a life-changing year for me. On 2 January, the VC hit the village that was home to one of our hooch maids, killing her brother and many relatives. Her brother had a small baby. It was the 5th birthday of my baby and I mourned his passing but realized that I would never experience the grief that was the daily menu of these poor people. The men put together some boxes of goodies for her and the village.

Beginning at O dark thirty on 3 January 1968, the 196th Brigade of the Americal Division began savage contact with the 2nd NVA Division near Hiep Duc and Happy Valleys, 20 minutes west of Chu Lai. The casualties were significant and on 3–4 January we were kept busy cleaning up the mess. My crew alone flew 15 hours on the 3rd and into the early morning of the 4th. Five hours were at night and included 41 landings. The 54th carried 214 patients and flew 33 hours on the 3rd alone. By the 5th, I slowed down to 4.5 hours. I hoped the worst was over. That night we sent a Dust Off to field standby at the 196th Brigade HQ on LZ West, or Nui Liet Kiem (mountain of Leeches) a 1,500-foot mountain overlooking Hiep Duc valley. The first few days of January were a rough stretch but we weren't doing badly. We had gone 40 days without a hit or Purple Heart. Six January was the Feast of the Epiphany and it was scheduled to be my day off.

33

6 JANUARY: THE FEAST OF THE EPIPHANY

I was awakened around 0700 hours that morning for a weather mission. Two Vietnamese soldiers were in serious condition at an outpost about 15 minutes to the southwest of Chu Lai in the Song Chang River Valley, deep in mountainous terrain at an isolated outpost appropriately called Lonely Boy. The valley was covered with fog about 400 meters deep. Other aircraft had made seven attempts to get in before they called me. My map recon showed a road just north of the PZ with a stream running south off the road right into the PZ. Once we got under the stuff we would have no trouble finding the patients. I grabbed a co-pilot and we headed out bearing 255 degrees.

Once en route I radioed for the situation and was delighted to hear an English speaking voice. He explained that the PZ had been mortared and they were under fire. I asked him to listen for my chopper, found a mountain clear of the fog, came to a hover at about 2,000 feet, and started down through the stuff toward the road. I found the road and the stream and had no difficulty getting close but missed the designated PZ. I landed in a confined area and we loaded the patients. That may have been a good thing since the selected PZ was clearly registered by the enemy mortars; and would be in the future as we learned. We did an ITO and headed for the hospital.

On the way out I heard a lot of chatter from LZ West 20 clicks up the Song Chang River to the northwest. Apparently they had some 70 casualties. Why aren't they being evacuated? I was told they could not be evacuated because of the fog and enemy action. I was astonished. Many had been in the mud all night. If the area was hot, it would have been better to get them at night although the fog would help. Two ships had already been shot down, one the night before, and many rescue attempts had been made.

I headed out to LZ West requesting the radio frequency and location of the casualties. They would not give it to me. I explained that we had just made a pickup down the river in identical circumstances and we could get them out. They still refused. I asked to speak with the brigade commander and landed at LZ West. I should add that the 101st, of the flare missions, was replaced by the 196th which may not have known our capability in night weather.

As diplomatically as a major can be with a colonel, I explained that we could get them out and needed to get on with it. In any event there was no need for them to die without us trying. He said it was impossible and turned away. He spoke to some medics who emphasized the seriousness of the wounded. He then actually asked my co-pilot if I could make it. My co-pilot said absolutely, and repeated that we had just made a pickup in identical weather and had done so before. I was beside myself. I had never before been denied the opportunity to try. I was beginning to question myself. This was one of those occasions when a willing co-pilot is so important. His confidence restored mine and brought me back to reality; I kept after whoever would listen to let us try.

Finally the colonel came back to me. He warned that the friendlies were surrounded and that the enemy had 16 12.7-mm anti-aircraft guns, often in sets of four, which had shot down the other birds. More importantly, he said that he would give me the frequency and location; but that he would not lift the artillery. That was puzzling since I had no idea what artillery had to do with my mission. I would learn later that he had lifted artillery at the request of gunships the night before while they tried to rescue a downed chopper crew. They failed in the rescue and he felt it was a tactical mistake giving the enemy some unwarranted slack from artillery barrages. Why in the hell didn't they call us? He was a World War II veteran and as such, enamored of the value of artillery. The chances of us getting hit in flight by an artillery round were beyond odds. I wonder why the other choppers requested an artillery lift. We would have never flown if we had to wait for artillery check fire.

I had what we needed. The call sign was Twister Charlie. That unit had been through hell. I loaded a medical team led by Cpt. Mike Scottie, another great field physician, and cranked up. The good news was that the patients were near the base of LZ West, only a few minutes away. The bad news was that they wanted me to take four other choppers with me because of the number of patients. I told them what I was going to do and to line up in trail. Once we got airborne I lost radio contact with them and was relieved to learn they all turned back. It could have been a mess in the fog with five birds and no inter-aircraft commo.

I hovered down the mountain away from LZ West and worked my way along a trail back toward the base. I was flying at about 10 feet and stumbled over a uniformed NVA unit. I was into the fog before they could hit us. They were probably as surprised as I was. Then some of the enemy popped yellow smoke hoping to lure us in. I was talking to the friendlies and knew it was a trap. We went around it.

I must have passed over the heads of the downed crew from the night before. I may have surprised one of them. They were still hiding in the mud near their downed aircraft. Their ship was within shouting distance of my PZ along the route we flew. One of the pilots insisted he saw a white helicopter hovering in the fog just above his head, like a ghost. He was sure it was a specially equipped secret chopper since no other pilots could fly in that stuff. There were no such choppers. I wonder if what he saw was the large white background surrounding the red cross on the bottom of our chopper? In any event, if he and his crew had a radio we could have easily gotten them out. As it was, three of the four crewmen spent years in cruel confinement in communist prisons.

With some guidance by the troops, we found the patients, dropped Mike off and loaded up. (We would later joke that this may have been the only time in history that an MSC [a medical administrator], left an MC [a physician] in a pile of shit; it was usually the other way around.) They were still in contact but there was no way anyone could see anything in that stuff. We were perfectly safe; I don't even remember begging God for help.

We did an ITO straight up through the fog. I heard that some of the troops on LZ West directly above us broke into cheers when they saw our chopper emerge from the fog. And the medical officer saluted as we landed. That was nice since he outranked all of us. We offloaded our patients for back haul to a hospital and went back. Again the four choppers tried to follow and again they turned back. This trip I moved my path off the road onto a stream to avoid the NVA. They might respond better this time. In all we made four trips in and rescued all the wounded, 54 to 60 depending on who counted. And we did it in about an hour. The tragedy was that they never called us the night before. It was the same area I had flown six hours of night two days earlier. It would have been as safe, safer at night, and we could have rescued the downed chopper crew as well. Twister Charlie was declared combat ineffective and removed from the battlefield shortly after we evacuated all their casualties. Thereafter the Hiep Duc and Happy valleys became known as Death Valley. But this valley had been killing people long before it became Death Valley. Included in those deaths was my stick buddy Bill Cawthorne who was killed within a few meters of where we made the pickups.

We had been airborne from LZ West only a few minutes when we got a call from Savage Golf on Fox Mike 60.20 for two urgent wounded. The unit had been in heavy contact and the voice on the radio was stressed and confused. The PZ was in a confined area surrounded by jungles and rice paddies with a village one click to the north. (I would learn years later that my operation folks were closely following my actions this day and taped some of the missions. It may be the only authentic verbal record of a Medal of Honor action ever. The recording does not pickup what was said on the ground but I will include some of my actual comments.)

Savage Golf was desperate to get the wounded out and called the PZ secure. I had long ago given up on discussing security with the grunts. Security meant different things to different people in different terrain. Some would lie to get a wounded buddy out; so would I. In truth there was no good definition. Someone had shot those guys. Where was he? That is what we needed, the truth. "Savage Golf, this is 55, got purple smoke, is that you"? I must have got a roger. I then asked, "Understand you received fire from the north, to your north, is that affirm?" I am not sure what was said but I was getting pissed: "Roger, now, do you want me to land to the north or not?" I must have got an answer, "Roger, we are coming down." As I came to a hover in deep grass near the smoke we initially saw nothing, no friendly, no patients just purple smoke. My crew then reported that the troops were prone in the grass under us!

But Charlie was not prone, he saw us and all hell broke loose. We were hit several times before I could get out. I flew to altitude to check the bird. We could not be sure of the damage as some rounds hit under the cockpit near the flight controls but we seemed to be flyable. Savage Golf came back on the air begging us to come back. "Savage Golf, this is 55, we are still overhead, we took several rounds. What is your situation down there, it seems that we were receiving fire from our left rear as we sat down" (that would be from the north if we had time to turn our tail toward the last fire, otherwise it was from terrain we crossed on the way in). Then more confusion on the ground as I tried to get their attention, "Golf this is Dust Off can you talk to me a minute?" My patience was wearing thin. Other units were on our frequency adding to the confusion and another mission was coming to operations for a plague patient with a malignant growth which amused my guys monitoring our mission.

Major Mac was worried about the condition of our bird and offered to relieve us on station. I told him I thought the biggest problem was the confusion and that I would give it one more shot. "Golf, are you going to have those patients ready for me?" More confusion. "Golf, if you want those patients out of there we are going to have to get on a frequency we can work on—do you have one? You come up my frequency so we can talk about this thing. Do you have those patients where we can get into them?" He must have said it was the same area we landed to before because I responded with some surprise (I was not sure where the fire came from) "Be advised that we took several rounds while we were sitting down in that area." I am not sure what he said next but my reply sounded a bit mournful: "Is that the best you can do?" which brought a loud outburst of laughter from my peanut gallery in the operation shack.

Then Dragon Six, Golf's boss, came on the air sounding a bit too incredulous for my confidence: "Dust Off, are you going in there again?" I told him we were and went back to Golf, "This is 55 we will try to make it in there again. We will be coming in the same way we came in the last time, (and a bit too sarcastically on my part) did you see which way that was?" Probably to ease his conscience (he was again calling the area secure), he offered the mad minute (constant firing). "Negative, I want you to hold your fire until I am on the ground. Now, if you start getting fire once I touch down, go ahead an open up, but let me know." I re-planned my route and went to the ground. Once I got my skids in the grass he again asked if I wanted covering fire: "Hold your fire until we get in there, if we hear any fire we are going to have to abort because we can't tell who it is." Savage Golf hoped I could find him without smoke (which exposed his position), "Negative, pop smoke I don't know where you are. Keep talking to me now, am I coming toward you (I wanted to use my FM homer to confirm that the radio operator was with the patients)." This time they got up out of the grass and we got the patients and got out, under fire, but we got out.

We landed at Chu Lai just as Boxcar (a Chinook helicopter) was stacking 16 KIA on the ramp; probably from Twister Charlie. My maintenance guy told me our controls were severely damaged and there was only a minuscule amount of metal between our controls and no controls at all. Another aircraft was down but that was a valuable mission; it gave me a definition of security. In the future we would use it as our standard. Don't talk to me about secure or insecure, just tell me where the enemy is or was; and promise to stand up and help load the patients. We got another aircraft, Pete Schuster jumped in and we headed out to an area with 12 wounded.

We managed to get the 12 patients in one load and were monitoring traffic from another "C" company (Twister Charlie was a "C" company) trapped in a minefield with six dead and all the rest wounded, including the commander. Injuries included traumatic amputations and severe head and body wounds. Immediate evacuation was imperative.

I am amazed at the fuss many elite make over the ways we kill each other. Torture is another issue but what difference does it make if we shoot or stab or bomb each other? We heard complaints about tear gas of all things—from the girly men that are charged to protect our country—and napalm. It is the killing that is bad and in my experience, mines are the worst. They don't always kill but what is left is always grotesque.

And they continue to kill for years after the war. Many years after the war I would meet an NVA soldier who had survived the French and the Americans and many trips down the Ho Chi Minh trail only to lose an arm and leg from a mine...in his vegetable garden. We had many mine fields in our area, few properly mapped and our guys became experts at traumatic amputations.

This minefield was in our route of flight and as we came over head I saw a Dust Off from a sister unit to our south sitting in the area. Before he could get the patients, a mine detonated near his aircraft killing two more soldiers. He left. I told him I was going in and he warned against it explaining that the mines were command detonated and "C" company was under fire. The key to landing in a mine field is to have a safe area around your skids and watch sudden power changes as the down draft could set off a mine. I had seen the exact spot where he was sitting and was pretty sure we would not set off a mine—since he didn't—if I could hit it. The spot was in good defilade and I was not too worried about enemy fire. I hit the spot and we landed safely. The crew looked at me a bit uneasily and I said simply, "Go get 'em."

And they did, Jim Coleman and Ron (Frenchie) Tweed actually ran into the mine field and began carrying the patients back to the bird. Things were going well until they set off a mine. I was watching them load over my shoulder when the mine blew them so high in the air I feared they might hit the rotors. Shrapnel ripped into the side of our bird as well as into Pappy and Frenchie and some of our lights turned crimson. Both of them, to my amazement, got up; although Pappy's uniform was smoking. He put out the fire and they finished loading. I am not sure why they both weren't killed outright. It may have been because they were carrying a large soldier on a litter and he must have taken most of the blast and shrapnel that didn't go into our bird. I think he was already dead as one of his legs was bent 180 degrees under his body.

The bird was flyable and Pete took the controls as I checked my crewmen. We headed for the hospital at a low level in case something stopped working. This ship was a mess with hundreds of holes in it so we got another bird and continued the missions on into the night. For seven of the missions I flew this day, I would receive the Medal of Honor which changed my life.

We got over 50 patients from Twister Charlie and another 12 in one load and counting the rest of the day and night, I must have been close to my record of 111 my first tour. I would break that record later. I am sure the five missions in the fog, the safest of all we flew that day, were the impetus for the Medal of Honor. They were essentially identical, illegal aviation wise, but they impressed the troops who watched us disappear in the fog and then rise through it. In truth we were never in any danger of crashing and, although reported to be under fire, never in danger of being hit. Later descriptions of how we got in were incorrect: "descended to tree top level, circled lower and lower" into the fog (this from someone who was actually on my bird; so much for the fog of war), and in the Medal of Honor citation: "...descended through heavy fog and smoke...turning his ship sideward to blow away the fog with the back wash from his rotor blades." How do you blow away fog? Where does it go?

One eyewitness statement said I found a hole. I never saw a hole in low valley fog but it does have an edge. The truth is you can see in fog or clouds and fly as far as you can see two reference points; but most aviators don't believe contact flight in such conditions is possible, hence it is illegal. As I mentioned, one of the downed pilots said such a flight in zero zero conditions was impossible and only a ship with secret special navigation aids could do it. I did have special navigation aids: my two good eyes, two good reference points and God's good will. And a number of soldiers are alive today because it is possible. And for that I am grateful; and I am grateful to the Lord for showing me the light in the fog, for my two epiphanies; and for those who took the time to write about these actions. As any soldier knows, the awards he wears are not his; they belong to those he cared for and who cared for him. The tragedy was those left to suffer in the field the night before and the downed crews. We could have got them out and saved some of them years of torture in POW camps.

January was busy. We were carrying 84 patients and flying 28 combat missions per day for the first time. During the 5th and 6th, when the combat was at its worst, I noticed that our average time for mission completion was 27 minutes. The weather was still bad and on the 19th I flew another flare mission. On the 20th, Schenck and Shannahan, with Pappy, landed in deep jungle to rescue a long range reconnaissance patrol (LRRP or "Lurp"). The Lurps were a gutsy bunch who went alone into enemy territory in small teams often without any support or commo. All five members of this team were wounded in an ambush deep in the jungle. Charlie landed as close as he could to the wounded but still some 100 meters away. We did not like to have our crew leave the vicinity of the aircraft but there was no choice in this mission. Pappy is not a big guy but was Hercules that day. The crew chief stayed to protect the ship while Pappy went into the jungle alone and carried all five wounded, one by one, on his back, to the bird. The crew came under fire during the rescue and was hit on departure. We were making up for the doldrums of December with six ships damaged by the enemy then on the 28th we totaled our first ship on our own.

After Sunday Mass I was enjoying a quiet breakfast when Dust Off Schenck came running in to tell me that 660 had gone down and was completely destroyed. Certain that we had lost a crew, I started to run toward operations with Charlie at my side.

"Who was in it?"

"Rock, Frenchie, and me." I stopped running. "You?"

"Yeah, me."

"Was anyone hurt?"

"No."

"Why in the hell am I running?"

"I have no idea."

Then I got pissed at Charlie for scaring me so bad.

Earlier Charlie and Rock departed LZ Baldy with four patients and two passengers en route to the 2nd Surg. They heard of an additional patient at Hill 35 and diverted to get him. While on short final to 35 at about 50 feet and 25 knots, they heard a loud bang much like a gun shot. Without warning the chopper began to spin to the right and the nose dropped. The tail rotor retaining nut had not been properly safetied and 660 lost one tail rotor blade, then the other, and finally the 90-degree gear box. With these losses went the loss of anti-torque and balance. The pilots knew immediately they had lost their anti-torque system and chopped the throttle. They kept spinning and feared the bird would spin into the ground on its nose. As they gyrated into the ground, Rock applied full collective and aft cyclic. Thank God they hit flat but the tail boom broke off and 660 then spun over on its left side and the rotor blades started to break it up. The engine was still running and they shut off the main fuel to prevent a fire. After being shot up seven times since Black Friday, 660 went out on a mechanical failure. Not a good end for a tough old war bird.

Thanks to the outstanding airmanship of Rock and Charlie, although Rock was knocked momentarily unconscious, everyone got out safely—a minor miracle. Two years later, one of our original aircraft, 664, (the bird Hook and Hyde were wounded in) also experienced a tail rotor malfunction and all on board, 12 souls, were killed. Perhaps our pilots were catching up with the enlisted in proficiency. However, had they not detoured for the patient at Hill 35, they would surely have been at altitude and their survival less certain. Unfortunately, we lost another ship and we would need all the ships we could muster—TET began the next day.

34

TET: AMERICA'S GREATEST VICTORY IN VIET NAM

TET is Viet Nam's biggest holiday, combining all the religious and national holidays we have in one. The three-day event, 29 January through 1 February 1968, ushered in the new lunar year, Francis' year, and the year of the Monkey. It was a time to celebrate family and friends and ancestors, correct one's faults and forgive those of others; a time when hope is the watchword, and peace everyone's wish. Peace was the furthest thing from the communists' minds. Their hope was that a massive onslaught during a TET truce would provoke a general uprising by the people who would throw out the government and the Americans. Accordingly, they petitioned for a scrupulous observance of a TET ceasefire in order to achieve the surprise necessary for a successful onslaught. The communists asked for a week. They got three days. TET was a go-for-broke, kamikaze, communist operation. They needed a victory to keep going.

As one should expect when dealing with the communists, they broke the TET cease fire and in fact had been planning to do so for months. They had previously violated cease fire during Christmas and New Year's cease fires. They used the Christmas cease fire to reload and make final preparations for their greatest assault to date. The Americal knew they were up to something evil and the TET cease fire in our AO was cancelled and combat operations went on as usual. TET was not a surprise. It was also their greatest defeat. Within the first hours of TET we heard reports of some 6,000 NVA killed and another 2,500 captured. Before it was over, 41,000 communists would be killed and 7,000 captured—out of a force of 84,000! TET must rank among the greatest defeats in military history. Communists' blood fertilized fields and farms across the country.

General Vo Nguyan Giap, supreme NVA commander, would later marvel at the mess we made of our victory at TET. He acknowledged we had won and could not comprehend our subsequent actions! Some have reported that Giap said he was ready to quit. (Many years later, Westy would send me to Viet Nam to meet with Giap and arrange a documentary wherein Giap would go on film with Westy and declare TET the disaster it was. I did meet with Giap but we never got it done.) Yet there was no follow up despite the begging of Prime Minister Nguyan Cao Ky, Defense Minister Cao Van Vien, and other South Vietnamese leaders. We can thank the likes of Uncle Walter (Walter Cronkite), the other U.S. mainstream media and the mediaphobes in the government for this monumental blunder. They rescued the communists from certain defeat.

Schuster and Shadrick started TET off by taking rounds on the 30th. That night Charlie hit Chu Lai with 48 122-mm rockets and many mortars destroying and damaging several aircraft. They also destroyed two bomb dumps and the ammo dump. I had never experienced such a blast. Being under such devastation engendered a new respect for the grunts who experienced it often in all our wars. It was terrifying. I launched our birds in case they hit Ky Ha. Several of our guys hurt themselves as they encountered generators and each other in a scramble to get in the bunker. We spent other nights in the bunker but none with the shock and awe of this one. We also had a surprise guest. Gertrude had somehow found her way into the bunker and was tip toeing around under our feet in an uncharacteristically passive manner. Earlier she had fallen in behind a formation and marched with the men. Could it be that this depraved creature was warming up to us?

My first missions during TET were highlighted that night by the explosions from the ammo dump which lit up the countryside. One PZ was inside the barbed wire of a nearby outpost. The troops warned that they were under attack as never before and would have to continue firing during the pickups. I was inclined to discount their concerns since exaggerations are common at night. In any event, I would be blacked out and not a good target. There were a multitude of casualties and we made several trips while they blasted away, not my favorite thing. As the sun came up we were able to see the barbed wire just outside of our blades. It was loaded with dead communists! I had never seen such an accumulation of dead, so much road kill, in such a small area. I would take these guys seriously in the future. We were now aware that something significant was happening.

We carried 2,624 patients in January, a quantum leap from all previous months. Unfortunately, 1968 would be the worst year for casualties—over 14,500 Americans dead. We set another record on the 31st, mid-TET, 294 in one day which included some of the 61 soldiers killed in our area that day. It would be some time before we broke this record but we would. My hope that the war would end before I left, ended. This month we added another category of patient, Scout Dogs, two of them. January 31 would be the deadliest day of the war with 245 killed.

They were unsung heroes in the war feared by the enemy and too often feasted upon by the puppy chow aficionados among the Vietnamese.

FAC Flory left us in January. We would miss Al. He was blessed with a set of magnificent ears much admired by all—and good for morale. Years later I would tell his lovely wife Dixie of heroic and herculean efforts on my part which undoubtedly saved Al's life. One of Al's ears fell out of bed during a mortar attack and much of the blood from his body rushed to the ear incapacitating Al. With superhuman strength I hoisted Al's ear back into the bed, he recovered, and we rushed him to the bomb shelter. Dixie was not amused.

35

FEBRUARY

TET continued into February as the communists held Hue. Our AO was teeming with casualties. We had five ships damaged in the first week of February with Schenck and Schwartz leading off on the 1st by landing on a booby trap and trashing 662. Pete and Buddha then destroyed 661 on the 7th followed by Greg and Norm mangling 663 a few minutes later. In 10 days we destroyed one third of our fleet and messed up most of the rest. In the middle of a hectic period, one of our NCOs got drunk and rolled a jeep. He crushed his fingers so bad they had to cut his wedding ring off. War doesn't change the disasters of our humanity.

Pete and Buddha as Dust Off 57 were called out for a downed chopper crew and other wounded near LZ Baldy. The last known enemy fire was out of the northwest. Pete came in low from the southeast. On short final the tail rotor was shot out. Pete watched the tail boom go by the windshield as 661 went into a spin and hit a dike. The bird was on its side in a tangled ball and the crew fell all over each other unstrapping and getting clear of the bird which was still under fire. Pete was hit by shrapnel as they ran into friendly lines. The pilot of the downed crew was dead but they needed medical supplies and Pete heroically took one of the grunts with him back across the bullet swept battlefield to get what meds were on 661. They managed to get back safely with the supplies.

Greg and Norm in Dust Off 58 were in the area on another mission and diverted to get Dust Off 57's crew. Pete waived them off as they were under heavy fire and no one was seriously hurt. Greg continued on the original mission. The area was reported as secure. During the approach, Dust Off took heavy fire and asked for covering fire from the grunts. They got none and continued to take hits. Gary Lowder, the crew chief, cussed aloud as each bullet tore up his bird. Eventually their hydraulics were shot out and both pilots struggled with the controls as they hit the ground hard splitting the skids but thankfully right side up. They crawled to cover in the friendlies' line behind a dike. Greg tracked down the LT in charge and asked why he had lied about the area security and did not give them covering fire. The LT said they were out of ammo. Greg was cussing him out when the LT took a round in one side of his steel pot and out the other. Greg grabbed the steel pot and led the crew to some secure terrain where they were able to direct gunship fire on the communists.

We were running out of aircraft and I went after the two downed crews who we desperately needed. I got Pete's crew and had landed for Greg's when a strange image appeared in my window. It was Greg grinning at me from under a bloody steel pot. I told him to get his ass aboard. He needed to change helmets and get back to work. On the way out, the cargo door flew off the wretched D model I was flying, whacking the tail boom but thankfully missing the elevator and tail rotor. It sounded like we were hit by a 12.7-mm. I had a door fly off my first tour and it was equally terrifying. They grounded all ships to fix it. Apparently they never got it fixed. Pete and Greg thought they were going down again; but we made it to Ky Ha where they jumped in some floats and went back to work. I flew 12 hours on the 7th making 37 landings. Some 73 great soldiers were killed in our AO alone this day. The next week over 500 Americans would be killed and 2,500 wounded.

The two-fold goals of the communists at TET, military victory and civilian uprising, were dismal disasters. Their military was crushed. They actually used two different TET calendars, one in the north and one in the south, to timeline the attacks! And many of the communists had never fought in a city and never trained for such. And it showed. So much for their media ballyhooed military prowess. As for the uprising, the people rejected them. And no wonder. The communists came into Hue with assassination lists. They would massacre some 3,000 civilians, non-combatant women and children. Included among the dead were six priests and five Brothers. Many of their victims were buried alive; others were clubbed to death to save ammo. One could search forever to find this atrocity fairly covered by our media. From TET on the VC were essentially out of it. The NVA would come out of the closet as they already had in our AO. The NLF, advertised as southern dissidents, was completely unmasked as a front for the North. They were Viet Cong, Vietnamese communists as everyone knew.

We had four more ships shot up before the end of the month for a total of nine in February. On one mission, Major Mac and crew were at Lonely Boy, under fire, waiting patiently for the grunts to move the patients to the aircraft. Bob Cronan was hit. Apparently the round had been fired from a half-mile away. This was the second hit for Bob; unfortunately it was serious and he had to be evacuated to the States. We lost another great soldier.

We were leaving a lot of ships in the field and it was not uncommon for the Chinooks to drop aircraft they were recovering. I always tried to ensure that our downed birds were in fact unflyable before I turned them over to the Hooks. I would take Sgt. Hodgdon to the downed birds and sit on a dike while he determined if we could fly it back. His word was gospel and I often let him fly back, but as always, we flew low so we would not fall too far if something went wrong. The worst part of losing so many aircraft was that we would fly much of the rest of the month in the dreaded D model floats, 200 horses weaker than our beloved H and without the muscle and agility needed for our kind of flying. But despite our travails, Huey continued to perform magnificently and celebrated its 13th birthday on the 23rd.

In February, we set another patient record, 2,683, and cut our flying time per mission to 34 minutes, about half of what it was when we started; and we got over five and a half patients per hour, our most efficient month of the tour. Our hits and patient load were growing. The 82nd, of my kangaroo patch, got some publicity for carrying 1,400 patients in February, about half of our workload. The 498th reported 32 aircraft hit in two and a half years before TET; we had more hits in five months and were carrying as many patients as they were with one fourth the aircraft. The week of 10–17 February was the worst for U.S. casualties thus far; 543 KIA and 2,547 WIA.

We lost a great medic, Jimmy Johnson, Super Medic, my faithful companion on flare missions, who rotated out on the 15th. We also fired another man who passed out on guard duty. There were some rumors of pot smoking but no one caught. We made it clear that there would be no second chances for anyone caught smoking dope. Nothing had changed in the local villages. Sex was the same price as 100 P Alley in Saigon—about the cost of a beer. I was not surprised to find that the communists were engaged in biological warfare, turning VD-infected women loose on the GIs. I had seen this tactic used in the Berlin Brigade where I was, unfortunately, the VD control officer; a job at which I failed miserably.

36

MARCH: MY LAI AND OPERATIONAL DEFINITION

M ARCH got off to a bad start when Pappy Coleman was hit for the third time on the second. Pappy was moving toward some Americans to get their wounded when a VC jumped out and shot him in his chicken plate. It knocked him down. He got up and was shot again. This time he shot and killed the VC from the prone and got up and loaded the patients. Several of the guys petitioned for him to be transferred out, three Purple Hearts in six months is enough. Pappy had not had enough and refused to leave.

By March we were about halfway through our tour and had amassed enough statistics in our AARs to determine trends and adjust our operations. We were getting pretty sick of landing in "secure" areas and finding friendlies who would not get off their ass. I had already visited several units and covered with them the discrepancies between the information they provided in the mission request, the front side, and the factual results, the back side. Things were slowly getting better but I decided to lay out in writing, for those we supported, our rules of engagement. We had already squared away the sequence of the EEI but I repeated that as well as our policy on patient classification, area security, and KIAs. The grunts were supported by several Dust Off units as they moved from AO to AO and they needed to know what to expect. The 54th rules were pretty unique among Dust Off units.

Aside from location discrepancies, understandable, the primary errors were over classification of patients and misinformation on security; also understandable but more dangerous. There is no way a soldier can determine the true medical classification of the wounded. If there is a medic present, yes, but even he will over-classify if he believes that a proper classification will delay the rescue. I would. One classic case of over classification involved a night hoist mission in bad weather—beyond the pale dangerous. The patient was reported as U.S. gunshot wound, extremely urgent. The crew managed their way through the weather and came to a high hover over triple canopy jungle. Hovering over one spot at night is difficult, in weather almost impossible; but they did it. The crew lowered the hoist and breathed a sigh of relief when the patient was reported secure and they raised him to the aircraft—where they were outraged to find that the urgent U.S. patient was indeed U.S.—but a Scout Dog! I am sure the grunts were happy to know their beloved companion was safe but the Dust Off crew was furious. However, realizing how dear the pooches were to the soldiers, they held their anger and delivered him to a veterinarian.

It was clear to me that the answer to over-classification is twofold: equal reaction to all classes of patients (even Scout Dogs), day or night, and constant education of those we serve. Very few soldiers will call a priority patient urgent if they know that Dust Off will get there just as quickly for either classification—and that a truly urgent patient may suffer if a limited resource is expended uselessly on an over-classified patient. We must make this point on a mission-by-mission basis: "Hey guys, this patient is not urgent, what if a truly urgent patient died while we were picking up this troop? Don't do that. We will come as fast as possible regardless of classification but

we need to know the truth to be efficient in our life saving efforts."
They were getting the message and we were cutting down on our
flying time per patient considerably.

What about night missions? Some Dust Off units were obsessed
with the dangers of night flying and feared adding their crew to
the number of wounded. They refused to fly other than "urgent"
patients at night. And some units used two aircraft at night, dou-
bling the maintenance drain. Unfortunately, combat goes on at
night and while we must respect the night, or any flying hazard,
we should not fear it. Again, why avoid something you must do?
Night-flying proficiency will come only with practice—not avoidance. Why not get good at it? The more you fly at night, the safer
you will become at night. And night flying is a training multiplier,
it adds to your proficiency in every aspect of flying. Additionally,
night missions, properly flown, are safer than day missions. Enemy
bullets are not as accurate, and many areas that are too "hot" in the
daytime, are readily accessible at night. By this time we were flying
some three missions per night, about five patients who didn't have
to wait in the mud for the sun to rise.

Night mission over classification was rampant when we began.
The grunts knew that some Dust Offs would not fly at night for a
non-urgent patient. Indeed, there were some Dust Off unit commanders, perhaps some of the old fixed-wing types, who would not fly
at night. For the grunt the answer was to call all night patients urgent.
As a result, many Dust Off pilots would push themselves fearing the
patient might die if they didn't, and they died instead; Tom Chiminello and Jack Lichte for example. In our AO we emphasized early
on that equal reaction time applied equally to all classes of patient,
at night as well as in the daytime. There is no need to over-classify;
we will come as quickly for ring worms as a sucking chest wound,
resources permitting—day or night. Using this system, our pilots
would know what the true condition of the patient was, act accordingly, and get help if necessary. We never hurt any of our people at
night, nor did we purposefully leave a patient in the field overnight,

although there were occasions when the commander, based on the tactical situation, would not let us land. Our guys were as proficient at night as in the day, many averaging a night mission for every day they were in Viet Nam.

Daytime signaling was pretty well understood (pilot identifies color, green in ripe rice paddies and red at dusk not as good as other colors) but signals are important at night. Almost any light that can be identified from the air is OK; flashlight, cigarette lighters, strobe light, and a combination of mirror and light work well. Red light is best in most terrain and the addition of a white light used in conjunction with the red light is even better. It was important to be able to blink or in some way control the light so the pilot is certain he is landing to the correct light. No flares during landing! If the area is dusty, the pilot may lose visibility as he nears the ground. It helps if the signaler shined a light on the touchdown spot in dusty areas.

But of all the EEI, the security of the PZ was alone the show stopper. This is problematic. *Who could believe that the grunt would call a PZ insecure if he fears you will then not come for his wounded buddy?* It was often amusing but always disturbing to hear, in whispered tones, that a unit had several troops suffering from gunshot wounds, but the area was secure. Somebody shot those guys and he probably was not far away. Security means different things to a grunt and a pilot. The grunt is happy to get a few yards clearance from the enemy. A pilot may use a mile on approach. And the grunt can get good cover from a few feet of matter. A pilot sits a couple yards in the air with no cover, completely vulnerable. Dust Off could live through bad information on many things, but misinformation on the area security can kill him. It killed Kelly and most of us had been almost dead from it many times. The 54th had already been shot up numerous times while landing in "secure" areas where the friendlies, who called us in, would not stand to help find and load the patients. By now the troops pretty well knew we were going to do all that was possible to get in. Still, we needed a standard.

Survival of the patients and the crew depended on clear and

honest communication and the ability of the pilot to use that info to design a safe approach. The key to communications must, as I never weary of preaching, not only be clear enough to be understood; *it must also be clear enough so that it cannot be misunderstood.* Uncertainty is rampant in combat but it need not lead to confusion, which will kill you. Good communication kills uncertainty and also will alleviate fear, which leads to terror an unconditional show stopper. Absolute honesty is of course the answer—lies kill, and we emphasized that. We also emphasized that we were not as interested as whether or not the area was secure as we were with where the enemy was and what weapons he had. Somebody shot the guy, right? Our pilots were getting more proficient at getting enemy data from the friendlies and using the terrain to get in. Our improvement in tactical flying was producing fewer and fewer multiple hits. Mostly Charlie got only a round or two in us before we got away. The standard would be, as I noted in the Epiphany mission, *If the area is secure enough for the friendlies to stand up and help load the patients, Dust Off will come in.* I have heard that the one in-country medical HQ at one time had forbidden Dust Off pilots to land in insecure areas. This was true for the MEDEVACs but no one ever challenged the 54th and our hit statistics were available to all.

I can think of few missions which engendered more trust, vital in our work, with the grunts than caring for their dead; but the policy on KIAs had to be clear. We did not want to be misused picking up "wounded" that had been dead for several hours, as had happened. As I mentioned, some ground troops had threatened Dust Offs who were in the area, found the "patient" dead, and refused to take him. The Dust Off pilot in that instance accused the grunt of lying to him. So what! They should not have to lie...ever. Would that pilot leave a dead loved one in the field? Does he not love the grunts? The regulation should not ever get in the way of service.

We were anxious to serve all our soldiers in every way possible. At times, removing the dead removes a terrible burden on the tactical commander. We were not required to carry the dead but there was nothing that said we were forbidden to do so. We told the troops that we would be happy to carry their fallen comrades (their angels) but asked that they first exhaust the designated resource i.e., quartermaster. Then if it would not interfere with our service to the living or present an undue danger to the crew, we would carry them. Major Mac once evacuated KIAs from a minefield, using a hoist. The 54th would average more than one KIA per day the first 10 months. I found that the dead did not decompose as rapidly as they did in the Delta (where the skin of those dead for a relatively short time would slide loose in the hands of the crew) but sanitation was still a problem. Bodily fluids leaked through the floor requiring that it be removed and the cables and parts underneath thoroughly cleaned. And all the nooks and crannies in the chopper had to be cleared so that patients did not come in contact with previous patients' overlooked body parts. Some crewmen, I was told, stuffed their nostrils with Vicks VapoRub to cover the smell of death.

Initially there were many instances of slicks and gunships picking up our patients. In any casualty situation everyone wants to show their compassion, admirable, but often a nuisance and not in the patient's interest. This problem improved once we explained that the key to survival depended on time to needed treatment, not necessarily time to a medical facility—unless that facility is a Dust Off aircraft! Dust Off has all that is needed to resuscitate and sustain life and, more importantly, a highly trained crew with exceptional experience in treating traumatic injuries and wounds. Slicks and Gunships have neither. If it is quicker to put an urgent patient on a Dust Off than in a hospital, he should be put there, even if it means an en route transfer. (Sadly, today some ASO do not realize this as I would learn later at the White House). And there was no need to put an urgent patient in a tent at a battalion aid station if we could have them in a hospital as quickly. This antiquated system never reared its ugly head in our AO except during the 1st Cav.'s visit.

Once again, I faced the problem of crews and gunships shooting.

I still remembered those hot shell casings down my back. Nothing had changed between tours. The enemy was still seldom seen, his gunfire sounded the same to me as the friendlies and the friendlies were all over the place, some not knowing where they themselves were. And the gunner had to shoot behind the target, which is hard. I settled on the quiet approach: no one shoots, not my crew, not the gunships, and no mad minute by the troops on the ground unless they had to. Just peace and quiet; then if you hear fire you know it is the enemy, dodge a bit, and try another route in.

The gunship pilots were as fearless as our pilots. They would follow us into the area shooting up every possible enemy location as they went; and then hover to our flanks, protecting us, as blatant targets, during the pickup. But they did not react as fast as we did and some pilots would wait for them delaying the rescue. I tried to sell the quiet approach because I was sure it was safer but most of our pilots wanted the gunnies, believing they provided security. They also believed that the Hogs provided a distraction for the enemy, an alternate target, if you will. One pilot rejecting all the disadvantages of the shooting, said simply it made him feel better. I couldn't argue with that and, as always, we left it up to the AC to decide how to complete the mission.

A mission went like this: reaction time was the same for all categories of patients, day or night—two minutes; KIAs (angels) welcome; tell us where the enemy is, stand up and we will come in; never leave a patient in the field at night no matter the weather (as they did on 5-6 January) but have flares on hand; load through medics door only, and load no hand grenades; have the patients ready and close to the PZ; and make sure there is a dedicated frequency exclusively for the pickup—no remote commo—we wanted to talk to the guy with the patient and we want him to observe and advise us throughout the pickup. Only he had the information we needed; no intermediaries unless there was no radio with the patients. Keep all others off the air. The Dust Off FM frequency was 46.9 primary, 45.7 alternate.

We also learned to carry less than a full fuel load, about 1100 pounds or less on heavy patient days. Our distances were short and fuel was plentiful and we could refuel hot (without shutting down) saving a lot of time; and best of all, no chamois cloth although we still had some fuel contamination. With a light load of fuel we were able to carry up to 20 patients, more if they were women and children (Don got 27 once). I never had to remove a patient from my bird, thanks to the H model.

I put most of this in a 20 March memo to those we supported emphasizing our ability at night and in weather, and charging them once again to never leave a patient in the field in any circumstances without giving us a call.

We got a new boss in March, Colonel Wallace R. Le Bourdais, a physician who fit the mold of Cass and Augerson. He immediately asked to fly with us. I told him we might have to leave him in an area (as we did with journalists who asked to fly with us) if he was taking space from a patient; unless he flew as a medic. He agreed to be the medic. The mission turned out to be hot, and he was great. But some of his underlings were not happy that I took him on a hot mission. They chewed my ass mercilessly. My retort was that it should not matter what happened to him: if he was a good leader he would have made sure all was in order in case he got zapped; and if he was not, they would be better off without him. In any event, he should be able to go where his people went. To be sure, none of his minions volunteered to fly with us.

I should add that although many were impressed with the dangers of our flying, the courage of our pilots and the fact that our guys went in after other ships were hit and kept going back until we got the patients—the dangers were a bit exaggerated. I had always believed, and taught, that the second mouse gets the cheese. For this reason, I was never particularly concerned with a clean up mission. Ships may have been hit on initial entry but that did not always excuse a mission abortion. Very often Charlie would "hug the belly" of the friendlies and lay low after the initial exchange knowing that he would be hit quickly by air and artillery barrages; or he would bug out as rapidly as possible. He frequently had little staying power. In any event, we were successful on post hit rescues and flew a lot of them. Of course ,terrain and darkness could make pickups possible regardless of the intensity of the battle.

On the day before Saint Patrick's Day, I made sure I was on duty so that I could take advantage of the special alcoholic dispensation God gave me the next day. I was anxious to try the wine Father Don gave me. I remember that Bobby Kennedy announced for president this day, his brother was an early hero of mine. The call was for several patients in the Bravo Sierra area just to the southeast in Quang Ngai province. The mission was unusual because the area was declared hot. That area, despite its revolutionary past, had been quiet to this point. It was near the minefield I went into on six January but I could not remember the last hot mission we had there. The coordinates took me to the Song My Peninsula and into the My Lai complex where the American, under Task Force Barker, was conducting an operation. The terrain was characterized by small tufts of villages seemingly floating in the heavily watered rice paddies that engulfed the area. This was a unit from the trouble-some 11th Brigade. I doubted the area was hot but took them at their word and started a low fast tactical approach when I spotted a bunch of troops in a river floating on air mattresses. Hot my ass. I pulled up and relaxed into the PZ. I saw nothing unusual in the terrain we covered and took the wounded to the hospital.

I think my experience on that mission explains the tragedy that took place there that day. Those troops were an example of when inexperience is dangerous in units in combat—with poor leaders. The 11th led the league in this regard. They had been in country a short time, had experienced little or no combat, and were over psyched from the stories they heard from those who had. The stories of women and children as suicide killers were grossly exaggerated. They were supporters and intelligence sources, but I never heard of one such incident.

My Lai, more than any other incident, allowed the media and their ilk to label our troops as war criminals. The truth is that no one knows for sure exactly what went on there. Initial reports of hundreds killed were inaccurate. No one knows or will ever know the true number. The murder of one innocent civilian is inexcusable, but it was the magnitude initially reported massacred at My Lai that was so horrifying. Equally as horrible was the tragedy that one murderer in this atrocity, William Calley, was pardoned. He should have been executed, preferably by firing squad. This incident also widened the rift between the military and the media, the two most essential elements in our society: one keeps us secure and the other keeps us free. My Lai gave rise to the belief by many soldiers that they need not fear the enemy, for he will only take your life; fear the media, for they will steal your honor.

Media treatment of the Viet Nam veteran would eventually outrage most Americans and we don't see similar defamation of today's warriors. Viet Nam is one reason, the other is that we bring our citizen soldiers with us today. And when we do that we bring over 3,000 American communities who will not allow their sons and daughters to be trashed. But there is no question that scorn for those in uniform is in the genes of many in the media. In Viet Nam we were war criminals; in Iraq we were torturers. The media did all they could to turn an obscenity, Abu Ghraib, into an atrocity. Viet Nam gave birth to the riffraff we have in our media today, a media characterized by Mike Wallace who said that given the choice to prevent the massacre of American soldiers, or allow the massacre for a story, he would opt for the story. He was, after all, not an American, he was a journalist. I could go on but enough said.

We were going into the hot season and I held a special briefing on the new dangers, i.e., density altitude, increased clear air turbulence in the mountains, and fuel load. I had not given any check rides since December and decided it was time to do it again. The WOPAs were around the magic 500 hours time frame and I wanted to destroy any delusions of grandeur. We had over-torqued three aircraft in six weeks, for no reason, not to mention the incredible number of tail rotors and main rotors we had destroyed. And some of the radio chatter was getting unprofessional. I was a fan of the football huddle as a communication paradigm. The fewest possible words to say in the clearest possible manner what needed to be said. Poor commo may be the greatest of all combat killers. Some of our guys talked too much. I got their attention by warning that I would revoke AC orders on anyone who did poorly on the ride. There was no greater threat than that. They would rather lose a limb than lose their AC status.

We lost Jerry Foust on the 20th. He volunteered to transfer to the Delta to help the infusion problem. He said he wanted to fly in the Delta because of my stories of flying there. I hated to lose him and did not like to hear I was the reason he left. Jerry was a jewel and had earned a chest full of ribbons for his extraordinary heroism. He would later make general and head up the entire MSC of the Army, the first and only aviator to do so. I am sure he would agree that his service in the 54th had a lot to do with his later success.

For the first time in one month, in March, we broke a thousand missions, 1,025. Our patient load was down a bit to 2,331 but we broke the half-hour barrier for mission time, 27 minutes per. We got two more Scout Dogs and no one was hurt even though seven ships were shot up. By now our guys were flying 28 combat missions, four at night, and 16 hours a day, carrying an average of 70 patients and getting an aircraft shot up every four to five days. They were under fire daily and the maintenance crews worked around the clock to keep us in the air. I was starting to worry about them. It was my experience that you can work a man pretty hard for about six months and then they need a rest. The good Lord recognized our problem and gave us Cu Lao Re at about the six months mark. Cu Lao Re was a 2x4 mile island about 20 minutes to our east in the South China Sea. Surrounded by white sandy beaches and bookmarked by two moss covered extinct volcanoes at each end, It was as beautiful as any spot on the planet. And it was secure!

The island was commanded by a navy lieutenant and used as a listening post. An old grass strip built by the Japanese for their Zeros was a perfect helipad. Our pilots found it on a mission and we quickly made friends with the LT who agreed to let our people do R&R there with the understanding that we would also bring some nurses. The Navy is famous for good chow and they had movies every night. During the day, our guys frolicked in the South China Sea and forgot the war. I understand there was even some water skiing...behind our choppers! I am not sure what I would have done had I known about that at the time, but I am glad I never did. We were now ready for the second six months.

My good right arm, Wayne, tried to sneak out for some R&R with his wife Jeanette just prior to a big inspection in March. Believe it or not, the starched-fatigue-man-among-men types insisted on disrupting even war to look for spit and polish. Some of it is necessary but we did not need it at this time. In the middle of our negotiations on Wayne's R&R, he got a care package from Jeanette, cake, candy, and fudge—yum! I thought this woman must be a doll (actually she is!). But much to my chagrin Wayne had the nerve to criticize her good faith efforts. He joked that the fudge broke a floor board when he dropped it; and Super Oink refused the cake. I was appalled. It was my duty to relieve him of her largess, which I did. I then proceeded to prove the fudge was not too hard by eating all of it—in front of him. The fact that I am a chocoholic had nothing to do with this just decision. Satisfied that he was repentant, I let him go on R&R. His stuff was always in order and the inspection was a breeze.

37

APRIL: THE MAN WITHOUT A FACE

THE rains returned in April and we had a ship hit on April Fool's Day. The medic on board was wounded. He was a conscientious objector (CO). Among the good people you get in medical units is the occasional CO. In my experience they have been exceptionally competent in every way—except weapons proficiency. Unfortunately a Dust Off medic has to be able to handle a gun not only for his own protection but for that of the crew and the patients. The famed Sgt. Alvin York was a CO, but he could handle a gun. The CO's ship was on short final when the pilot spotted a sniper in a tree on the medic's side. He ordered him to open fire. The medic would not pickup his weapon and instead dove for the center of the bird. He was too late and took a round right in his ass. We would be more careful in the future to insure medics who refused to use weapons were routed to the hospital.

Missions have way of running into each other and get lost in the many caverns of our memory. I have forgotten even some of the missions for which I got an award. I do remember the terrain, though; and one mission in April I will never forget. Although my queasiness for blood as noted was absent on the battlefield (and only there; I suffer from this affliction to this day), I came close to a relapse on that mission. Only rarely does the medic ask the pilot for help. He is, after all, the real expert. "Sir, what do I do with this one?" It was a hot pickup and I was busy. "What do you mean?" I asked sharply. "Look." The patient was a big man. His hands were folded on his chest where I noticed a wedding ring. He had no face. Two flaps of skin near the holes where his nose once was were gently moving. He was alive. I was reminded of Robert Service's *Les Grands Mutiles* and his poem *The Faceless Man*. One nurse at the hospital said she was praying that he died. I could not get past the ring; I prayed he would live. What worthy wife could refuse her man, a man who gave what this man gave, no matter his looks? Service's faceless man feigned his death to spare his wife and daughter the horror he saw in his own grotesqueness. Our faceless man died.

On the 28th we all got a letter announcing a possible reduction in forces (RIF). There was no doubt aviators would be the prime target.

Viet Nam required that many majors filled the role of peter pilot, no command, no real responsibility. Not a good thing for promotion. And we had far more pilots than would ever be necessary in peacetime. I had other responsibilities but a good LT could do my job. With my background, I was toast. But a RIF would at least get me an honorable discharge.

April produced another 1,000 mission month, 1,102. We carried 2,522 patients, 2.3 per mission, and 4.3 per hour. Our mission time went up five minutes from March to 27. Only one of our guys was shot and four ships hit. A chaplain was shot at Easter services but could this be the beginning of the end? Not so; the worst was yet to come.

· 38 ·

MAY: MAYHEM

BY the beginning of May we were flying almost continuously. The second week we had five ships hit and carried 1,000 patients—another record. We were ravaged with alerts. Our guys were getting a taste of a grunt's life, waking in the middle of the night to tremendous terrifying explosions. Some, who had been shot at in choppers almost daily, said they were never more afraid. As usual, our maintenance crews, led by John Hodgdon and Don Goody, were working around the clock. John was now into his ninth month without a break. I believed John was truly a maintenance superman and I loved him dearly but he needed a break. I ordered him to Cu Lao Re. He refused to go unless I went with him.

So I went. We spent two days exploring up and down, in and out of the volcanoes and following the beach around the beautiful Island. We discovered a Buddhist temple in a cave on the north side of the island. Entry was possible only when the tide was right. It was an eerie place, smoke filled and quiet. We almost got trapped in there. On a trek through a village I spotted two ancient cannons in front of the police station. It turned out they were from the Napoleonic era. I had to have them. John could communicate in Vietnamese and he made a deal, two cases of C-rats! We had a helluva time getting them to and on the chopper; but we did and they made a nice display in front of operations. John was one of the finest human beings I have ever known. I will always treasure that time with him, a quiet time before all hell broke loose.

· 39 ·

VIET NAM GOLGOTHA

IN February 1968, Captain John White of the Australian Army Training Team, Viet Nam, took command of the 11th Mobile Strike Force company or Mike Force at Da Nang. Mike Forces were indigenous troops under the Green Berets. The Mike Forces at Da Nang were organized into companies of Vietnamese, Montagnards, and Nungs. The Nungs were of Chinese ethnicity and, although residents of Viet Nam for generations, were treated as non-citizens and could not be drafted. Many earned their living as mercenaries augmenting their income by bounty per captured weapon and enemy killed.

White's 11th Mike Force consisted of 122 Nungs, two Aussie warrant officers, and three U.S. Green Beret sergeants. He was given two weeks to train his new command and move to an area south of Kham Duc to monitor the movement of the 2nd NVA Division which was thought to be moving east off the Ho Chi Minh trail in Laos onto Route 14 which flanked friendly forces in I Corps. Kham Duc was one of the last remaining Green Beret outposts monitoring the Ho Chi Minh trail near the Laotian border. It featured a 6,000-foot all weather airfield, inaccessible by road, originally built to facilitate big game hunting by the ruling elite in Viet Nam.

The 11th Mike Force was airlifted to Kham Duc and in mid-March began to work their way south along Route 14 in search of the 2nd NVA Division, about 50,000 strong. About five miles south of Kham Duc they came upon an old French Foreign Legion fort. It was perfectly disposed to serve as a temporary base for their mission, only six miles from the Laotian border. Unlike the familiar triangular French forts, it was rectangular and lay north east/southwest. The fort consisted of two rectangular breastworks, six to eight feet high, one inside the other surrounded by dense jungle and mountains. The inner area was less than half the size of a football field. A foot bridge connected the fort to an old French parade field, smaller than the fort, to the south which became their Helipad. An abandoned airfield lay a couple hundred yards to the north. Route 14 surrounded the fort on the south, east, and north where a hole in the breast-work opened to it. Captain White named it Ngoc Tavak after a nearby mountain. From the air, Ngoc Tavak bore an eerie resemblance to a skull, perhaps even a sad skull if that is not redundant.

White was assigned the call sign Bangor Stylus, which was how I knew him for 35 years. The 11th Mike Force dug in and began patrols in search of the communists somewhere to the south. For several weeks they enjoyed their jungle habitat filled with wild elephants, tigers, and other exotic animals including deer which made an excellent addition to their diet. A batch of pigs was parachuted in to further augment the drab C rats that are the fate of soldiers in the field. And White found a Montagnard garden a few miles from the fort. Ngok Tavak was a mini fat city, but not for long.

In late April, Mike Force made their first contact with an enemy patrol and began to hear explosions as the enemy cleared Route 14 toward Ngok Tavak. Intelligence reports confirmed the enemy's intention and White, realizing he was overmatched, decided it was time to melt into the jungle and begin surveillance of the enemy. Then, inexplicably, a detachment of Marine artillery was helicoptered in. They brought with them 44 Marines, two 105-mm howitzers and a heavy load of ammo. Neither the Marines nor the howitzers, were suited for melting into the jungle. In fact, the terrain made the howitzers practically ineffective. The only round that would have been effective was the Flechette which White requested but was denied. White's whole mission was now compromised. He was outraged and made it known to his higher HQ. He was ordered to stay put and was reinforced by a platoon of CIDG from Kham Duc.

The CIDG in this case were not mercenaries and they were not commanded by the U.S. or Australians. They were conscripts, the dregs of the area, some from jails in Da Nang sent to Kham Duc because there were no roads out, no way they could desert. But they could defect to the enemy and provide him intelligence. Shortly after their arrival, Mike Force communications and claymore mine wires were found cut. White was certain the CIDG platoon was infiltrated by the enemy and put them on the north outside the fort perimeter. White now had a ragtag force of Vietnamese, surely containing enemy troops, Chinese, many who were teenagers, Aussies, American Green Berets, and Marine artillery men. If that were not bad enough, he had to command and control this motley gang in several languages. The sounds of the enemy grew closer and White dug in for a battle he dreaded. His one hope was air power which was severely limited by extremely cruel weather in his AO.

On the 9th of May, the CIDG announced they were going back to Kham Duc. White was glad to get rid of them but they quickly returned after being "ambushed" two kilometers north of the fort. Despite reporting a prolonged fire fight they suffered no casualties and asked to be deployed near the howitzers. White put them back on the outer perimeter. That night as White made his rounds, he could hear the enemy in the jungle nearby and he alerted his men. Shortly after the moon set at 03:15 on 10 May, there began a fight in that old French fort, in an area half the size of a football field, which must match in intensity any fought anywhere.

The battle began when a group of CIDG soldiers approached the hole in the north perimeter saying, "Don't shoot, don't shoot, friendly, friendly." They were not friendly and immediately wiped out with grenades and satchel charges the sentries guarding the entrance to the fort. They were followed by masses of NVA troops who attacked the howitzers with flame throwers setting off the ammo stored nearby. Some of the defenders were killed in their sleeping bags while others joined the fight in various levels of undress. The Marine artillery commander jumped in a hole where he came face to face with one of his Marines. An explosion blew him out of the hole and when he crawled back he checked his Marine who appeared to be dead. The enemy fought their way to White's command bunker at the southern edge of the fort and climbed on the roof from where they pitched inside grenades and satchel charges. White and his men threw them out as fast as they could but they missed one grenade. White's teenage body guard covered it with his body saving White and the bunker with his life. The enemy command post was actually set up within 10 meters of White's. Enemy records claim they overran the fort in eight minutes.

In the midst of the chaos, White manned the radios and begged for help. Help finally came in the form of "Puff the Magic Dragon," a retrofitted C-47 Dakota, full of flares and massive fire power also known as "Spooky," and much feared by the enemy. White gave orders in English and Chinese for everyone to dig in, knowing those left standing spoke Vietnamese and would be the enemy. He then directed Puff to strafe the entire fort and its perimeter. Puff cut loose with mini guns at 6,000 rounds per minute. It could cover an area the size of a football field and not leave an inch unscathed. The NVA had been repulsed in their attack on the parade field and White ordered his Aussie platoon leaders to turn their fire inside the fort. The tide of battle began to turn. But when Puff ran out of ammo the dreadful hand-to-hand combat continued amid exploding ammo, the screams of the dying and wounded—and squealing pigs.

In the midst of the bedlam, friendly killed friendly as the Marines mistook Asian Nungs for enemy Asians. But most Marines and Nungs fought gallantly, two Marines earning the Navy Cross. The communists deployed tear gas which drifted into their own lines and forced them back. At the first light of dawn, the two Aussie platoon leaders were ordered by White to start a counter attack from the parade field north through the fort. Initially their Nungs refused to leave their holes. The Aussies went alone. When the Nungs saw their heroic action, they joined in and the enemy was driven out of the fort. The last communists stopped to pick up a pig on the way out. The delay proved to be his death warrant. Daylight brought U.S. fighter planes to bombard the enemy positions. But nothing could suppress a steady barrage of NVA fire from the mountain jungles down into Ngok Tavak and chaos continued in the fort. The Marine thought dead by his commander woke up and began to fire hysterically into friendlies. He had to be silenced by his fellow Marines. Two Marine CH-46 Chinook style helicopters bringing reinforcements were destroyed on the helipad.

White assessed his situation. The sad skull was crying blood. In that half football field, hundreds of warriors had clashed for hours leaving stacks of dead and wounded friendly and enemy everywhere. Some three fourths of White's force was dead or wounded. One hapless troop was found dead with his member in his mouth. Earlier he had made the mistake of comparing his to one of the less endowed CIDGs. One Marine, believing he was ordered to kill the wounded enemy, emptied a clip into five helpless NVAs while one tried to throw rocks at him in self-defense. Two wounded communists were left behind. White raised a white flag. The enemy ceased fire until they could recover their wounded, but resumed the bombardment immediately after. There was no doubt the enemy were determined to wipe out Mike Force 11. Two NVA dead were found with live grenades under their bodies. It was clear to White that he had no recourse but to escape and evade through the enemy line. Permission was again denied. He was ordered to stay and fight, assured that more reinforcements were on the way. He would persist to seek permission to retreat but he could not leave the wounded. Leaving the dead would be unfortunate but essential. His immediate concern was the wounded. He called for Dust Off.

Early in the morning of 10 May, the Friday before Mother's Day in 1968, Don Sewell and I got a call for urgent patients at coordinates VC964009. It was a valley beyond our usual AO and neither of us had been to those coordinates before. The call sign was Bangor Stylus and the voice on the other end had a distinctly British accent. As always, I listened to the tone and demeanor of the voices from the battlefields. I could often learn as much about the true situation and my chances of getting accurate information from a voice as anything else, perhaps more. I must admit that I derive more confidence from a voice with Celtic tones than any other foreign accent; perhaps because of my heritage. Bangor Stylus sounded like a man who would exhibit no verbal panic even with his dying words. He sounded like my pencil mustached friend from my first tour. I knew he was a professional who would give us accurate information without embellishment or exaggeration. He said he was surrounded and doubted we could get in. (Many years later John would tell me he actually believed they had absolutely no chance of getting out alive, yet, in the manner of all leaders, he projected a demeanor of confidence that inspired his men and led to their survival.) We asked if they would stand and help us load the wounded. He said they would. We said we would give it a try.

The area was stunningly beautiful, decorated with graceful rivers occasional waterfalls and a canopied jungle that glowed a luminous mossy green. The usual blanket of ground fog was absent. My enchantment with the landscape was interrupted when we came around a mountain into the valley and spotted the fort. There were two Air Force fighter bombers strafing the jungle above the fort. This was not a good LZ. It was surrounded by high terrain on all sides allowing the enemy to shoot down on us. As we got closer, we could see what appeared to be two Chinooks sitting on the spot we were to land. We thought that was a good sign and I dropped down for a high-speed, low-level approach. As we were setting down Don exclaimed: "Holy shit, both of those choppers are destroyed!" or words to that effect. He had my attention. One of the birds had been hit by a mortar or RPG which meant the spot was probably registered. I then noticed rocket fire from the jungle above us streaming into the fort. I had never seen that intensity of fire in daylight and I longed for the low valley fog.

But the patients were there and so were soldiers to help us load them. Bangor Stylus' voice remained composed and it calmed me as we sat there, an easy target between two destroyed helicopters, enemy registration marks, while the wounded were loaded. Bangor Stylus told us he had more patients and needed to get them out as rapidly as possible so he could get his men to safety. Seventeen severely wounded patients were quickly loaded and we departed for Kham Duc where they would be backhauled to medical facilities. We would set up a round robin for the rest of the patients.

I am convinced to this day that the only thing that saved us from a rocket was the red crosses on our bird, especially the one on the top. The only reason that they didn't take us out was that they chose not to. They clearly had us zeroed in. This had happened before. Dust Off escaped unscathed while all around were shot up. I am convinced that some, and I emphasize some, of the disciplined enemy troops respected the Red Cross. I was happy to get in the air safely and studied the terrain around the camp for the next pickup. I was not going to trust or test the continued discipline of the enemy and land on that bull's eye between the downed choppers again.

On the way out, I noticed a V-shaped spot between a cleared area down the hill on the north side of the fort where the trees at the bottom came up almost to the top of the hill. It was a perfect place for us to hide. The terrain to the west was lower than that on the other sides of the fort which worked in our favor. We couldn't land but we could put a skid on the side of the hill and hover the chopper there while the patients were loaded. And that is what we did while they literally threw the wounded aboard. It was a bit tricky to keep the skid on the side hill without hitting anything but it worked flawlessly. We came in low level from the west and slipped down the hill behind the trees and were in perfect defilade. I had been on few battlefields where I felt as comfortable. I doubt if the enemy could see us and even if he knew where we were, I didn't see how he could hit us with any direct fire weapon. It would take a miraculous shot by a mortar to get us. After loading we would be vulnerable as we hovered up above the trees but only for a short time while we picked up air speed at low level across the jungle and cleared the battle area.

I am not sure how many trips we made but Captain White said later we took out over 70 patients. White said he started with 250 and got out with about 45. Whatever the numbers were, a lot of people died there. Bangor Stylus organized the patients for evacuation and was extraordinarily cool throughout the operation despite the fact that the enemy was at the gates. He told us that they would abandon the outpost after we made our last pickup.

During the Dust Offs White persisted in his efforts to convince his HQ he should abandon the fort. They remained adamant that he should stay and fight again promising reinforcements and ignoring White's lament that there was absolutely no safe place to land the reinforcements. Higher HQ knew the real target of the communists was Kham Duc. With the publicity of TET still in the public mind, the communists hoped to overrun Kham Duc and turn it into an American Dien Bien Phu. The anniversary of their defeat of the French there was 7 May. The communists had a thing about Mary's month, May. An earlier attempt to Dien Bien Phu Khe Sanh failed miserably after President Johnson ordered, "I don't want any damn dinbinfoo," at Khe Sanh. The 10th of May was the date scheduled for the beginning of the Paris peace talks. It was also the date the Communists kicked off a mini TET with an assault on 119 cities towns and camps in South Viet Nam. The 2nd

NVA Division was actually equipped with filming gear to record the overrun and turn it and their mini TET into a propaganda victory for leverage at Paris. The propaganda nature of this battle may have reinforced the reason they never destroyed my chopper. A destroyed red crossed helicopter would not look good on film.

White's superiors hoped that he could slow down the onslaught on Kham Duc. White had less than a platoon left and knew for certain one onslaught would be over Ngok Tavak. He would not commit suicide to slow down a force that outnumbered him about a thousand fold. He was getting out while the getting was good. He remembered the Montagnard garden and decided it would be a good pickup point. He had the downed CH 46 pilots to help guide in rescue choppers. But how to escape through the surrounding enemy? He then devised a truly ingenious plan. He would call for the Air Force to walk a path of napalm through the enemy lines to the northeast. He hoped the enemy would believe they would try to escape northwest toward Kham Duc where the NVA had set up ambushes. With a bit of luck, the communists would think the napalm was aimed at them and retreat from the area. It was the exact path of the main attack of the communists only hours earlier, their strongest position.

As he finished his plans, the final Dust Off arrived. The last wounded were loaded. White knew that Dust Off would have taken the dead but there was no time. They would remain behind. As the last Dust Off departed, he saw one of the Marine chopper pilots grab the skid. Seeing the Marine example two Nungs grabbed the skid also. In his mind they were deserters and, fearing they could harm the chopper and set a bad example, he ordered them shot off the skids. He then destroyed anything the enemy might use and departed through the burning napalm and communists bodies in a circular route to the Montagnard garden. On the way out, the rear echelon was hit with a mortar and sustained casualties. A heroic medic, Tom Perry (full name, Thomas Hepburn Perry, nephew of Katherine Hepburn), went back to help. Neither the medic nor the wounded were ever heard from again although the enemy reported capturing four this day. But White's plan worked flawlessly. The enemy actually thought we had mistakenly napalmed the fort and hesitated. But not for long. The NVA main force had moved on toward Kham Duc leaving three companies, some 450 men, to clean up Ngok Tavak.

The remnants of Mike Force 11 were picked up in the Montagnard garden without incident but the last load was a challenge. The chopper could not get off the ground and the pilot ordered three or four of White's men to get off. A medic on board had thrown four Nungs off earlier. This medic later confessed to me, tearfully, that he took the place of those he had thrown off. By now the enemy was hot on their heels and White, as the commander, knew he would be one of those who had to get off. He refused. The crew, fearing they would be stuck on the ground, began to strip weight from the bird, ammo, guns, gear, everything, even clothing. One Marine stripped to his skivvies. That may have made the difference. The shuddering chopper made it out with a cockpit full of flashing red lights.

Before the last trip we had gotten all of the seriously wounded out and only a light load of routine patients remained. I got an up and we lifted slowly to the top of the trees. I then made a hard turn and broke for the low ground on the top of the trees to get some air speed and become a moving target. Almost immediately, I heard a scream from the back that there were three people on the skids. The medic was laying on the floor with both hands out the cargo door. We quickly searched for a hole in the jungle. Within seconds I found one but not before I heard my medic yell twice, "there goes one!" There was a chance we were landing in the middle of the enemy and the crew got ready. One of the three had hung on and we set down carefully so as not to hurt him. We would learn later that he was a Nung. He was not wounded but I will never forget the look of undiluted fear on his face as we pulled him in the chopper. I can see his face as I type this and it has always been for me the very definition of horror.

We rose to the top of the jungle and retraced our flight path at a hover, searching the terrain below, hoping to find the fallen troops. I called Bangor Stylus this time getting a gruff U.S. voice. They were leaving the outpost at the time and their route was very close to where we were. I told him what happened and asked if he could send some troops to help in the search. I have never forgotten his response. His exact words were, "F**k 'em; they were supposed to walk out with us." I thought that was harsh, but his outpost was about to be overrun and he was entering a jungle full of the enemy. His only concern was to save the surviving soldiers.

I would learn later that the three on our skids included two Nungs, one who fell and one of the Marine helicopter pilots who also fell. None of them were wounded and must have grabbed the skids in a panic. We had plenty of room and there was no danger in waiting. My crew was sick after this mission. It could not have been more than 30 seconds from the time we noticed them on the skids and when we landed. How could it be that one could hold on and the other two could not? For 30 seconds? It would be 35 years before I learned the answer.

To this point, I had only one person die in my chopper that I knew of. I know I did lose two people off my skids that Friday and I have never quite gotten over it. Our job was to prevent death not cause it. We heard later that the Marine chopper crews had drawn straws to see who would go with us. Marine chopper pilots were more conscious of their chopper loads than we were. They limited the load on the 46s to nine or ten passengers. We routinely took twice that many. We could have taken them all. It was such a waste. Our crewmember who watched the two soldiers fall into the jungle never flew with us again and had to be reassigned.

Soon after White cleared Ngok Tavak, B 52s obliterated the fort and the surrounding areas to include all the bodies in it. There were left behind many skulls in this Viet Nam Golgotha. The search for those bodies would go on for 37 years but the U.S. never gave up and there was a very moving ceremony for the remnants at Arlington on 7 October 2005. The son of Thomas Perry, the heroic medic, sang all the words to the national anthem a cappella, the most moving rendition I ever heard.

White would be called to task by his higher HQ for disobeying the command to hold the fort. White then denounced the leadership for converting a mobile survivable and valuable reconnaissance force into sitting ducks. They had promised help and none came. They had forced on him defenders, none of whom were trained in defense. The unfortunate officer listening to White made the mistake of smiling during White's diatribe and got a knuckle sandwich for his blunder. Fortunately, White was not subject to the U.S. Uniform Code of Military Justice or he could have been court-martialed for disobeying a direct order, not to mention punching a fellow officer. But had he obeyed, he would surely have been dead along with all his men, a complete Custer-type wipeout.

Later a Marine colonel sought out White to denounce him for leaving the Marine dead. The Colonel gave the impression it would have been better to leave the wounded Nungs and evacuate the Marine dead. White was outraged. What about the other dead? He pointed to Ngok Tavak on a map. "Colonel, why don't you get off your ass and go get them yourself? Then you can become a KIA and get some other Marines killed looking for you." The Aussie leadership agreed with White. They were disgusted with the U.S. leadership in this mess and moved all the Australians out of I Corps.

Meanwhile, the 2nd NVA moved past Ngok Tavak, wreaking havoc on their way to Kham Duc. Initially, it appeared U.S. leadership made the same mistake at Kham Duc as at Ngok Tavak; they reinforced with a battalion from the Americal, a hopeless situation in a useless piece of terrain, dug in, and braced for a fight. The friendlies were now only outnumbered five to one. This was exactly to the liking of the communists. They now had more U.S. forces to capture and kill for their propaganda film.

By the morning of 11 May, they had the camp surrounded and were steadily bombarding it. This was exactly to the liking of the

U.S., a perfect "bait and blast" situation. They had a huge force of enemy, more or less sitting ducks—if the weather permitted. It did. Then began a massive bombardment in I Corps the likes of which I had never seen. With the blessing of an unprecedented three days of clear skies, hundreds of U.S. fighters, bombers, and gunships from all services flew thousand of sorties dropping thousands of tons of ordinance on the hapless communists. Still the NVA fought on hoping for cloudy skies and a film of their capture of the camp. The communists had counted on bad weather to stop our air assaults. The U.S. command, realizing they had pushed the weather gods to the limit, ordered the evacuation of Kham Duc on the 12th, Mothers Day. That day was the mother of all heroics for those who flew the evacuations.

The area became a graveyard for 14 downed U.S. aircraft. But most of the pilots were rescued as were all the surviving defenders of Kham Duc. In the worst air disaster of the war, (in fact, in history to this point) the communists shot down a C-130 full of civilian women and children, killing some 150. Army aircraft evacuated half of the forces at Kham Duc, over 700. The Air Force and Marines got the rest. The last pickup was made by Joe Jackson in a lumbering C-123 just prior to the communists' overrun of the airfield. He was able to land amid the burned out aircraft on a runway damaged and littered by enemy ordinance and downed U.S. aircraft, and rescue the last three men. Jackson and his crew watched in horror as an enemy rocket hit the runway and rolled under their nosecone. It failed to ignite. But their rescue was successful, so characteristic of the many heroic rescues that day. Miraculously, his C-123 did not receive one enemy round and Jackson earned the Medal of Honor. Twenty minutes after the Jackson rescue, weather closed in on Kham Duc making further air operations impossible.

Dust Off was not as fortunate as Jackson. Two of our new pilots were hit by a 12.7-mm on the 10th and McWilliam and Schwartz were shot up on the 11th. Don and I would get hit with 12.7-mms on the 13th; so much for the 2nd NVA respecting our red crosses.

The countryside was filled with casualties and the 54th Dust Off began its most intense period of rescue ever, perhaps the most intense ever for any Dust-off unit. It was the mother of all Mothers Days. We flew 45 hours and carried over 300 patients, many of them escaping from Kham Duc (but I am not sure how many were included in the 700 evacuated by army choppers). I carried what was a record for me on that day, 125. Between Ngok Tavak and Kham Duc, I flew 22 hours and made 61 landings, probably an average for all the 54th pilots in our rescue efforts during that time. But we didn't get them all. Major Mac watched a pilot bail out of his burning aircraft but another chopper beat him to the downed pilot. And he listened helplessly as a wounded GI on one of the outposts around Kham Duc pleaded with his commander that he could not stop his bleeding and asked when someone was coming to help him. That would prove to be Major Mac's worst moment in Viet Nam. The NVA were overrunning the poor soldier's position as he spoke.

And they would eventually overrun Kham Duc and capture a bunch of burned-out aircraft and equipment. There is no telling how many hundreds, thousands by one estimate, of casualties the communists suffered and no leverage for Paris. There would be no propaganda victory at Kham Duc. They did kill 25 U.S. troops at Kham Duc and scores of helpless civilians. Thankfully there were no U.S. media there (they covered many battles from hotels in Saigon) to record the massacre of the NVA or they surely would have turned it into a victory as they did the massacre of communists at TET. One of the most intense actions of the war got very little coverage. The dynamic duo of Uncle Ho and Uncle Walter would have little grist for the communists' cant.

The 2nd NVA division would later boast, and be praised by survivors of Ngok Tavak, that it was their policy not to shoot red crossed helicopters. As I have said and taught, I am sure that was true on occasion certainly during our initial landing at Ngok Tavak. But, as noted, we had three choppers shot up in the three days after

Ngok Tavak, two by 12.7-mm all in encounters with the 2nd NVA Division. Perhaps the enemy figured there would be no propaganda film and it didn't matter anymore. And we would have nine of our Dust Offs shot up in May, which tied for the highest number in any one month.

As a result of the Kham Duc rescues, we heard most of those involved received significant awards, except Dust Off. As far as I know we did not receive one award for that action even though it resulted in our biggest month—bigger than TET. In May, we carried 3,084 patients, averaging over 100 patients, 35 missions, and 19 hours per day (a far cry from my first month in Viet Nam when the 57th's total was 178). But we were well remembered award wise on most occasions and by now the reader should better understand awards. And despite all the hits we took that month, we had only one man wounded, very seriously. He was a jewel, one of the finest men I have ever known. I would rescue him and in an extraordinarily timely manner. But to this day I do not know the why of it.

· 40 ·

WHERE IS THE WORM?

ON the 27th, our Johnny Carson, Frank Zuber, was on a mission at Lonely Boy. Frank was neither a medic or crew chief, but he volunteered to fly many missions. He urged Major Mac: "Sir we need to get out of here." "Sit tight, Bob, we will but there are some more patients." This conversation went on for a while until Mac a bit aggravated asked, "What in the hell is your hurry?" "G-- Damn it, sir, I been shot." And he was. Zuber had lived through the crash with Schenck and Rock but we would lose him to his wounds and the quality of the unit as well as the morale suffered from his loss. Cronan was also shot there, from a great distance. The commies had that place zeroed in. Lonely Boy was getting to be a pain in the ass.

On the 29th, Dust Off Schenck and I were busy working routine missions along the coast. We had another ship out; the Worm, in Dust Off 54, was working the valley. For reasons that cannot be explained in natural terms, I was worried about him. Chuck shared my concern. I called control, "Have you heard from 54?" "No, 55, they are in the valley, but everything is quiet out there." "Do you have radio contact?" "No, they are behind the hills." "Give me the frequency and I will call." I could not get through. A few minutes later I tried again. Nothing! "Control, any word on 54?" Control sounded annoyed at my repetitive inquiries. "No 55, but things are still quiet out there."

I could not let it go and was upset that control was not as concerned as I was. "Control, 55, where are they?" "Lonely Boy, 55." That did it. In addition to Cronan and Zuber, it was the same pad I landed at my first missions on the feast of the Epiphany. That pad had been under attack on and off for three days. Ordinarily this would have been a waste of time, two birds in an area where one could do the job, but I could not shake my concern.

We refueled and headed out to the mountains and just as we cleared the crest, our radios were filled with screams of chaos and confusion. "Where is Dust Off?," I demanded. The voice said he was down at the north end of the strip, hit by a mortar. Norm came on the mic. "Five five, Hook is serious, the whole crew was hit except me, they're not bad, but Hook is bad." My heart sank. Good Lord, not Hook. Thank God I had Norm there to help get them out. If it was a mortar then they had the downed Dust Off registered and we would be an easy and sure target if we landed near it. They had mortared this pad on 6 January and many times before. I missed it in the fog or we might have been hit that day.

There was no time to move the patients. Chuck and I decided we needed to change Charlie's registration point. I told Worm to gather the patients at the north end of the pad and be ready to load quickly. I then landed at the south end and imagined the enemy re-registering his mortars on us. My ears were burning like crazy. When I could stand it no longer, I scooted to the north end as mortars impacted behind us. They threw the patients on. Hook was a mess. He took 14 pieces of shrapnel in his brain and his arm was a bloody mangle, a frag having severed his brachial artery and nerve. Lowder, though wounded himself, went to work on Hook, performing the CPR and mouth to mouth resuscitation Hook had taught him on the fruit cocktail mission. He kept Hook alive! It may have been the difference; Hook may have been responsible for saving his own life.

Dust Off 54 had been called for a mission at Tam Ky for a baby born without an anus and was deferred to Lonely Boy for an ARVN with a frag wound in his thigh. They were about knee-high off the ground when the mortar went off. It blew Hook out of the bird 25 feet away. Worm's co-pilot was hit in the back of the neck. Phil Holdaway was hit in the left thigh and the right shoulder and was bleeding seriously when he spotted Hook lying in a pool of blood. He thought Hook was dead but he and Lowder ran through the fire fight to rescue him. As Phil grabbed Hook, his blood and Hook's caused Hook to slip out of his grasp and fall. They recovered and got Hook into a ditch. My crew arrived within minutes. If we had not gone out there, on a whim (or at God's urging), and they had to call our operations, the delay would surely have been fatal for Hook.

I was emotionally out of control as we took off and I bent the bird past the red line in my rush to get Hook to the hospital. I heard a loud screech from the back and looked around. It was the Worm letting off steam, a primal scream. He saw the tears in my eyes and he also broke down. Charlie gently took the controls away from me, eased back, and guided us to the hospital.

The good Lord was working overtime this day. It was truly a miracle that we decided to check on Worm's ship, but it took another miracle to save him. The one neurosurgeon in the country just happened to be visiting Chu Lai on that day, for one day. He was able to save Steve but it would be months before he was operational again and his arm was never quite right. We lost one of the finest soldiers I have ever known, a man I have called the Charles Kelly of enlisted medics. Father Don scrubbed in and watched and prayed while the surgeons opened Steve's skull and removed most of the mortar frags but not all. Some are still in there.

Near the end of this horrible month, one of our medics, Richard

Sanders, fell out of a chopper on takeoff. It was a signal that we needed to tighten up crew coordination. In the rush of exceptional action, we sometimes forget the basics. I jacked the troops up on coordination. We had lost those men off our skids at Ngoc Tavak simply because we got an up when we shouldn't have. Details are life and death and need constant attention. Sanders was a great medic in the mold of Tiny, Hook and Pappy. Tiny died for lack of crew coordination. Sanders lived through his fall but he would be the first member of the 54th killed in Viet Nam. He died on my birthday, and Hook's, the 1st of October 1968, when the 54th, which had gone through a year without a fatality, lost seven KIA in one month.

In addition to the 3,084 rescues, and nine ships shot up in May, we again flew over a thousand missions. One ship was hit by mortars at Duc Pho where they took 1,000 rounds of rockets and mortars in one night. Finally, in an act as dastardly as the shooting of the chaplain on Easter, the communists destroyed our PX. May would be the deadliest month of the war claiming 2415 lives.

· 41 ·

JUNE: AMAZING STATS

O N the 13th of June 1968, Viet Nam became the longest war in American history. It was also on this date that we covered a tragic accident, not only in terms of all those killed, but in terms of one of those killed. We were flying near the My Lai complex in the midst of extensive combat operation. The sky was full of fighters, helicopters, and an Air Force fixed wing FAC. The sun was bright and low making visibility difficult. I was anxious to clear the area. Suddenly the FAC went out of control and came together with a Huey in mid-air. Both aircraft plummeted to the ground, the Huey breaking up on descent. We spotted the FAC in a pond and we went to a hover on top of him. Almost immediately we started to receive mortar fire. The communists were actually trying to mortar us at a hover. It would have been a remarkable shot, and they were good; some of the rounds actually impacted nearby in the water. We saw some blood surfacing and were sure the pilot was dead. He would later be recovered with a bullet hole in his head.

We jumped over the water into the rice paddy near the blazing

Huey. Burning bodies were scattered across the rice paddy. The crash was so devastating that it would be some 26 years before one of the pilots was identified. One of the dead was LTC Frank Barker of Task Force Barker and My Lai, one man who could have shed considerable light on what happened at My Lai when the scandal broke later. He died only minutes from My Lai. Barker was in the area to rescue two of his companies pinned down by the VC. Our crew got out, doused the fire on the dead soldiers, and we took them to the morgue.

On the 15th I inspected my aircraft, expecting to fly that day. I was called away for a meeting and Buddha Shadrick jumped in throwing my helmet on the floor and headed out on a mission. My helmet was like an old friend. It still had the kangaroo from my days with Kelly on the back. I have a large, hard-to-fit head and it fit perfectly. I had soaked it with my wife's perfume as a reminder and to cover the smell from gallons of sweat. A newer helmet came out promising better ballistic protection and the pilots, Shadrick among them, tried to get me to buy in to it perhaps more for the smell than concern for my protection. I resisted.

During the mission, Buddha and the Worm went into a hot area and took several rounds, one passing undaunted through my helmet into Buddha's arm. When I returned from the meeting, I was told Lester was seriously wounded in the hospital. I ran to his ward where he greeted me a bit sarcastically I thought for a WOPA addressing a real officer: "Thanks a lot for wearing a ballistic helmet and saving a guy's arm." This was the third time he was hit. He miraculously survived the bullet through his helmet, but not the one through mine. He had a million dollar wound and would go home. We lost a great pilot who survived hundreds of dangerous missions. He would later be killed in a civilian helicopter crash. (I highlighted with paint where the bullet went into my helmet with an "in" but no "out" and some still wonder if the bullet is in my head.)

June was a bit of a relief from the mad house that was May. We were down to 2,386 patients, only 780 being GIs, our lowest since

December. I took my last hit on the 23rd in an area I hated the most, a terraced rice paddy, with some guys shooting down on us. Norm and Pete got shot up pretty badly with one round hitting Pete in the leg just as it expired. It scared the hell out of him but did no damage. We had seven ships hit and a medic wounded when an RPG hit the top of his ship at night. He came out of it with a broken arm and multiple frag wounds. The ship was badly damaged which was not unusual for us, what was unusual was they never woke me up for the incident. For this entire tour, I could hear the radio from my bunk and monitored our missions continuously. We had lost 25 percent of the original 54th and a combination of our pros and the FNGs handled the incident. And they did a good job. They didn't need my two bits worth. Nonetheless I was a bit upset and somehow felt left out. It was like someone ate my beanie weenies.

As I prepared our first newsletter the end of June, I was amazed at what we had been through and accomplished in nine months. The 40-man detachment had been or would be awarded 26 Purple Hearts, none, thank God, were for KIAs. They earned, by the John Kerry definition, many more but had refused to take the time for the administration. We had been awarded and recommended for: one Medal of Honor (this went in as a DSC, my second, but was later upgraded), one Distinguished Service Cross, 16 Silver Stars, 27 Distinguished Flying Crosses, 2 Bronze Stars for valor, 4 Air medals for valor (regular Air Medals don't count, they were in the hundreds), and 4 Soldier's Medals.

We would leave many eye-witness statements for awards that our successors neglected. In addition, we had been recommended for a Presidential Unit Citation (the highest unit award) and a Valorous Unit Award (both of these awards were also neglected and I am still looking for them. I hope this book will help). Individual awards are fine, but the unit awards are more representative of the true team the 54th was. In addition to neglecting our awards, our successors lost or destroyed all the MRFs, which constituted a complete record of every mission we flew. When I asked a commander who succeeded me about these records (which were nowhere to be found in official archives) he didn't know what I was talking about. I wondered if he wrote the mission requests on his hand!

Wow! If you count the Purple Hearts, that is 78 awards for valor! But as impressive as that number is, it was only a sample of the totality of their valorous acts. Surely this was one of the most highly decorated 40-man units in the history of warfare; and also one of the most effective and efficient. By the end of July, in ten months and seven days, we would evacuate 21,435 patients in 8,644 missions while flying 4,832 hours. Included were 8,904 civilians, 531 enemy troops, and seven Scout Dogs. In other words, we flew 16 hours and carried 69 patients in 28 missions each day. Four of those 28 missions were at night. Before Kelly, Dust Off flew one night mission every three days! I wonder what our total night combat time was. I would bet that many of our pilots had more night time than the total time of some commanders. Don Sewell and Rock both broke 1,000 hours of combat time in their tour; perhaps the only Dust Off pilots after Ernie to do this. The 54th achieved all this with an average of three aircraft available each day due to maintenance and enemy action which damaged 116 percent of our aircraft each month.

July would be our most efficient month in terms of time per mission, 24 minutes. As further tribute to our efficiency, the average time per mission for all aeromedical evacuation aircraft was 55 minutes with 2 patients per mission; it was 33 minutes for the 54th with 2.4 patients per mission or 4.4 per hour, twice as many as the norm. At the height of the conflict, each medical helicopter flew four missions per day; as noted the 54th averaged 28 mission per day or about 9 per duty helicopter. Altogether a great 310 days work.

Major Mac left in June and I took command on the 21st. I would not have been able to command if he had not talked the brass into it. They knew my record, he didn't, and they were prepared to bring in another commander for the few weeks I had left. I hated to see him go even though I would get to command. We had our differences but the men loved this man. I did too. They put up with me. Together we made a great team, a kind of good cop bad cop thing. I never minded being number two as long as I was heard. I was blessed in both tours to have men like Kelly and Mac as commanders—one who taught me the proper attitude for Dust Off flying and the other who let me execute to my full potential. I would never have been successful in some of my rescues if Mac had not given me my head. There were few other commanders who would allow the kind of flying we did and stand by the men through all their mishaps. And I know of none who would have allowed, let alone gotten in with me on the first flare missions (although he tells me that he still has nightmares about those missions).

On a tragic note, Francis our beloved monkey, fell off a bike and cracked her skull on the 20th. We rushed her to the hospital (where she was well known) and five doctors examined her taking numerous X-rays. Fortunately the neurosurgeon was again present and he operated. She recovered but was walking with a limp when I left. On another tragic note, Bobby Kennedy was assassinated on the 6th.

· 42 ·

JULY: A WEDDING, A MEDAL, AND MY LAST MISSION

BY the first of July 1968, the U.S. had suffered more casualties than in all of 1967. This war was not getting better. But I was getting short and was anxious to see my family. Yet you cannot spend a year with a bunch of soldiers and go through what we went through and not be concerned for them. You wonder how they will do without you. My concerns were relieved as I monitored a mission on the 8th. Rock was called out on an urgent mission for soldiers wounded by enemy hand grenades. The area was called secure but they had requested gunship support. Rock got to the area, did not wait for the gunships, but asked only where the last location of the enemy was and that they hold their fire if possible while he went in. He got bad information and was driven out of the area by heavy fire. The Six in a command ship came on and asked Rock to wait for the gunships. He did and this time went in with the gunnies. The fire was so intense he could see, in daylight, the tracers flying past his doors. I was second up and left for another mission. Rock was getting low on fuel and I asked if he needed help. His reply was that the guys were badly wounded and he was going back in. He went in for the third time and got them—and they were serious. He did everything right this mission. Security was not an issue—they had been wounded by grenades, you have to be pretty close to do that. All he asked was that they stand up and give him accurate information on the enemy location and weaponry. Some pilots would say call us when there is no fire. Not Rock.

Not only was I impressed with our pilots, it was impossible not to be impressed with the courage of the grunts. Day after day, they humped in impossible terrain and weather with an ungodly load. These men saw more combat in less time than any soldier in any of our wars. I will never forget landing in a paddy one day and looking out my window to see a young man up to his hips in the paddy, one arm missing holding an IV with the other. As it turned out, he was not up to his hips—*he had no hips.* He had lost both legs and an arm and he was conscious—and smiling; as if to say, I got it made I am going to the land of the big PX.

The carnage was difficult but so, too, were the death rattles, the last words of crashing pilots, or troops about to be overrun, which we would occasionally hear on the air. Often it was a message of affection to be passed to a loved one but more often it was an admonition or prayer to God; in one case, a dear friend's plea: "God above, God help us, I'm sorry God, I'm going to die, I know it." And he did, at night in weather and there was no good reason for it. I was sorry to lose him but pleased that he was thinking of God at the end. Then there was the guy who left his bunker to relieve himself and was seriously wounded. He blamed God for making him have to urinate.

On 11 July at 10:00 hours, General Creighton Abrams, who replaced Westy as MACV Commander on 1 July, presented a DSC to me for the flare missions. He had earlier ordered that pilots quit wearing the jungle boots. There was a danger of the plastic in the boot burning into the skin in a fire. Pilots were to wear leather boots which were heavier and hotter. Some ignored the order. I noticed as he approached me at the ceremony his eyes immediately focused on my feet. Thank God I was wearing leather boots; otherwise he might have taken the award away.

His only words were, "That was a great thing you did." It was a great thing for me to get my DSC from General Abrams. I would serve under this remarkable soldier later at the Pentagon as he died from cancer. He had special praise for Dust Off at a gathering of aviators: "...a special word about the Dust Offs...Courage above and beyond the call of duty was sort of routine to them. It was a daily thing, part of the way they lived. That's the great part and it meant so much to every last man who served there. Whether he ever got hurt or not, he knew Dust Off was there. It was a great thing for our people."

After the ceremony, COL Le Bourdais ordered me to cease flying immediately. I disobeyed that order knowing that he was a soldier who would understand why. He may have been one of those concerned with the cliché that the odds that one would get hurt built with each mission. Hence the hundred mission thing with the Air Force. I believed that the odds started over with each mission. They don't accumulate, what does accumulate is sloppiness and that is what kills. I made my 20th and last combat landing of the day on the 18th of July, my next-to-last day in country. For the last time I flew over the beautiful terrain in our AO. A few years later, an Air Force pilot would be shot down near that terrain giving rise to the legend of Bat 21. Eleven warriors would tragically die in his rescue, a rescue that any pilot from the 54th could have executed without mishap. Unfortunately the 54th and all Dust Off units had left the area when the pilot went down.

Two days after the Abrams visit, we had a wedding. One of our WOPAs married a nurse from the 2nd Surg. There were 10,000 men in our area and 20 nurses. She showed good taste picking one of our guys. She outranked him, much to the delight of the international media which covered the wedding worldwide. Earlier the unit gathered to decide on an appropriate wedding gift. We settled on a honeymoon cottage on the banks just east of our area overlooking the South China Sea. Kennedy and Johnson dusted off their tools and we went to work. The finished product was spectacular as was all their work. The cottage was built of beautiful mahogany plywood, three rooms, air conditioned, private bath and shower with one wall a Plexiglas window (for protection) overlooking the ocean. We even built them their own private bunker.

The groom asked me to be his best man and Ken Cass gave away the bride. Father Don recruited some Vietnamese Boy Scouts for altar boys and married them. We flew them to and from the wedding in a chopper emblazoned with "Just Married" on the nose and streaming smoke bombs. The cake was cut with a Bowie knife and the Americal Division band played "Tenderly," their favorite song, at the reception. We barbequed some 200 pounds of lobster and steak around the pond in the center of our area. The booze was plentiful, too plentiful. I may have been the only sober person there, save the duty crews. It was a grand affair. I wish it had ended that way.

During the celebration some of the WOPAs asked if they could shivaree the wedded couple. I said not only no, but hell no. Our commander, Colonel Le Bourdais, was there and thus far had a very high opinion of our unit. I didn't want that changed in the few days I had left. I was just settling into my bunk when I saw a flare go off. Oh, shit! That was the signal. Then all hell broke loose. I ran from my hooch toward the honeymoon cottage taking care not to step on the drunks that littered the area. One soldier ran toward me shouting that we were being invaded. He had seen bodies in the ditch between our area and the Morgue. There were bodies for sure, but they were only more drunks. I knew what was happening. The flare was the signal to begin the revelry. The shivareers scattered as I approached the cottage. The bride groom was on the porch in his skivvies cursing to a fare-thee-well. The revelers had used real bullets for the shivaree and some of them had gone through the cottage, more than likely taking a lot of romance out of the evening.

I checked to see if the Colonel was awake. Thank God he was not. He must have been well into his cups. And neither were any of the others in our yard. I got on the radio and squelched any rumors of an invasion and ordered the miscreants to be in my office at first light. I was as pissed as I had ever been and they knew it. As I got into bed, one of the malefactors appeared at my door. He was troubled. "Sir, you said that no matter what we did, if we raped a nun, as long as we never hurt the mission you would stand by us." I did say that but I explained that if what they did got to Le Bourdais or caused a reaction from other units, it would have hurt our mission. You don't shoot live rounds in a compound in a war zone unless you are shooting at the enemy—much less shoot up one of our buildings! I could not believe it, less than a week to go and I could have had a reaction force from the Division attacking my area. The next day I hit the shivareers as hard as I could, I revoked all their AC orders. I then told the new commander that if he was smart, he would put them back on AC status when I left. They were all outstanding pilots, far superior to any of the new pilots. He did.

But I was impressed with the eagerness of the new pilots and spent as much of my last month as possible flying them under the Hood simulating IFR flight. Bad weather was just around the corner and this training could save lives. I also flew as many missions as I could with them. One mission gave me insight into the quality of these FNGs. It was a night weather mission with Renis Fox one of the new WOPAs shortly after his arrival. We were able to make it to the PZ VFR and I shot a blacked out approach to a tight confined area, a maneuver requiring some skill. His only comment was, "Not bad," meager praise I thought for a FNG; his unimpressed attitude pissed me off a bit. But as I thought about it, it became clear that this guy was a Kelly twig. And he was. He had the perfect Dust Off attitude. You may be a legend in your own mind, Double Nickel, but just watch my smoke. Tragically, he would be killed earning his second Silver Star in the same crash that killed Sanders. He had been shot down on his initial approach near Lonely Boy. He was then evacuated but got another bird and went back. He got the patients but took heavy fire on departure and crashed and burned.

Tragically, the new 54th would have seven men killed before the end of October 1968, but none in weather. In fact, although our successors in the 54th would lose 21 crew men in three years, only four of them were killed at night in weather. That crew flew into Nui Dong Tranh Mountain, a few clicks from Chu Lai. The new commander, who had far more time than I did, asked me to demonstrate a tactical approach. I was happy to do it and know that he had heard of such a thing; but not impressed with his enthusiasm for it. He would be promoted out of the unit to a desk, probably a good thing.

My departure from the 54th would be a far cry from that of the 57th. Although nothing ever came of it, the 44th Medical Brigade was kind enough to nominate me for the Chamber of Commerce Man of the Year. Several media people interviewed me, one professing on film that I was a legend (which, to this day, I don't let anyone, including my wife, forget; and later, much to the chagrin of my fellow aviators, *The Encyclopedia of The Viet Nam War* would proclaim I was the top helicopter pilot in Viet Nam). And this time I would receive an appropriate end-of-tour medal. The totality of my medals in Viet Nam would result in one publication ranking me number five among our county's most decorated servicemen (but I must add that efforts to rank "Most Decorated..." are a fruitless folly. It cannot be done fairly or accurately and one wonders why it is so often tried). My OERs were not written to damn with faint praise and did not question my loyalty. It was likely that this combat tour, unlike my first, would make it possible for me to finish an honorable military career free from challenges to my loyalty and threats of dismissal. But above all the medals and accolades, I had helped save over 5,000 souls in my two tours.

The troops had a nice farewell party for me in the bunker (we spent a lot of time in there). They presented me with a plaque featuring the golden winged 54th emblem and their nickname for me engraved on it, "Craze." I knew they called me that although this was the first time they did so in public. They also called me "Mother." I am sure they often appended the Motherf****r; this was a group only a mother could love—and I surely did love them. But "Craze" was not far from "Mad Man" and it did not offend me. (Unfortunately, "Craze" followed me to the States. One aviation commander took it to mean I was a loose cannon addicted to reckless, even irresponsible, flying. He actually grounded me and put me through a flight evaluation period after a crewman complained that, during training, *I was shooting night approaches without lights!*)

Craze was happy to be numbered with the irreplaceable Wayne, the Worm, Rock, KIA, Buddha, Dust Off Schenck, Frenchie, FAC Flory, Combat/Pappy, Mac, Speedy/Batman, and all the rest in one of the most effective and efficient combat teams ever. I am sure Mad Man Kelly would be very proud of this unit which he once commanded; which was full of Kelly twigs. In fact, in the official military history of Dust Off, the 54th was singled out as the one unit that most closely mirrored the Kelly tradition and the legacy of the Lafayette Escadrille (American fighter pilot volunteers to France in World War I, renowned for their flying and libation skills—not unlike the 54th). Later the same book, in describing Dust Off in the most difficult, demanding and dangerous conditions, reads: "Most important, the Kelly tradition had survived in full force in the 54th...[and] the courage of these pilots...had made the Dust Off system an object of reverence in the ever shifting battlefields of Viet Nam." Our pilots certainly experienced this reverence if they went anywhere with the Golden Winged 54 on their shoulder. Many of them still wear it.

I will end this with some thoughts on Kelly and what I learned about leadership from him. He is most remembered for his physical courage in combat lifesaving, but it was his moral courage that saved Dust Off, the greatest lifesaver the battlefield has ever known. Dust Off shattered the Golden Hour resulting in the fact that less than 1 percent of all wounded who survived the first 24 hours, died! Thanks to Kelly, a soldier shot on a battlefield in Viet Nam had a greater chance of survival than a civilian in an accident on a highway in America. And it is well-known that soldiers fight better if they know they will be cared for if wounded. Kelly and Dust Off contributed immeasurably to the great fighting spirit of the Viet Nam warrior. I have known many with blinding combat courage who would later cower before the outrages and onslaughts of bureaucratic salt mines; and bend in the unending wars we all wage between our security, our desires, our passions and those wonderful things called—our ideals. Kelly was unique in the degree to which he possessed all forms of courage, which is, of course, the bedrock of leadership.

Kelly was a man of humble beginnings and humility is a constant mark of great leaders. Loss of humility also marks the disintegration of leadership. Kelly was a humble man who drove home for me the incredible treasure that is courage. In many ways, we are not all born equal; certainly in terms of ability and opportunity, we are not equal. In fact, there may be only one way in which we are all equal—courage. Each of us can have all the courage we want. God has made this incredible gift infinitely available to all, you can't use it up. And it is the key to success in life, the great equalizer. It clearly marks failure and mediocrity as the fruits of choices not chance. Courage produces great people from those among us without great ability or who were not privy to great opportunity. Kelly fit the mold. He certainly was not born with a silver spoon in his mouth nor was he blessed with great ability (I did not think he was technically a particularly outstanding pilot) but he was a great man.

I also found in Kelly what for me is the key to courage—faith. I have not known many people of *constant repetitive* courage who were not also people of faith. Kelly was a man of deep faith founded in World War II and fostered throughout his life. He did not wear his faith on his sleeve but it was evident to all. The sacrifice of a soldier like Kelly is a sacrifice without a bottom line, no material rewards, no quid pro quo; all it does is increase one's capacity for more—sacrifice; and also for responsibility, for leadership, indeed for happiness itself. Just as exercise builds muscles, sacrifice builds human effectiveness—and is the key to happiness. I would define this sacrifice as love in action. If you agree with that definition, it is easy to see that a soldier's love is the foundation of the security of our nation. No one loved our nation, its flag, and his fellow soldiers more than Kelly.

The contrasts in this man were sharp. He was quiet, even shy, but as loudly decisive as anyone I have ever met. He was colorful, even flamboyant, but so aware of his humanity, really almost meek. He did not take himself seriously, but he was very serious, even fanatical about his mission and responsibilities. He seemed to have no insecurities. Inside this modest man was a volcano of certainty about what he was about. He could not even pretend to be phony. I am sure if I looked hard enough I could find flaws in this man—but I don't want to. And that is what a real leader will do to his subordinates, which is the difference between a leader and someone in a leadership position.

Today there are many monuments and memorials to this man, but none grander than those in the hearts of his men. His last words, "When I have your wounded," set a standard for excellence that was both monumental and memorable, unmatched in the annuals of life saving. Kelly was one man who made a difference. He was a leader, a man who provoked openness, honesty, and caring—who lived beyond his lifetime. The great thing about true leaders like Kelly is that they never leave us. Dead or alive, the noblest part of their being remains behind, becomes a part of our being—as soldiers, of our profession, of all those things that make our way unique. "When I have your wounded"—what a great way to die; and really, not a bad way to live.

· 43 ·

DUST OFF DÉJÀ VU

SO where is Dust Off today; after all the blood and sacrifice? I am afraid that Charles Kelly is turning over in his grave. The Army has done what he died to prevent. They have put the Dust Off mission under the control of Combat Arms Aviation. Soon to follow will be the end of the MSC aviator. The portable Red Cross and the dreaded ASO have emerged from the dust bin of history. Mission requests now go through a long and tortured evaluation process while the patient waits. Launch authority is vested with REMFs remote from the Dust Off and onsite weather—and common sense. These folks are obsessed with risk analysis and obstacles; much like some of Kelly's successors. Reaction time and the Golden Hour are a joke.

In a recent visit to troops at a USO, I had a soldier turn his back on me when I told him I was once a Dust Off pilot. When I could get his attention he said that a friend had died because the Dust Off took too long to get there. This is but one of many stories I have heard from pilots in the field (who will not speak out for fear of retribution) who said patients have suffered because of delays in launching Dust Off, delays that are inexcusable.

Not only does the tortured decision process needlessly delay a Dust Off launch, it sometimes prohibits it. During the famous Black Hawk Down incident, a Dust Off was less than 10 minutes from the downed Black Hawk. The Dust Off pilot was preparing to launch when an ASO forbid him to leave the ground. Why? There were other helicopters in the area. There were gunships to support the rescue. Another chopper landed and dispatched two soldiers (who were killed earning the Medal of Honor) to rescue the downed crew. Why was Dust Off not given the opportunity to try, at least to try, the rescue? I have seen photos of the area and am convinced a Dust Off could have made the rescue if they were dispatched in a timely manner. Only the ignorance of the ASO and other REMFs could explain this fiasco.

What caused the changes? Has Dust Off failed to do its job? I recall some incidents that caused me concern. A soldier was left overnight in the cold on a mountain in Afghanistan. The enemy was on the other side! The man could have easily been rescued if Dust Off had simply hovered up the safe side of the mountain. In another instance, two birds, an air ambulance and a chase aircraft, were sent at night for one patient. One bird crashed and the patient was rescued by a non-medical aircraft. They sent four engines to do the job one did in Viet Nam. We have gone from two pilots, one engine, to four pilots and four engines—and can't get the job done as efficiently. Imagine what that does to maintenance. Has the night phobia returned?

I was told that the Dust Off helicopters were the oldest in the fleet; backwards from Viet Nam. Why was this allowed? The current MEDEVAC aircraft, the Black Hawk, will not react like the Huey. Not only does it take forever to get airborne, it is not quick, and has a tail low attitude promoting poor visibility and awkwardness in tight terrain. I have very little time in one but would not want to make a snake approach in combat, let alone do a death spiral in it. To make matters worse, they put a carousel in the back to hydraulically lift and position patients (possibly in deference to upper body weaknesses with some soldiers but adding weight and space problems, not to mention time on the ground). This bird, unlike the Huey, was not designed for patients—let alone for Dust Off operations. At the time the Medical Department was considering the Black Hawk, many of us advised that they add an engine, a radar altimeter, spruce up the Huey and keep it. On the medical side, I have seen some indifference on reaction time. I actually found some Dust Off units without a reaction standard, and one with Hueys used seven minutes! (In 2009 15 minutes was set as a standard). Yet despite some negatives, it has been my observation that the Dust Off pilots have done their best to continue the tradition they inherited; and they excel in aviation standards of safety and maintenance—and have the awards to prove it.

The truth is that the changes are driven by obsessive command and control issues and ignorance among the ASO; the lack of a champion and leadership in the Medical Corps are contributing factors. Dust Off in Viet Nam by any measure was the most effective and efficient Battlefield Operating System in that war. The battlefields of today do not dictate a change. If anything, the jungles and mountains of Viet Nam were more difficult to fly than the deserts of today. Tragically, many of the ASO (and the Medical Corps) have no knowledge of Kelly and the proven system he died to preserve. More tragically, unlike many changes in the Army, subject matter experts (Wise Men, White Hairs) were not consulted on the change. Had they consulted any experienced Dust Off crewman, especially those of the Kelly era, they would have found universal scorn for the changes. They would learn that the changes have been tried and they failed. Incredibly, I heard there was not even a test of principle, usually required. The change was rammed through.

Let me give you a startling example of the ASO's ignorance behind this change. Once again I was in the White House for a Medal of Honor ceremony. While there I had a conversation with a high-ranking ASO. He related with enormous pride a rescue made by an Apache crew. An Apache is a gunship. There is room for two people in tandem. The ASO described how the Apache was present at a casualty situation. The Dust Off was en route but encountering radio problems. The Apache crew decided not to wait. One pilot would get out and they would put the patient in his seat. I do not know what the condition of the patient was but if he was a litter patient they would have had to cram him in the seat; and because of his position and since there was no way to monitor him en route to the hospital, his condition would worsen and he could die.

Clearly, if the patient was urgent his treatment should not have been interrupted. He should not have been separated from the medic on the ground. And Dust off had extensive life-saving skills and equipment worth waiting for, skills and equipment not found in the seat of an Apache. On the other hand, if the patient was not serious why not wait for Dust Off and let the Apache do the mission it was designed for? In Viet Nam, we made it clear to the gunships that if it took them 20 minutes to get to a hospital but only 10 minutes to rendezvous with me, we would rendezvous and he would get back to shooting the bad guys. And, unlike the Apache, there was room for a litter in the gunships of Viet Nam. Not since the Korean War have we treated a patient like this. The worst part of this story is that the ASO had no clue, he praised this travesty. Equally tragic was the fact that a high-ranking civilian was present and raised no concerns. I did not confront the ASO because of the occasion. I wonder if the Apache pilot was put in for an award?

What is missed by today's ASO is the uniqueness of the Dust Off mission. There is no comparable aviation mission. The skills are acquired from repetition (next to cleanliness, next to Godliness), day in day out, over and over analyzing terrain, landing under fire, determining patient needs and destination. Perhaps the best example of non–Dust Off aircraft attempting a Dust Off mission is the Bat 21 debacle which I mentioned. The Air Force called it the largest search-and-rescue mission in their history, 11 days at a cost of 11 lives—*to rescue one man*. In fact, it was not a search and rescue mission. There was no search; they knew where the downed pilot was—*and they had radio contact with him*.

This tragedy took place near the 54th AO but all the Dust Offs had deployed. Any Dust Off pilot in the 54th would have had that man out post haste. If it was too hot in the daytime, they could have got him at night. But knowing that terrain, it is hard to imagine that a safe tactical approach could not have been made in daylight. Additionally, it was perfect terrain for a hoist if the pilot was in dense jungle; there was no high terrain around him, no one to shoot down on the Dust Off. It is hard for me, and most Dust Off pilots, to imagine that *there was a man on the ground moving about for 11 days, in radio contact, and no helicopter could pick him up*. Yet, I have had some, who are aware of the details, tell me it could not be done, that the area was simply too dangerous for helicopters. Army helicopters and Dust Off flew this area for years. There were no areas in Viet Nam that choppers could not fly and did not fly for 11 days! These are people who do not understand Dust Off's capabilities, who would put a wounded man in the back seat of an Apache, who have no concept of tactical helicopter flying, reaction time, and the Golden Hour. According to the Department of Defense, the Army "has implemented the aeromedical evacuation standard of a one hour mission completion time" Forty seven years after Dust Off, they rediscovered the Golden Hour.

It may be that battlefields of the future, and the current ones, do not require the medical efficiency of past wars. We have become a nation that cannot stomach casualties and will fight accordingly. Additionally, I am told we have more highly trained (super) field medics in every unit who mitigate quick reaction time and the Golden Hour. Time will tell but I cannot imagine that we would implement a system that is unproven, untested, and guaranteed to lengthen the time of getting wounded soldiers to a hospital. And that is what is happening. None of the rationale I have heard for the changes included one mention of the patient. Not one. And no one can explain to me how these changes will benefit our wounded soldiers. For several years, I have highlighted this issue to anyone who would listen including two Secretaries of the Army, numerous four-star generals, and a member of the Senate Armed Services Committee. They have given me their ears on the issue but only lip service on the solution. The solution begins and ends with patient needs; totally absent from the rationale for the changes in Dust Off operations. Recently, the former Vice Chief of Staff for the Army, General Peter Chiarelly, a combat veteran, has worked hard to change the focus on the patient and make needed changes; but until this medical mission is returned to medical control, patient needs will suffer.

· PART 4 ·

AFTER WAR

44

WHY SOLDIERS FIGHT

"War is an ugly thing, but not the ugliest of things. The decayed and degraded state of moral and patriotic feeling which thinks that nothing is worth war is much worse."

—John Stuart Mill

After the betrayal of our allies in Viet Nam and the horrible treatment of the veterans of that war, I would occasionally reminisce with fellow old soldiers, and friends from my youth, about the changes in America. Many of us feel that we have become aliens in our own country, a country we dearly love. We see courage, sacrifice, patriotism, honor, military strength, family, traditional morality, modesty, even chastity, and faith, especially Christianity, being derided or redefined. We believe that our lives have meaning only if lived to benefit the next generation. We see problems in that generation. And just as alarming, we have witnessed the disarming of our military as if war were obsolete. War may have had its origin with Cain and Abel. There you had a good man interested only in doing what was right, who saw no reason to protect himself, who found himself helpless before an evil man who was better armed than he was. And he got killed. We also see the essence of war—the evil in people that is with us always.

How can anyone not know that sooner or later we will have to fight, ergo, we better be good at it. All the sheep in the world would like for everyone to be vegetarians, but that will never happen; there are too many wolves out there. If the history of the world comprised a single day, we would enjoy only an hour and a half of peace, the rest often devoted to re-arming. We fight because we have no choice. It's fight or be sheared like sheep; fight or lose your freedom and become slaves. We are becoming a nation of sheep in wolves clothing, indeed, Mr. Obama tore away the clothing. The greatest threat to peace is the mindless spin that there is no threat. Strength and peace are inseparable.

Which brings us to the indispensable ingredient of peace, the GI—once the most lethal force on any battlefield. There is an old saw that goes something like this: soldiers do not fight because they hate those in front of them; they fight because they love those behind them—America. I would also add that they fight because they love those beside them. I would have gladly given my life for the America I served while in uniform. Obama was fond of saying, "That is not who we are." I pray *he* is not who we are—or are becoming. I would not give a drop of blood for the America we are becoming—the America of the *New York Times*, the Obamas, the Pelosis, the Reids, the Ginsbergs, the Ivy League professors, and others in our axis of evil: the courtrooms, the classrooms, the cloakrooms and the newsrooms (C3N).

A soldier's love and sacrifice (love in action) is essential to our future. But we must be a lovable people to earn that love. I am positing that evil is not lovable. In the years of my life and since I folded my uniform I have seen a transformation of the lovability of our country. Sooner or later soldiers will not fight for a country they do not love. During Viet Nam we saw the cowards of that generation who hated America, who would not fight, who deserted those who fought and died for them, and who ran to Canada. Unfortunately, we are becoming unloveable, a transformation led by an assault on traditional morality bought into by half the country. (Remember, we twice elected a man who forever defined down fitness to be president.) Not only must soldiers love their country; to be motivated to fight for it, they must be *able* to fight.

BEYOND HOLLOW: THE DISARMING OF AMERICA

There is a story about a three-legged pig that illustrates some of what has happened to our military. A farmer was asked why his pig had only three legs. He replied, "You see that pig? One night our house caught on fire while we were asleep. Without regard for his own life, the pig raced into the house squealing away. He went from bedroom to bedroom waking us up. He dragged our baby out the door and saved all our lives."

What has that got to do with the three legs? "Well, dummy," said the farmer, "you don't eat a pig like that all at once." While Bill Clinton loathed the military, Barack Obama tried to destroy it. Not only did Obama leave the pig with only two legs, but worse, he tore its heart out and castrated it.

Obama moved our military beyond hollow to a point where the foundation, the ethos, its morale and traditional values were attacked. Obama created what I call a quad-sexual military with its LGBT policies, and he put females in foxholes, both of which are readiness killers. His defense budget language mandates equal opportunity to all "regardless of their gender, their race, or their self-identity." The military has led the league in unbiased opportunity, but what the hell is self-identity? Can I now identify myself into showers with young females?

I lived through a hollow military. The term was coined by a former Army Chief of Staff as a warning against the cuts of the Carter administration after the Viet Nam War. It is not unusual post-crisis to witness the political class mania to enfeeble the heroes of the crisis and divert resources to where they see votes — despite the certainty of future crises. We are often surprised by crises, but in the past we had a foundation—a force structure, contingency plans, weapons systems, training standards, and an ethos—that allowed quick recovery and response to any threat. The ethos was sacrosanct.

No longer. Men and materiel are replaceable, but not morale and ethos. Ethos is key. Obama was determined to transform our military to be more like his vision of America. That is a fool's errand. Although civilian control of the military is essential, civilianization of the military is madness. A military is designed to kick ass, and our civilian leadership are too often wimpy-assed can kickers.

It is easy to blame the assault on our military on a merely incompetent man who has taken leadership to dithering heights, who confuses corps with corpse, who coined the term *leading from behind* (the king of all oxymorons), who trades terrorists for a traitor, and who dared not speak the name of our enemy. Some believe he hates America like many of his fellow lounge lizards, the elite who "mock the meat they feed upon." But I believe his motives for military ruination went beyond incompetence or hatred of America.

Obama promised to fundamentally transform America. Some of those efforts have been thwarted by a pesky Constitution. Unfortunately, there have been fewer obstacles to his remaking the military, where the Commander in Chief reigns pretty much supreme. He had a Congress that, like him, was devoid of military experience and fortitude. So there was no one to stop him. If one is to transform America from what we are, to Obama's image and likeness, one must begin with the military, the protector of what we are, the vault for our values. And the key to our Military is its ethos. Destroy that and you are well on the way to transforming America—just as Obama promised—and putting our head on the block for all the axe men of the world.

I believe it was all premeditated, a part of the Obama's promise to transform us, a Pontius Pilate kind of doctrine. He washed his hands in the Iranian riots, in Syria where he became Putin's pretzel, in Iraq, in Benghazi, and on every battlefield where he put victory in the hands of the enemy by announcing a date of withdrawal. It is not quite a "hell no, I won't go"—the key is, if we were weak enough, Obama could say we would like to go, but can't. He never realized that his failure to enforce the red line was viewed by the entire world as a yellow streak down our back. Our adversaries immediately crossed the line and kicked sand in our face.

By any objective measure of readiness, our military is not ready. When is the last time we won? Much of our society is obsessed with comfort, and it has seeped into our military, comfort which Khalil Gibran called, "That stealthy thing that enters the house as a guest, then becomes host, and finally master."

In 1940, before the disasters of Kasserine Pass in WWII or Task Force Smith in Korea, General Douglas MacArthur warned, "The history of failure in war can almost be summed up in two words: *Too late*. Too late in comprehending the deadly purpose of a potential enemy. Too late in realizing the mortal danger. Too late in preparedness. Too late in uniting all possible forces for resistance. Too late in standing with ones's friends..." Barack Obama will be known as the too late president.

I have known heroes, to include Medal of Honor recipients, from as far back as the Indian Wars. Those heroes were real men, so much tougher than we are today. Hardship, misery, and privation, not comfort, was their schoolhouse. These were men with a moral foundation and sense of honor. We hear so often that we have the best military in the history of the planet. There is no way to know that, but take the soldiers of WWI, WWII, Korea or Vietnam, with modern equipment, and I believe they would kick our ass.

No matter what Obama did to the country, if he hasn't destroyed the military, we can survive. We can only pray that president Trump will turn our military around as he has promised. But that is only half of the battle. We must also turn our society around if it is to be worth fighting for.

E PLURIBUS DUO

We hear often about a great divide in America defined as being between liberals—mostly Democrats—and conservatives—mostly Republicans. Actually it is a divide between good and evil. At the foundation of this divide is an assault on morality, an abandonment of God. It is a fundamental, irrefutable fact that God is the essence of goodness. No God, no goodness, you can't have one without the other. It is impossible to define evil if there is no good, no God. It is that simple.

Pride, the sin in the fallen angels, is the root cause; we want to be our own gods, free from consequences for anything we choose to do, as we each define what is good and evil. As Archbishop Fulton J. Sheen once said: "If you do not worship God, you worship something, and nine times out of ten it will be yourself." Since we don't hold ourselves to any absolute standard, we cannot discern good or evil in the acts of others either, for we have no objective standard of good and evil. Therefore, tolerance of evil becomes mandatory for us; what we cannot tolerate is the good. To us, if it feels good, it is good. Morality, even truth, becomes relative.

These doctrines of non-consequence and non-judgmentalism—a great evil—have been drummed into our youth by those who go by names such as progressives, liberals, and the like. But there is nothing wrong with being a liberal, an elite, or a progressive. As any soldier knows, it is important to accurately identify the enemy, so I will call these agents of evil the fascist left. My first memory of politics as a child was simply: *I am a God-fearing, Irish Catholic Democrat, wanna make something of it?* The fascist left, with its evil policies, resides in the party of my youth—the Democratic Party. A word on evil. It is not proper for any of us to label anyone as evil. It is not the person; it is what the person does that is evil. Only God knows if the person is evil, and His judgment is perfect. We must absolutely love the sinner, but hate the sin. This simple truth is beyond the comprehension of the fascist left. They cannot separate the two and so, for example, anyone who denounces the policies of Obama is called a racist, or who sees sodomy as a physical evil is called a homophobe. But there cannot be evil without consequences—here or in the afterlife, or both. So if I slip and call someone evil, forgive me.

E Pluribus Unum, "out of many, one," is now out of many, two. The two sides are what Jimmy Stewart called "the uncommon

common man" (of course, that includes women) and the fascist left. We are divided and, as such, cannot survive. The fascist left I speak of, epitomized by Obama, is best defined as those who believe they were born with boots and spurs and the rest of us with saddles on our back. They believe they are better and know what is best for the rest of us. Power is their god, and they are sprinkled generously throughout our most influential forums, which I called the axis of evil—the C3N.

The fascist left seldom are found in boardrooms, factories, farms, the military or veterans' cemeteries. There is little they would physically fight for. Traditional morality, even chastity, is denounced, as is marriage, and toleration of evil is good. They can rationalize evil, claiming it is a disease. These people would kill a baby on its birthday and believe you can marry your cat. These facts alone put feigning moral outrage off limits to these baby killers. They are the mill stoners Jesus spoke of—the atheists, the humanists, the amoral, and the immoral. They believe they have a right to persist in any evil that suits them.

For the fascist left, patriotism is hokey and the flag is merely a cloth. Defecating on the flag, which has happened, is protected speech, but prayer is not—and the Ten Commandments are dangerous. Pornography is a "lyric" and terrorists are misunderstood freedom fighters. The *New York Times* is their Bible. They have an irrational fear of guns. Many are from Ivy League schools sympathetic to socialism, even communism, but hostile to free enterprise, the military, and Christianity. They believe the Constitution should live and breathe their values and opinions. They decry amendments by the people, protecting our flag for instance, instead promoting changes only by their fellow travelers in the courts. (Don't ever play cards with these folks; they will change rules in the middle of a pot.)

The fascist left is obsessed with change, but only change that involves them. Technological changes, advances in medicine, and logistics can be good. Proposed changes in morality are not good. In fact, it is impossible to change morality. The Golden Rule, the Decalogue, and the Sermon on the Mount define a morality that is immutable.

On the other hand, the uncommon common Americans accept the fact that they may have been ridden hard and put away wet. In their ranks are those who have been fodder for the forces of freedom. Their sweat lubricates the machinery of America, and their blood nourishes the tree of liberty. These uncommon common Americans fill veterans' cemeteries. Those veterans didn't believe they did America a favor by their service and sacrifice, they believed God did them a favor by allowing them to be born in this greatest of countries. They know there are worse things than war, and they all come (as Hemingway said) with defeat. Peace is the ultimate victory of all warriors—but they will fight. God is their supreme good. The Bible is their Basic Instructions Before Leaving Earth manual. They cling to their guns. They cannot rationalize evil. They believe the Founders meant what they wrote in the Constitution about life (especially innocent life), liberty, and the pursuit of happiness—and that only the people should amend it. They are patriots and proud of it. The uncommon common American possesses the three sources of American exceptionalism: they are courageous; they are compassionate; and they are competitive—all three of which are essential if we are to remain exceptional. Members of the fascist left don't believe in American exceptionalism; in fact, some of them hate America.

THE GREATEST EVIL

Alexander Pope, a great English poet who could say a lot in few words, wrote about America three hundred years ago in his poem *An Essay on Man*: "Vice is a monster of such frightful mien, As to be hated, needs but to be seen; Yet seen too oft, familiar with her face, We first endure, then pity, then embrace." But before I identify the greatest evil, or vice, full disclosure. I am an orthodox Catholic, not condom or cafeteria. I emphasize Catholic, not Christian, because some Christian denominations condone abortion and homosexual "marriage." I believe in heaven and hell and final judgment. I believe in sin and that the seven deadly sins are at its root. I believe this life's only purpose is to save our souls and those of the people around us.

That is my truth and I am sticking to it. I may be wrong, but I am not willing to take a chance. But none of that influenced my judgement in this issue; nor does the fact that some holy people, given a vision of hell, tell us most of those poor souls are there for sins of the flesh.

As a Medal of Honor recipient, I spend a great deal of time with our youth, and I am often asked about the keys to success and to happiness in life. Frequently, they will ask what is the greatest evil, the greatest vice? Sex outside of marriage between a man and a woman, I tell them. Wow! Can you imagine the C3N reaction to this? Think about it.

Spare me the religious zealot crap. I am talking cold, hard, measurable facts, not sin. Measure the social costs of single unwed mothers and their children. Measure the costs of sexually trans-mitted disease. Think of the costs of homosexual priests and others who abuse our children? Consider the human tragedy of sex outside marriage in regards to divorce, crime, prostitution, even in poli-tics. Oftentimes it leads to the horror of abortion. St. (Mother) Teresa believed abortion was an assault on peace itself. At the 1994 National Prayer Breakfast, she said: "I feel the greatest destroyer of peace today is abortion, because . . . it is really a war against the child, a direct killing of the innocent child, murdered by the mother herself. . . . And if we accept that a mother can kill even her own child, how can we tell other people not to kill one another?" She added: "Any country that accepts abortion is not teaching its people to love, but to use any violence to get what they want."

Abortion is an assault on a mother, her child, and our civilization. We have joined other civilizations that killed and enslaved those it deemed lesser persons and that practiced human sacrifice. We are no longer the last hope of mankind. Abortion is a Trojan horse within the "shining city on a hill." It is tragic that the Democratic Party has as its icons the Clintons—one a serial adulterer, and the other an advocate of unbridled abortion.

We need to educate our society, especially our youth, on the con-sequences of sex outside of marriage between a man and a woman.

45

AMERICA'S AXIS OF EVIL

THE NEWSROOMS

The Ninth Commandment says, "Thou shalt not bear false witness against thy neighbor" (Exodus 20:16).

Let me begin with what I believe is the axis of the axis of evil: The Newsrooms (media). But it is important to know that the two most important elements in our society, if we are to survive, are the military and the media. One keeps us secure and the other keeps us free. The military lives by the duty, honor, country code. Today's media does not. It is duty bound to tell us the truth about ourselves. They don't do that. It is dishonorable (even evil) to bear false witness against our neighbors. The media does that. No one should do anything to jeopardize the security of our country. The media has and will publish top secret documents that could jeopardize our security and kill innocent citizens. (This fact alone makes those who do this an enemy of the people.) The media uses unnamed sources often in security issues. Remember, at the source of the source is a coward. The media and their sources are of the same ilk.

Mike Wallace, a media icon, once said that if he were a journalist with an enemy patrol covering the ambush of American soldiers, he would cover it as any other story and not warn the Americans. Peter Jennings agreed. They were journalists before being Americans and therefore, by definition, dishonorable people. F. Scott Fitzgerald famously said the rich are different from the rest of us. So are many in the media; they are part of the fascist left.

The word *news* originated from an acronym for information from north, east, west, and south. And that is what it used to be, information from all over, good and bad and ugly. The purpose was to tell us the truth about ourselves. But the news media have turned news into a C-lettered word: chaos, confusion, conflict, cover-up, conspiracy, corruption, color, crime, catastrophe, and the biggies: combat and casualties. (Someone once suggested copulation, too.) We are not a C-lettered society. Again, news today is about pushing an agenda, rather than telling us the truth about ourselves.

No element of our society spews more evil than Hollywood. They are almost devoid of artistic talent, certainly of morals, and depend on sex and violence to sell tickets. Car chases are a major art form, often followed by casual copulation to confirm and justify the lifestyle of many celebrities and to indoctrinate our youth. Evil, like misery, loves company.

The fascist left in the news and entertainment media is clearly an enemy of the people. Some believe it is their job to control what we think. What I call the greatest evil is their primary message: they are waging a sexual jihad against America, promoting fornication, which ruins lives. In the past, the media perpetuated the myth that we should not argue with anyone who bought ink by the barrel. In other words, the uncommon common man should just take their shit and keep quiet. That has changed. Now all Americans, by virtue of technology, own ink by the barrel, as President Trump is teaching us. We only need to be informed and not apathetic, and we can bring the media back to their mission as intended in our precious Constitution.

THE CLOAKROOMS

The Eighth Commandment says, "Thou shalt not steal" (Exodus 20:15). In a discussion of the 2016 election, a friend denounced the incivility of all the politicians. They certainly fall short, spending more time off raising money than performing their duties. It is not civility, however, but honor that is the problem with our politicians. Look at the candidates who, in that historic election, pledged on their honor to support their party's nominee for president—and yet who broke their pledge. They lied to our faces. Look at senators Lisa Murkowski and Susan Collins, both women who voted against a nominee of their party, a woman, to appease their donors. The examples are legion.

My favorite example of honor among politicians of our past is the duel between Andrew Jackson and Charles Dickinson, a man who insulted Jackson's wife. Never mind that Dickinson was the best shot in the state, and had killed 26 men in previous duels. Jackson challenged him to a duel. Jackson knew he was outgunned and had little hope of survival, so he wore lose clothing and let Dickinson shoot first, hoping it would not be fatal and that he would live long enough to kill Dickinson.

Dickinson did shoot first and put a bullet in Jackson that broke two of his ribs and lodged inches from his heart, where it would remain the rest of his life. Jackson miraculously remained on his feet long enough to kill Dickinson. Reflecting on the duel, a doctor remarked to Jackson, "I don't see how you stayed on your feet after that wound." To which Jackson responded, "I would have stood up long enough to kill him if he had put a bullet in my brain." Is there a Jackson anywhere in our Congress? For many politicians today, a vote, or a donation, is more important than their honor.

Saint Thomas Aquinas, renowned philosopher and theologian from the Middle Ages, defined the commandment, "Thou shalt not steal." One type of thief he described was a person who buys promotions to position of power, using the money of constituents for his own benefit and self-aggrandizement and to the detriment, or contrary to the wishes, of those who gave him the money. Too many of our politicians today meet St Thomas's definition of a thief, and of someone who once said there is no honor among thieves. We can only pray that these people do not represent who the rest of us are as a people. The Irish have a saying about honor: "A man lives after his life but not after his honor." We are in the swirl around the drain, and politicians without honor will flush us down. Some would sell their own soul for a vote.

THE COURTROOMS

Fulton J. Sheen, Roman Catholic Bishop of the diocese of Peoria, Illinois, who later became an archbishop, denounced those who rationalize evil, those who would take an obviously evil act and call it good.

Nowhere is this more evident than in our lawyers and judges. The armor against humans' insatiable lust for power in our Constitution was the division of powers, but there was one chink: the lifetime appointment of judges walled from the will of the people. Thomas Jefferson said: ". . . the germ of dissolution of our Federal Government is in the constitution of the Federal Judiciary—an irresponsible body (for impeachment is scarcely a scare-crow), working like gravity by night and by day, gaining a little to-day and a little tomorrow, and advancing its noiseless step like a thief, over the field of jurisdiction, until all shall be usurped from the states and the government be consolidated into one."[1]

I am amazed at the reverence some have for the Supreme Court. Many of these people are political hacks, there ostensibly to do the will of those who appointed them. I once watched a discussion involving a Supreme Court justice, who was exposed as the lightweight in the room. One Supreme Court justice supported lowering the age of sexual consent to twelve years—and the legalization of

---

1 From Thomas Jefferson to C. Hammond, August 18, 1821, https://founders. archives.gov/documents/Jefferson/98-01-02-2260.

prostitution. This judge is OK with twelve-year-old prostitutes! Another justice banned the ROTC from her campus.

None of these people have ever met a payroll, created a job or served in the military. Some believe the Constitution means whatever they say it means. They all attended Harvard or Yale. Only one is from the West. Too many are among the fascist left, totally ignorant of everyday America. It is difficult to have common sense if you never had a common experience. A further mark of the quality of these folks is how often they turn on the hand that fed them, e.g., John Roberts, Anthony Kennedy and David Souter. President Eisenhower said he made two mistakes and both of them were on the Supreme Court. These people have torn the blindfold off Lady Justice.

Our laws and court decisions should not only reflect our values, they should serve as teachers for our children. But look what the courts teach our children: flag burning is protected "speech," and so is pornography, but prayer is not, and the Ten Commandments are banned from the public square. Many judges seem horrified, almost as vampires are, with the cross, yet they think nothing of usurping the role of God by redefining His definition of marriage. They believe it is protected speech to fraudulently wear military decorations, (something few of them ever earned), even the Medal of Honor. What would they do to someone who pretends to be a lawyer?

What I have called our greatest evil has ties to the Supreme Court—which brings us again to abortion. Surely these lawyers know intent is everything in the law. What is the intent of an abortion? Simply to kill a human being. I never heard that Stalin or Hitler or Mao ever personally killed another human being. Perhaps they never had the guts to kill a human face to face; but they are monsters because they were responsible for the massacre of millions. How is the Supreme Court different in the case of abortion? You can say, or do, the most hateful things just about anywhere, but don't do them on the Supreme Court Plaza or burn a flag there.

They will put you in jail. Hypocrisy is their hallmark.

It is hard to point out any social or moral malevolence in today's America that does not bear the fingerprints of some judicial decision. I will not say that some of these people are evil, but I would not like to be in their place at the Judgement. It is time strip them of their robes, take them off their thrones and put them in working clothes at the same level as those they are supposed to serve. We left Europe to get away from elites in robes sitting on thrones, and these elites are helping to ruin our country.

THE CLASSROOMS

President Trump, among others, has said education is the civil rights issue of our time.

I recently saw a photo of an Arab child playing in some dismal street with the burning twin towers emblazoned on his T-shirt. In that photo were both the cause and the solution to both the deadly threat of radical Islam and the curse of the fascist left in America. Radical Islam will continue to kill as long as the Muslim children are taught that the United States and other infidels are the great Satan. The doctrine of the fascist left will survive as long as American children are taught we are the great Satan. The entire fascist left movement has its roots and hope in our classrooms and they are the movement's hope for the future. The great horror of the fascist left is a thinking, logical, virtuous, voting public. Many professors will fight to eliminate such a public.

As I travel on behalf of the Medal of Honor Society's Character Development Program, I spend a lot of time with teachers, mostly middle and high school teachers. We often discuss the main topic and purpose of education in a democratic society. The topic is patriotism and the purpose is to grow patriots. A patriot is not someone who says he loves our country; a patriot is someone who proves he loves our country by supporting and defending that country. Support and defend are the key words. How can any democratic society survive if its citizens who ostentatiously rule the country will not support and defend her? In ancient times, morals were taught, but then were lost over the ages. Thomas Jefferson believed morals should be taught, that citizens should be good people to be good rulers. So dedicated was he to education that his tombstone does not list his accomplishments as president, but rather declares him to be the "Author of the Declaration of American Independence" and "Father of the University of Virginia."

Morals are out of bounds in many of our public classrooms. As is patriotism. Academia is turning too many of our children into snowflakes, limp wristed, safe spaced, spaced out, crybaby "victims" who have no idea how America runs, who runs it or what it has done for the world. Evil is not a decision, it is a disease. Above all don't think—feel. Facts, unfortunately for them, have no feelings, and our children are ill equipped to deal with a world that runs on facts. The greatest assault on free speech is in academia, and PC (and BS) is the greatest assault on the truth. If you can control speech you can control minds—which is the objective.

Academia is creating an entitlement generation—young people without gratitude for the bounty of America, who demand to be cared for, who denounce competition and merit-based outcome, who strive for a life participation trophy. The entitlement mind-set is a vice, but even worse, these people are devoid of gratitude, which is essential to happiness.

In the military, we have a litmus test for leaders: would I want this person with me in combat? I have met, or read about, few professors I would want with me in combat. They can't control riots and chaos on their own campuses. Academia is almost devoid of leadership. Leaders are patriots. Service to our youth is the highest form of patriotism, but for too many in academia, patriotism is a joke. And therein lies the greatest threat to our future. No democracy can survive unless we grow patriots, and much of it must be done in our classrooms.

CONCLUSION

In my faith, there is a doctrine of grace. It teaches that there is a treasure chest filled with grace, and that it was filled by the sacrifices of Jesus and the saints. It's available to all of us to help us as we struggle to do what is right. We can all draw from that chest through no particular merits of our own, but simply because of God's love for us. Our freedom is, like grace, a treasure chest. It was filled by the sacrifices of our great heroes and patriots, particularly by our military. We all constantly draw from that chest of freedom, through no merits of our own, but simply because of their love for us.

The chest of grace is inexhaustible because it comes from God. Not so the chest of freedom. It must continuously be replenished by the blood, sweat and tears of our military—the grunts, whose blood, sweat, and tears are the holy trinity of our freedom. But there will be no blood for an unlovable, immoral people—and too much blood is shed by a military that is unfit to fight. America stands at a stark and final crossroads. Either it continues on its post-moral path toward the garbage bin of history, to end up like so many other once-great nations, or else it experiences a desperately needed national and spiritual revival, for which every "uncommon common American" hopes, works, fights, and prays.

EPILOGUE

OVER the years I have tried to get the 54th guys together at the annual Dustoff Association meetings. Thanks to the work of Hook, Rock, and Wayne we have found quite a few. It was some years before I realized what an exceptional group of men we had. If it were not for the record keeping of Wayne, which I found after a few years, this book would not have been possible. I wanted the men to know what an extraordinary unit they manned. Most of the guys went on with their lives healing their wounds and forgetting Viet Nam. The media treatment of that veteran made us want to forget. Some have died, others don't care, and a few can't afford the reunions (we will use some of the proceeds from this book to help if they agree to join us). Over all they have joined the quiet heroes who, in war and peace, make our country what it is. America has no kings or queens, but we do have a nobility: our nobility is called veterans. These men were heroes, not celebrities and much of America no longer knows the difference. A true hero does not feel he did America a favor by his service; he feels God did him a favor by allowing him to be born in America.

Five out of the original 40 are in the Dustoff Hall of Fame; and, based on the core requirements of the HOF, (medals, missions, rescues) most of the crewmen in the 54th should be. In fact, I don't know of a single crewman of the 54th whose deeds are not a match of some member of the HOF. Some of them are a match for those of us who wear the Medal of Honor. Three members of the 54th are in the Army Aviation Hall of Fame. And one member of the 54th is the only Army aviator in the National Aviation Hall of Fame, me. Hodgdon Hall, home of Flat Iron (the MEDEVAC unit at Fort Rucker, the home of Army Aviation) is named for John Hodgdon, a personal hero of mine. A few of the WOPAs had enough sense to become RFO. Mac retired as a colonel as did FAC Flory and Jerry Foust became a general. Sgt. Rock, a practitioner of many trades, and master of most, found time to play Morgan Earp in simulated shootouts at the OK Corral in Tombstone, Arizona, where he also tended bar in a local saloon. Rock suffered a stroke a few years ago and came to stay with me a couple of times. He always came not with a can of beanie weanies but with some Irish whiskey and several cases of boiled peanuts, which he knew I loved. I made the mistake of mentioning to him that I was getting a concealed carry permit. He then sent me not one but two pistols in the mail, both loaded! He is in a home and when I talk to him he calls me sir, but I am not sure he really knows who I am.

Years later, I would meet the troop whose wife mailed him her wedding ring. When I asked if he ever remarried, he held up five fingers! He obviously recovered from the ordeal. Some of his wives were featured in catalogs from several foreign countries.

Super Medic, Jimmy Johnson, got an education to the level of a doctorate, came back in and retired as a major. He served in the Gulf War spreading the Kelly attitude and his exceptional leadership skills everywhere he went. Don Sewell made international news when, as a helicopter policeman, he heroically protected the White House from a runaway chopper. Charlie Ramirez, after being shot twice in combat, survived a pencil bomb that exploded on his bus in San Francisco. Charlie is now in an area of northern California where he continues his caring ways with his neighbors. The area is so remote that he built a helicopter pad for emergencies. Hook, after months of hospitalization, became a postmaster in Iowa; one daughter has a doctorate from Duke, the other a masters from the University of Northern Iowa (they had a smart mother, Pam). KIA has disappeared into the forests of Washington where I tried but failed to find him.

It took us 38 years to find Pappy Coleman. He was in ill health living in obscurity in North Carolina. For family necessities, he left the military. He was within two years of his pension, which he sacrificed for his family. He had children and grandchildren who needed care and his career came second. He would have been a shoo-in for sergeant major as he was for the HOF. Pappy defines hero for me—as with Kelly—when goodness and courage combine in a person, that person is a hero. Goodness is essential.

Three years ago I got a call from Rose, Pappy's wife. She said he was dying and wanted me to take care of his funeral. He died a few hours after her call. Arranging a funeral in Turkey Creek, Kentucky, was a challenge, but burying that marvelous soldier was one of the great honors of my life.

I often tell the story of the time I screwed up an assigned task pretty badly. I was feeling awful. My boss tried to cheer me up: "Pat, don't feel bad, no one is a total loss—they can always serve as a bad example." And that is where I am along with many of my contemporaries. We have been in the arena but our time is past. We cannot correct all the mistakes we made but we can still live our lives over again—through our youth. As the reader will know, I am not locked into the experience thing—I think caring is more important—but good judgment may be related to experience; which may be related to bad judgment. We need to pass on to our youth the path around bad experiences.

The bad example of my military career may be instructive. My record up to major was a disaster. In fact, it was a minor miracle that I made major; after all, I was not a "shoo-in" to captain. The Medal of Honor certainly helped my career but it is not the golden parachute many think. It can be a burden and I have often said that it is harder to wear than it was to earn. The greatest part of the Medal is simply to know that someone cared enough about you to recommend it. Although I have often preached about the merits of hard times in hard places, it never occurred to me until I started writing this book that the greatest adversity in my professional career—being kicked out of Intelligence School—was a blessing. If that had not happened I would not have gone to flight school, saved those lives, and earned those medals with the blessing they brought on me and my family. The lesson from my bad experiences is that seeming disasters need not be show stoppers. The military, for the most part, is peopled with extraordinarily fair people, tested often and hard, but people who pull for the underdog and will do all they can to make winners of their subordinates. I am truly nothing without the Army and the soldiers who were my comrades—and my faith.

I cannot emphasize enough the role my faith played in any success I have had. It was the source of whatever courage I had, a constant source of comfort, of calm and of the confidence that allowed me to do things that for me would have otherwise been impossible. For reasons that escape me, the Good Lord has seen fit to bless my life in so many ways, not the least of which was saving lives. There is no greater joy; those who flew Dust Off know the thrill of a walk off-home run, a game-winning shot and a playoff winning-putt—all at once. You not only save that life, you save a son, a husband; you bring happiness to a marriage and life to children who would not otherwise been born.

Whatever happens to our bodies as we age, our minds are not devoid of romance and we still dream. In my dreams, I am again a captain, not a general, hurrying into the mist of a moist morning fog—or inky blackness; climbing into the cabin surrounded by the sweet smell of JP4; strapping in; to the detent, the trigger, the whining turbine, then the bumpy roar—and off across tracer marked terrain; voices in my ear begging for wounded comrades—hurry Dust Off; then the signal, the terrain, the enemy, the highway; down on the collective, forward on cyclic, kick it out of trim, hard over to the ground; dodging trees, dipping into paddies, snaking forward, swiftly; stop, hard left pedal, steady right cyclic, a fast flat turn, no float, down to the ground; confusion, we got them, clear on the right, the left; oops, the sharp crack of gunfire snapping through our bird, crew ok, no red lights, up steady, right pedal rotating into translational, speed then altitude then more speed, full bore ahead into the caring hands of a physician—and life.

THANKS AND THOUGHTS

IN my efforts to document the bright and shining truth of our extraordinary humanitarian efforts in Viet Nam, I have focused almost entirely on my personal recollection and records and those of many actual players in this magnificent but largely untold narrative. There is no way I can name all those I need to thank but I must thank some. In no particular order, these folks were especially helpful: Armond "Si" Simmons, who shares my love for Kelly; Ernie Sylvester, who shared his diary; Jessie Kelly Morris, Major Kelly's beloved wife; and his wonderful family; John White (who physically resembles Kelly); Jim McLeroy and other great warriors from Ngok Tavak and Kham Duc; Bob Richter for his editorial genius; Wayne Aurich, who is as responsible for this book as I am; Steve Hook, who has worked tirelessly to find our men; and many members of the Golden Winged 54th. I will add thanks to my daughter, Meghan Smith, herself a fine soldier and member of the second-greatest generation—today's troops. Meghan is alone responsible for all grammatical errors.

There is a tendency among some veterans to exaggerate the

importance and uniqueness of our personal experiences. We have all met those who cannot tell us what they did in Viet Nam, lest they be required to kill us! And I have been amazed at stark differences in recall among those who shared identical experiences. With this in mind, I have done my best to sort out the truth and not exaggerate—but the numbers do not lie. It has been awkward, but I have gone to great lengths not to demean any individual, by name, although there are a few who through ignorance, cowardice, or both deserve demeaning. But none of us are consistently heroic in all areas of our humanity. I have also not identified certain crewmen on certain missions because they are unknown or because they did not provide input and may not have the same recollections I have—or they may have underperformed.

Herein I have highlighted the Dust Off crews, but no aviation combat function ever can match the performance of the everyday helicopter crews in Viet Nam. They flew 11 million hours of combat. In WW2 aircraft losses were 16 percent, in Viet Nam, 43 percent. I am told that in WW2 some pilots completed a tour after 25 missions averaging 4 hours per mission! By way of comparison, Mike Novosel, a Dust Off MOH recipient, and I were playing golf one day with a famous fighter pilot celebrated for having flown 100 combat missions. Between us Mike and I had over 5000! Needless to say we brought this to his attention as he leaned over some important putts.

Once this book is on the street, I am sure I will get plenty of corrections, which may be fodder for future editions. But hopefully, this book will nudge others to bring to America's attention the magnificent quality of our Viet Nam vet and the goodness of his humanitarian work for the wonderful Vietnamese people. Who could not love those people? And, of course, we owe our veterans a humanitarian memorial somewhere on the battlefields in Viet Nam.

And I would add another memorial near the Viet Nam Wall. On that wall, a Wall of Shame, I would put the names of every congressperson who voted to betray our allies in Viet Nam by defunding, indeed, disarming them, in the face of a ruthless communist enemy.

ABOUT THE AUTHORS

Major General (Ret) Pat Brady served over thirty-four years in the Army in duty stations across the world: In Berlin during the building of the Wall; as commander of the DMZ in Korea, in the Dominican Republic; in the Pentagon as chief spokesman for the Army and for two years in Viet Nam. In two tours in Viet Nam he rescued over five thousand wounded and flew over twenty-five hundred combat missions. He is identified in the Encyclopedia of the Viet Nam War as the top helicopter pilot in that war and is one of two Viet Nam soldiers to earn both the Medal of Honor and the Distinguished Service Cross, our nation's second highest award. Some pundits also identify him as the most decorated living veteran. His awards include: Two Distinguished Service Medals; the Defense Superior Service Medal; the Legion of Merit; six Distinguished Flying Crosses; two Bronze Stars, one for valor; the Purple Heart and fifty-three Air Medals, one for valor. He is a member of both the Army Aviation and Dust Off Halls of Fame. General Brady is the first and only Army aviator in the National Aviation Hall of Fame. Brady is a former president of the Congressional Medal of Honor Society and a past Commissioner of the Battle Monuments Commission during the construction of the WWII memorial. General Brady has a bachelor's degree in psychology from Seattle University and an MBA from Notre Dame University.

Meghan Brady Smith was commissioned a second lieutenant Medical Service Corps from the ROTC Brady Battalion at Seattle University where she earned dual degrees in Journalism and the Humanities. She also has a master's degree in education. She served in Germany, Kosovo, Kuwait, and Iraq, during the Operation Iraqi Freedom invasion where she earned the Bronze Star. She married Matt, an Army aviator, and left the military as a captain. She is now a homeschooling mom with four children homesteading in the wilds of Vermont.

GLOSSARY

A-1E. Douglas Skyraider, heavily armed with great staying power used often to protect downed pilots.

AC. Aircraft Commander, in charge of the aircraft.

AO. Area of Operations.

ARVN. Army of the Republic of Vietnam, good guys.

ASO. Aviation Staff Officers, at the time, a danger to common sense, efficiency and effectiveness.

C-123. Called the Provider a multi-use Air Force plane.

C-RATS. C rations, food for soldiers in combat.

CIDG. Civilian Irregular Defense Group.

CIA. Devised program to counter communist influence and protect locals. Later transferred to Special Forces with expanded combat role.

Dust Off. Radio call sign for aeromedical evacuation via army non-divisional helicopters.

EIA. Eaten in Action, soldiers killed by tigers.

FNG. F****** New Guy.

G-2. Command intelligence officer.

G1. Command personnel officer.

H-13. Bell helicopter made famous in the MASH series.

HQ. Headquarters.

IFR. Instrument Flight Rules, Flight by instrument and rules thereof.

IP. Instructor Pilot a teacher of pilots.

ITO. Instrument Takeoff, aviation takeoff using aircraft instruments without reference outside the cockpit.

JP4. Gas for choppers.

KIA. Killed in Action.

L-19. Cessna single engine Army observation aircraft called the Bird Dog.

Landing Zone. Designated landing area for helicopters.

MEDCAP. Medical civic action program. Targeted medical care by physicians and other medical specialists often in rural areas.

MEDEVAC. Call sign for helicopter ambulances in direct support of Divisions.

NCO. Noncommissioned Officer.

OER. Officer Efficient Report, report card for officer's performance, key in promotions.

POW. Prisoner of War.

PZ. Pickup Zone for patients.

R&R. Rest and Recuperation.

REMF. Rear echelon mother f*****. The scourge of operators.

RVN. Republic of Viet Nam.

SF. Special Forces, elite military teams.

TOE. Table of Organization and Equipment.

VC. Viet Cong or Vietnamese communist.

VFR. Visual flight rules, flight using references outside the aircraft and rules thereof.

VNAF. South Vietnamese Air Force.

WETSU. We Eat This Shit Up.

WHAM. Win the Hearts and Minds necessary in Guerilla warfare.

WIA. Wounded in Action.

WOPA. Warrant Officer Protective Association, mythical, playful union to protect warrant officers from RFOs or Real F****** Officers. WOPAs nickname for Warrant Officers.

INDEX

A

Abrams, Creighton: 281–82

Afghanistan: 290

After Action Report (AAR): 172, 240

aircraft commander (AC): 6, 322

Allen, Charles: 77, 93

Anderson, Dick: 3, 7, 32, 75, 82

Anderson, Webster: 190, 202

Area of Operation (AO): 31, 44, 103, 160–62, 177, 180, 191–93, 205, 233, 236, 238, 241, 242, 245, 258, 261, 282, 293, 322

Army of the Republic of Viet Nam (ARVN): 4–5, 26, 39, 46, 49, 51, 61, 65, 95, 121, 163, 273, 322

Army Times: 145, 148

Atrocical Division: 207

Augerson, Bill: 176–77, 205, 208, 247

Aurich, Wayne: 150, 157, 319

Aviation Digest: 146

aviation staff officers (ASO): 132, 322

B

Barker, Frank: 276

Beckwith, Charlie: 144

Benny, Jack: 99

Berlin: 36, 38, 54, 93, 121, 132, 188, 239

Black Death: 18

Black Virgin Mountain: 35

Black, Charlie: 136

Blonien, Joan: 24

Bradley, Omar: 131

Brady, Nancy: 22, 141, 145

Brown University: 151

Burwick, Brian: 177, 189

C

Cambodia: 38, 40, 70

Camp Wolters: 56

Casals, Pablo: 15

Cass, Ken: 205, 247, 283

Cawthorne, Bill: 33, 56, 78, 224–25

Chiarelly, Peter: 294

Chiminello, Tom: 145, 169, 242

Chu Lai: 157–60, 171, 185, 192, 217, 219, 221, 227, 233, 273, 285

Cider Joe: 12, 42

Civilian Irregular Defense Group (CIDG): 30, 163, 190, 258–60, 322

Clausewitz, Carl Von: 109

Coleman, James (Pappy): 150, 178–79, 189, 195, 199–200, 228, 240, 316

Columbus Ledger-Inquirer: 136

conscientious objector (CO): 252

Copenhagen: 89

Craze: iii, 286

Cronan, Bob: 199–200, 238, 271–72

D

Desert One: 144

Detachment A: 32, 59, 62, 71, 74, 77–78, 82, 84, 92, 94–95, 100, 102, 112, 116–18, 121

Devil Brigade: 30

Distinguished Flying Cross (DFC): 187, 277

Distinguished Service Crosses (DSC): 47, 187, 188, 277, 281, 282

Dominican Republic (DOMREP): 135–36, 139–40, 166, 211

Donlon, Roger: 121

Donovan's Brain: 104

Dooley, Tom: 23

Dragon Six: 226

Drunken Sam: 87

Duke University: 316

E

Eisenhower, Dwight: 131–32, 310

essential elements of information (EEI): 171–72, 241, 243

F

F***** Up Beyond All Recognition (FUBAR): 191

f****** new guy (FNG): 8, 11, 13, 28, 37, 110–13, 117, 123, 124, 164, 196, 277, 284, 322

Father Damien: 19, 25

Fergusson, Robert: 188–89

FitzGerald, Barry: 145, 152, 158

Fitzgerald, F. Scott, 307

FitzGerald, Marion: 145

Flory, Al (aka FAC Flory): 147, 153, 175, 189–90, 194, 234–35, 286, 315

Fort Benning: 127, 157, 163

Fort Rucker: 144, 315

Foust, Jerry: 147, 164, 175, 178, 194–95, 199, 250, 315

G

Gabaldon, Bob: 178

Garza, Jim: 178–80, 182

Giles, Henry: 75–76, 82

Golden Hour: 10, 286, 289, 293

Goody, Dan: 150, 164, 171, 186, 254

Green Berets: 21, 30, 256, 258

Grider, Jeff: 77

Guam: 3

Gulf of Tonkin: 136

H

helicopter ambulance (HA): 3, 46, 118–19, 132, 134, 136–38, 158, 175, 191, 323

Hepburn, Katherine: 264

Hiller the Killer: 16, 141

Ho Chi Minh: 4, 30, 49, 124, 227, 256–57

Hodgdon, John: 143, 147, 150, 177, 181, 186, 238, 254, 296, 315

Holy Angels Academy: 22

Honolulu: 3

Hook, Steve: 150, 164, 173, 179–80, 182, 195, 208–9, 231, 238, 272–74, 314, 316, 319

Hope, Bob: 124, 208

I

Instructor Pilot (IP): 111, 323

Instrument Flight Rules (IFR): 111, 323

instrument take off (ITO): 185

J

Johnson, Jimmy: 186, 239, 315

Johnson, Johnny: 165, 283

Johnson, Lyndon: 135, 263

K

Kane, Chuck: 135, 137

Kelly, Charles: 5–7, 10, 22, 32, 36–37, 41–44, 46–47, 49, 51–52, 58–62, 70–86, 92–96, 103, 109–13, 116–19, 121, 123, 125–28, 134–35, 138, 142–43, 146, 152, 159, 161, 166, 174, 195, 243, 273, 276, 278–79, 284, 286–89, 291, 315, 316, 319

Kelly's Krazies: 95, 117–18

Kennedy, Anthony: 310

Kennedy, Bobby: 248, 279

Kennedy, Jim: 165, 283

Kennedy, John F.: 30, 35, 104

Kham DUC: 256–58, 262–65, 267–70, 319

Killed in Action (KIA): 13, 45, 151, 180, 190, 227, 239, 241, 244, 245, 246, 267, 274, 277, 286, 316, 323

King's Pond: 132

Korea: 5, 44, 61–62, 84, 163, 187, 292, 301

L

Landing Zone (LZ): 16, 26, 35, 75, 89, 102,

189, 190, 191, 201, 220, 222–25, 230, 236, 261, 323

Laos: 23, 47, 134, 256

Lawton, John: 188–89

Le Bourdais, Wallace: 247, 282–84

Lichte, Jack: 145, 169, 242

Liteky, Angelo: 145

Lonely Boy: 221, 238, 271–73, 284

Lowder, Gary: 178, 208, 237, 272–73

Lucas, Jim: 72

Lynch, Nick: 135–36

Lynch, Patsy: 135, 145

LZ West: 220, 222–25

M

Marines: 44, 123, 163, 258–60, 267–68

Markey, Keith: 31

Martin of Tours: 213

MC: 224

McDaniel, Jim: 177

McWilliam, Bob: 147, 177, 268

Medal of Honor: 107, 121, 123, 137-138, 145, 187, 190–91, 225, 228–29, 268, 277, 290, 291, 301, 305, 310, 311, 315, 317

MEDEVAC: 119, 132–34, 137–38, 152, 191–92, 201, 244, 290, 315, 323

Medical Civic Action Program (MEDCAP): 29, 31, 323

Medical Service Corps (MSC): 7, 36, 92, 122, 145, 149, 151, 224, 250, 289

Mike Force: 256–58, 260, 265

Mission Request Form (MRF): 171–73, 277

Mitchell, Billy: 78, 93

Montagnards: 18, 20–21, 23–24, 26, 30, 32, 95, 256

N

Napoleon: 88, 131, 167–68, 255

National Liberation Front (NLF): 4, 238

Nett, Bob: 145

Newsday: 15

Ngok Tavak: 257, 260, 264–67, 269–70, 319

Notre Dame: 23

Nui Ba Den: 35

NVA: 5, 136–37, 190, 210, 219, 223–24, 227, 233, 238, 256–57, 259–60, 264–65, 267–70

O

Officer Efficient Reports (OERs): 54, 285

P

Paddy Control: 105

Patterson, Alicia: 15

Patton, George: 131–32

Peacock: 184–85

Perry, Tom: 264, 267

Philippines: 3

Pickstone, Earl: 75, 82

pickup zone (PZ): 9, 27, 39, 67, 70, 97–99, 103, 105–6, 108, 137, 164–65, 171, 173–74, 177, 179, 184–85, 188–89, 194, 199, 204, 207, 221–23, 225, 234, 243, 246, 248, 284, 323

Plain of Reeds: 38, 105

Platz, Jean: 24

Pleiku: 4, 7, 13, 15, 18–19, 21, 26, 29–33, 35, 37–38, 95, 157, 216

Popular Forces: 163

Presley, Elvis: 104

Puerto Rico: 139

Purple Hearts (PH): 47, 121, 240, 277–78

Q

Qui Nhon: 4, 7, 32, 158

R

R&R: 77, 124, 139, 251, 323

Ralph, James "Doc": 67

Ramirez, Charlie: 178, 194, 196, 199–200, 315–16

Reduction in Forces (RIF): 253

Regional Forces: 163

Republic of Viet Nam (RVN): 29, 323

S

Sacrament of the Last Rites: 213

Saigon: 4, 8–9, 12, 23, 32, 34–35, 37–38, 40, 49, 59, 67–68, 70–71, 73–74, 79, 90, 95, 110, 112–14, 116–18, 120–22, 160, 168, 239, 269

Savage Golf: 225–26

Savior of Mothers: 22

Shaw, George Barnard: 98

Schexnayder, Chuck: 5

Schuster, Pete: 147, 151, 175–76, 189, 227, 233

Schwartz, Greg: 147, 151, 175, 177, 236, 268

Seattle University: 22

Semmelweis, Ignaz: 22–23

Service, Robert: 83, 84, 211, 253

Sewell, Don: 147, 151, 153, 157, 175, 194, 211, 261, 278, 315

Shadrick, Lester "Buddha": 147, 151, 168, 175, 177–78, 199, 206, 233, 276

Shannahan, Norm: 147, 151, 153, 157, 175, 181, 198, 230

Simmons, Armond "Si": 40, 82, 92, 319

Simmons, Wayne "Tiny": 93, 133, 150

Sinatra, Frank: 104

Smith, Pat "Doc": 22–25, 79

SOC Trang Tigers: 87

South China Sea: 6, 250–51, 283

Southern Mississippi University: 92

Special Forces (SF): 21, 29–30, 32, 68, 163, 322, 323

Steinbeck, John: 15

Stilwell Hooches: 12

Stilwell, Joe: 12, 42–44, 46, 52–53, 57–58, 73–74, 77, 84

Street Without Joy: 49

Stylus, Bangor: 257, 261–63, 266

Super Oink: 167–68, 251

Sylvester, Ernie: 60, 82, 319

T

Tam Ky: 178, 273

Tan Hiey: 70

Tan Son Nhut: 4–5, 34, 51

Taylor, Ed: 102, 143, 145

Taylor, Rose: 145

Taylor, Elizabeth: 135

Temperilli, John: 4, 43, 147, 206, 263

TET: 24, 231–35, 238–39, 263–64, 269–70

Time magazine: 125

Trung Lap: 68, 120

Tucker, Stan: 149, 157

Tuffy: 87

Tweed, Ron: 166, 228

Twister Charlie: 223–24, 227–28

U

Uncle Ho: 49–50, 160, 269

University of Northern Iowa: 316

University of Washington: 22

USS *Card*: 35, 168

Utility Tactical Helicopter Company (UTT): 43

V

Versace, Rocky: 107

Viet Cong (VC): 4, 30, 49, 68, 238, 323

W

Wallace, Mike: 249, 307

We Eat This Shit Up (WETSU): 30, 323

Westmoreland, William (Westy): 42, 46, 77

WHAM: 29–30, 59, 62, 323

White, John: 256–60, 263–67, 319

Wobbly Ones (W01): 162

WOPA: 147, 150–51, 165, 167, 170, 174–75, 198–99, 204–5, 212, 215, 249, 276, 282–84, 315, 323

Wounded in Action (WIA): 13, 45, 239, 323

Yards: 21

Y

York, Alvin: 252

Z

Zenc, Bruce: 151